A **CENTURY** OF **TOMORROWS**

A **CENTURY** OF TOMORROWS

HOW IMAGINING THE FUTURE SHAPES THE PRESENT

GLENN ADAMSON

BLOOMSBURY PUBLISHING

NEW YORK · LONDON · OXFORD · NEW DELHI · SYDNEY

BLOOMSBURY PUBLISHING
Bloomsbury Publishing Inc.
1385 Broadway, New York, NY 10018, USA

BLOOMSBURY, BLOOMSBURY PUBLISHING, and the Diana logo are trademarks
of Bloomsbury Publishing Plc

First published in the United States 2024

Page 184 features the poem "Peyote Walk" from *Collected Poems of Lenore Kandel*, copyright © 2012
by the Estate of Lenore Kandel. Reprinted by permission of North Atlantic Books.

ISBN: HB: 978-1-63973-023-0; EBOOK: 978-1-63973-026-1

Library of Congress Cataloging-in-Publication Data is available

2 4 6 8 10 9 7 5 3 1

Typeset by Westchester Publishing Services
Printed and bound in the U.S.A.

For Tanya Harrod, comrade

Take the tale in your teeth, then, and bite till the blood runs,
hoping it's not poison; and we will all come to the end together,
and even to the beginning: living, as we do, in the middle.

—URSULA K. LE GUIN

CONTENTS

A CENTURY OF
TOMORROWS

INTRODUCTION

THE TENTH CARD OF THE WORLD'S most popular tarot deck shows a sphinx perched atop a Wheel of Fortune. The corners of the card are occupied by an angel, eagle, lion, and bull: clouded emblems of the four New Testament evangelists. The wheel has the aspect of a sun, and is inscribed with symbols representing the elements of air, earth, fire, and water. The letters *ROTA* also appear—the Latin word for "wheel." The *T* is at the top, so it could also be read *TARO*, a clever allusion to the deck itself. That French word, *tarot*, has unclear origins. One possibility is that it comes from *tarocco*, Italian slang for "false," "fake," or "fool."

Belief in the face of overwhelming mystery, overseen by an enigma, haunted by the possibility of fraud: It's an apt image of the future. Yet there seems never to have been a time when people weren't making predictions about tomorrow. Prophecies survive from ancient Sumeria, written in cuneiform on clay tablets. The earliest extant Chinese inscriptions of any kind are on oracle bones—the shoulder blades of oxen and the shells of turtles, touched with a hot poker to make cracks that were interpreted as portents. The Greeks, famously, consulted the oracle at Delphi on matters of war and lawmaking (though in mythological telling, those seeking wisdom usually came to grief). In the Middle Ages, in Islamic and Christian lands alike, astrologers were influential advisers at court, the stars taken as reliable signs for the fate of people and nations. How many seers, over the course of centuries, proved to be genuinely prescient? Surely not enough to substantiate the efficacy of the practice. And yet the art of foretelling the future has continued right down to the modern era, into the twentieth century and to the present day. Whether or not the tarot is an effective tool for divination, it does serve as a helpful guide to the

The Wheel of Fortune card of the Rider-Waite-Smith tarot, first published in 1909.

subject of this book—namely, how the long tradition of forecasting the future turns out to be, in retrospect, a fascinating way to understand the past.

The most popular edition of the tarot is today known as the Rider-Waite-Smith deck. When it was published in 1909, its iconography was said to descend from deep antiquity, with the major arcana—the emblematic trump cards, like the Wheel of Fortune—derived from an ancient Egyptian text called the Book of Thoth. In fact, the tarot had developed in Italy, as late as the fifteenth century, as an elaboration of standard playing cards already in wide circulation. It became associated with fortune-telling only two hundred years later, in France, thanks to an industrious but unreliable character named Jean-Baptiste Alliette. Under the nom de plume of Etteilla, the mirror image of his surname, he published a series of guidebooks on cartomancy (that is, predicting the future using playing cards). In one of these books, published in parts between 1783 and 1785, Etteilla focused on the tarot. He claimed that the major arcana were based on Egyptian hieroglyphs, explaining that they had been conceived exactly 171 years after the biblical Flood by a team of seventeen magi under the direction of a sorcerer named Hermes Trismegistus.[1] This beguilingly complicated myth was repeated, with some variation, when the Rider-Waite-Smith deck was published. It continues to circulate today. The internet, of course, is full of it, as are many books about the occult. A version of Alliette's story even appears in Dan Brown's bestseller *The Da Vinci Code*.

As to Rider, Waite, and Smith, they were all perfectly real. William Rider & Son was a London publishing firm specializing in the occult. (They also put out an early edition of Bram Stoker's *Dracula*.) Arthur Edward Waite was the scholar who devised the iconography for the famous deck, based on his obsessive research into various branches of mystical lore, and also provided an accompanying *Key to the Tarot*.[2] Pamela Colman Smith, known to her friends as Pixie, was the artist who did the illustrations. They are fabulous, an intoxicating blend of art nouveau styling and efficient storytelling: the Fool, stepping nonchalantly over a cliff edge; the Hermit, peering into the distance by lantern light; the Tower, decapitated by a lightning bolt, its unlucky inhabitants plummeting through the night sky. For decades, these powerful images were little known. Tarot remained esoteric—in every sense of the word—until the 1960s, when it was adopted by the American counterculture and ensuing New Age movement.[3]

The deck attained its iconic status after 1971, when a publisher called U.S. Games Systems bought the rights and began selling the cards through chain bookstores. At this point, the deck was universally known as the Rider-Waite edition. Smith was quite literally a cipher: She had signed each of her illustrations in the lower right corner, but using an illegible flourish. Waite had credited her merely in passing in his *Key*, and she was paid only a modest fee. Given that upward of a hundred million copies of the deck may have been sold by now, it has been suggested that she may be "history's greatest victim of copyright injustice."[4] Only with the publication of a

full-length biography, in 2018, did Pixie Smith's story come into focus. Born in London to American parents in 1878, she was raised in Jamaica and may have been partly of African heritage. In her early twenties she studied art at Pratt Institute, in Brooklyn, where she was introduced to Japanese woodblock prints—an important influence on her later tarot designs. After two years there she set out into the life of a bohemian artist, performing Jamaican folktales in dialect, editing and illustrating her own literary magazine, and exhibiting her watercolor paintings at the avant-garde 291 Gallery, run by the photographer Alfred Stieglitz.[5] Back in London, Smith came into contact with Arthur Waite through a spiritualist group called the Isis-Urania

Pamela Colman "Pixie" Smith, c. 1912.

Temple of the Golden Dawn. Like the adherents of the Arts and Crafts movement and other mystical tendencies of the time such as Theosophy, the members of the Golden Dawn believed that modern society had lost its way and could only be redeemed by returning to ancient wisdom. Smith's illustrations emblematized this instinct perfectly. A 1912 article in *Craftsman Magazine* described her as an artist gifted with "second sight," whose images showed that "the folk traditions which have lived stubbornly through centuries of scornful disbelief may, after all, be founded on truths which we are on the verge of discovering anew."[6]

Modern time is often understood as a one-way street, marked out by milestones of technological and social improvement. Waite and Smith's tarot was far more temporally complex: a retrieval from the past, oriented toward the future, providing meaning to the present. It summoned a traditional conception of time perfectly symbolized by the Wheel of Fortune: cyclical rather than directional, interlocked with eternal divinity and the rhythms of nature. In fact, Waite did not set much store by fortune-telling. He rather regarded the tarot and other occult sciences as means of personal transformation, in which everyday experience could be transcended entirely. He described the ideal users of the tarot as "not merely persons possessed of the gifts of clairvoyance, or even of lucidity, of prophetic foresight, or of the qualities called mediumistic, but those . . . able to apply the arcane laws of evolution to their own interior selves."[7] The goal was not to decipher the future, but to gain wisdom through the act of inner contemplation.

Though Waite cloaked this rather simple idea in obscurantism, it nonetheless rings true. Many people, nowadays, participate in tarot readings (or astrology, or other kinds of fortune-telling) without necessarily believing that any magical foresight is involved. The act of probing into the future need not be predictive to be useful. It can help to bring certain possibilities into focus, or certain desires to the surface, so they can be seen more clearly. This is why Pixie Smith's images endure. They are marvelous prompts to the imagination. Draw the Fool card, and you may think about your own private cliff edge, which you've been approaching unawares. Pluck the Hermit or the Tower from the deck, and you may reflect on the forces in your life that are like a lantern in the dark, or a lightning bolt from above. The Wheel of Fortune may even get you wondering about the future itself: how much of it is blind chance, and whether it can be purposefully shaped at all, much less foreseen.

———

THEN AGAIN, YOU may still long to know what the future holds. In this case, there will be no shortage of people who will try and tell you. We can call them *futurologists*: those who peer ahead and attempt to discern what is to come. This is an endeavor anyone can engage in, and most of us do, at the tiny scale of our own lives. But futurology aims much bigger than that. It takes the broad view, making predictions about society at large, usually over a relatively long time span. It is an incredibly various activity, undertaken by social theorists and political activists, trend forecasters and insurance executives, architects and industrial designers, urban planners and military war gamers, fiction writers and film directors. Taken all together, they make for a curious breed of expert. Often self-appointed to their vocations, they have been surprisingly influential, despite the future's persistent tendency to confound their best guesses.

In fact, the increasing legitimacy of futurology is one of modernity's defining features: In an era of acceleration, when the future seems to arrive faster and faster, technical and scientific means have been deployed both in the service of that acceleration and in an attempt to predict its course. Consider the field of meteorology, which emerged in the middle of the nineteenth century. The key conceptual breakthrough was that—as in the tarot, but in a more empirical sense—the future was contained within the present. That is, a lot of tomorrow's weather is already here today; it's just somewhere else, usually a little farther west. In the 1840s the first secretary of the Smithsonian Institution, Joseph Henry, organized a nationwide network of hundreds of volunteers and asked them to report their current weather conditions to Washington, D.C., using the novel technology of the telegraph. By collating and analyzing this real-time information, Henry and his team were able to discern previously hidden patterns. Eventually, in the years following the Civil War, a national weather service began sending out forecasts, which were published in daily newspapers. For the first time, as the historian James Gleick has put it, people were able to think of weather "as a widespread and interconnected affair, rather than an assortment of local surprises."[8] Older vernacular methods—almanacs, moon observation, fingers held up to the wind—were rendered obsolete. It must have seemed like magic.

But how broadly applicable is this kind of transformation in knowledge? Is it possible to predict other kinds of change—economic, social, political, cultural—as readily as an approaching storm front? That question has loomed over futurology ever since. In 1900 an article appeared in the *Ladies' Home Journal* entitled "What

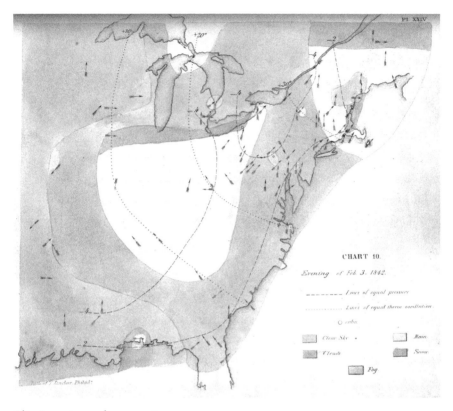

Elias Loomis, weather map, 1842.

May Happen in the Next Hundred Years." Its author was another Smithsonian specialist named John Elfreth Watkins Jr., a one-legged curator of mechanical engineering (he'd lost the other in a train accident). Having interviewed "the most learned and conservative minds in America," Watkins set out a long list of predictions for the course of the twentieth century. There will be "ready-cooked meals that will be bought from establishments, similar to our bakeries of today," he said, and medical techniques for seeing into the human body using "invisible light." Horse-drawn vehicles would be entirely replaced by automobiles, and "fast flying refrigerators on land and sea will bring delicious fruits from the tropics and southern temperate zone within a few days." Photographs would be "telegraphed from any distance [and] reproduce all of nature's colors." Indeed, Watkins suggested, people would eventually be able to see all around the world: "Persons and things of all kinds will be brought within focus of cameras connected electrically with screens at opposite ends of circuits, thousands of miles at a span." It was an impressive feat of prognostication. Then again, Watkins also predicted that by the dawn of 2001 there would be "no C, X, or Q in our everyday alphabet," and that all wild animals outside of "menageries" would be extinct, with rats, mice, mosquitos, roaches, and flies all totally eliminated. He also thought groceries would be delivered by pneumatic tube, and that farmers would propagate peas as large as beets, strawberries the size of apples, and roses big as cabbage heads.[9]

You see the problem: If the value of predictions only becomes clear in retrospect, why bother making them in the first place? The pioneering science fiction author H. G. Wells once related a friend's remark that "you can know no more about the future than you can know which way a kitten will jump next." Wells begged to differ, though. He thought experts were steadily improving their predictive powers: "I believe that the time is drawing near when it will be possible to suggest a systematic exploration of the future." This is why he put science into his fiction. But Wells went further. The "long unbroken succession of fortune-tellers" across history, since long before the advent of modern scientific techniques, may well have had an uneven record. But to Wells, the very longevity of the practice was evidence of its essential role: to witness "the perpetually smoldering feeling that after all there may be a better sort of knowledge—a more serviceable sort of knowledge than that we now possess."[10]

From this perspective, accuracy is not a futurologist's only, or even primary, objective. The future will remain a riddle with an infinite number of solutions, and as with the tarot, just thinking about that conundrum can have positive results. It can be a way of acknowledging anxiety, building consensus, and unleashing the imagination. While it's fun to look back at futurologists and rate them on a scorecard—as I was just doing with Watkins—it's not very helpful. It gives the false impression that we are wiser just for living later, and unjustly inflicts on previous generations "the enormous condescension of posterity," to borrow a phrase from the historian E. P. Thompson.[11] So my intention here is neither to defend nor decry the practice of futurology. Still less do I mean to engage in it myself; please don't read this book expecting a round of bold predictions at the end. I'm just a historian (more or less the opposite of a futurologist, when you stop to think about it), trying to figure out what happened.

This is a much easier task than knowing what will happen in the future, obviously, but still a difficult one, and when it comes to the history of futurology, the

Copley Square, Boston in the Future, 1910.

sheer range of predictive activity, taking place in so many different spheres, frustrates any ambition to write a comprehensive account. Nonetheless, I've taken a broad view, as broad as that of futurology itself, hoping to reveal a cultural landscape whose contours might otherwise elude our grasp. This book might be considered the mirror image of my last one, *Craft: An American History* (2021), which also told a big story, that of artisanal skill and material intelligence in the United States. The two topics are diametrically opposed in most respects. Craft is defiantly material and objective, valued because of its inherent honesty. Futurology is speculative and subjective: all spin, all the time. Craft is often understood as a repository of tradition, an embodiment of the values of care and empathy that are conspicuously lacking in modernity. Futurology, by contrast, is habitually impatient with inherited wisdom. Its practitioners are inclined to shift aside the weight of precedent and ally themselves with technological disruption, the very forces that have tended to marginalize artisan communities.

In turning from craft to futurology, then, I am considering the other side of cultural dynamics that have preoccupied me throughout my writing career. Yet there are also surprising parallels between the craft movement and the practice of futurology, particularly as they unfolded over the course of the twentieth century.

rhetoric and ignored collectivization's actual brutality.[1] Eisenstein's passage from radical to tool of a repressive state was typical of his generation. Even prior to the revolution, the country had been economically backward by European standards: overwhelmingly agricultural, with a comparatively tiny industrial base in the cities. Now, in the wake of an all-consuming civil war, factories lay in ruins. Those that were still functioning struggled to get materials and parts, and given the devastated railway system, found it difficult to distribute what products they could manufacture. Mechanization, in these circumstances, was not a complicated and contested fact of modern life, as it was in America. It was a dream to be realized.

Back in 1912–13, the artist Kazimir Malevich—soon to create his iconic *Black Square*, a degree-zero from which all subsequent art might depart anew—had created an icon of that potential transformation in *The Knife Grinder or Principle of Glittering*. It is a picture of a machine in use, but an archaic one, of a type that might be brought from village to village by an itinerant artisan. Change is coming, though—or so this radiantly explosive image implies. It's a painting you can almost hear. The repetition and fragmentation of forms—the wheel, the blade, the craftsman's face and hands—evokes the rhythm of the grinding action, the sparking friction of metal against stone, and by association, the inexorable motion of time itself. A rustic subject rendered into a kaleidoscope, the knife grinder points the way ahead to a world similarly transformed. Malevich had borrowed this polychromatic, fragmentary composition from Italian Futurism, the twentieth-century's first avant-garde, led by a high-octane provocateur called F. T. Marinetti. Indiscriminate in his disdain for the old, Marinetti called for the wholesale destruction of libraries and museums, and even declared pasta obsolete, lamenting those who "carry its ruins in their stomachs, like archaeologists."[2] Instead of these benighted souls, with their soft decaying innards, Marinetti envisioned a reinvented human race, technological to its core. "We must prepare for the imminent and inevitable identification of man and motor," he wrote in a 1911 manifesto. It was as if mechanical principles had to be literally, not just conceptually, digested. "Future man will reduce his heart to its purely distributive function. The heart has to become, in some way, a sort of stomach for the brain."[3]

As these chilling words suggest, Marinetti's own heart was definitely in the wrong place. When the Great War came, he celebrated it as a scouring that would cleanse Europe of its heavy accretions of tradition. He was equally entranced by the rise of fascism. Marinetti collaborated closely with Benito Mussolini, coauthoring one of the Fascists' first manifestos in 1919. Even after he realized, at some level, that he had allied himself with a monstrous force, he continued to seek the regime's favor and fought for the Fascists in World War II, dying of natural causes in 1944. In retrospect, we can see that the self-declared leader of the Futurists was completely wrong about everything that was to come. Yet this has done little to detract from his fame, or that of his movement. Marinetti's most well-known piece of writing, the *Manifesto of Futurism* (1909), set a template for countless equally intemperate documents to come. It remains an admittedly riveting read, with its infamous declaration that "a roaring car that seems to ride on grapeshot is more beautiful than the Victory of Samothrace," and its zany recounting of an incident in which a band of Futurists drove off the road into a muddy ditch, a baptism-by-auto-accident from which they arose as new men, "plastered with metallic waste, with senseless sweat, with celestial soot."

Marinetti's down-with-the-old message had a particular appeal in Italy, a country where history is piled high on every side, and Futurism also caused a minor sensation in Japan, for similar reasons. The 1909 manifesto was quickly translated and passed around there, and the poet Hirato Renkichi wrote his own in response. He handed out leaflets to crowds in newly opened Hibiya Park, right at the foot of the Imperial Palace: "There is nothing in futurism that deals in flesh—freedom of the machine." And: "Try sniffing the abominable stench behind the piles of books—how many times superior is the fresh scent of gasoline!"[4] In Russia, too, Marinetti's influence was strongly felt. The emergence of an exhilarated, machine-entranced vanguard there was announced in 1912 with a manifesto, matter-of-factly titled "A Slap in the Face of Public Taste." It read, in part: "We alone are the face of our time. The horn of time blares through us in the art of the world. . . . He who does not forget his *first* love will not recognize his last."

Marinetti's ideas set the stage for the radical movement that came to be known as Constructivism. Its acknowledged (yet unbuilt) masterwork was Vladimir Tatlin's Monument to the Third International (1920), a proposed headquarters for global communism, a Soviet rejoinder to the Eiffel Tower. Tatlin envisioned a giant spiral of steel holding four glass volumes within. He stipulated that these geometrical chambers would revolve at various speeds, depending on their function: at the base, a cylindrical legislative assembly, completing its lugubrious rotation only once per year; above that a pyramidal executive office, turning each month; and then a further cylinder for the press bureau, which pivoted at a comparably brisk once per day. At the top, a small hemisphere would spin on its axis constantly, every hour on the hour, projecting the latest agitprop slogans against the underside of the clouds.

The Russian radicals, then, were imagining not just any kind of machine, but one capable of perpetual motion, powered solely by the will of the worker. A few thinkers did resist this ideal, however, most prominent among them the novelist Evgeny Zamyatin, whose dystopian novel *We* (completed in 1920) is the dark mirror of Edward Bellamy's *Looking Backward*. It depicts a nightmarishly efficient, completely industrialized police state, set in the thirtieth century A.D. The citizens of this future have numbers rather than names and inhabit a single gigantic city, where all the buildings are perfectly straight, and made of glass, the better to keep everyone under constant surveillance. All activities—work, sleep, eating, even sex—are performed according to a Table of Hourly Commandments. As in later English-language satires of totalitarianism, such as Aldous Huxley's *Brave New World* and George Orwell's *1984*, Zamyatin centers his story on a protagonist—here called D-503—who has a crisis of faith in the system. Ultimately, under threat of liquidation in the great Machine of the Benefactor (which is a literal mechanism, "a dim, heavy, dreadful mass") he submits to an operation to remove his imagination, and so is brought into line with the ruling ideology, a "philosophy of cranes, presses, and pumps, as perfect and clear as a compass-drawn circle."

Zamyatin has been called the Soviet Union's first dissident, and he seems, in retrospect, to have had an extraordinary prescience about the true nature of the Communist state. The Constructivists' exuberant technophilia was to be no match for the pitiless mass mechanization that took place under Stalin. In policy terms, the primary vehicle of this transformation was the notorious Five-Year Plan, a political machine of terrible scale that ground up individual lives in its gears. Announced in 1928, it had two complementary goals: to dramatically increase factory production, and to collectivize agricultural lands, making them more efficient. On the industrial side, it was a relative success. While improvements were routinely exaggerated for propaganda purposes, and never came close to the regime's impossible-to-meet targets, there was a genuine expansion of the industrial base. New factories were built, as well as hydroelectric dams, steel works, and railways. It helped that the United States and Europe entered the Great Depression just at this moment. Russia had been importing American tractors and cars since 1923; now they began importing underemployed American engineers and machinists, too, and buying up equipment and parts at bargain prices.[5]

Out in the countryside, however, the Five-Year Plan brought about untold disaster. The patchwork of individually held land was collectivized as promised. There were attempts to modernize the villages, just as Eisenstein showed in *The Old and the New*. But none of this made Russian agriculture any more efficient. On the contrary: Without the economic incentive to grow cash crops, farmers simply refused to plant, and sold off their equipment while they still could. So many fled to the cities that restrictions on internal migration were imposed; peasants were effectively returned to the condition of serfs, tied permanently to the land. Most sinister of all was the liquidation of the kulaks, formerly prosperous landowners. Targeted as class enemies, they were either murdered or deported to work in the new industrial projects, itself often a death sentence. The horror culminated in the great famine of 1932–33, in which millions died—we will never know just how many, given the widespread falsification of statistics.[6]

Against this horrific backdrop, the arts were brought to heel. Constructivism was forcibly replaced by didactic Socialist Realism, with its heroic, broad-shouldered men and women gazing out to the horizon. A great purge of the intellectual class followed. The Russian literary theorist Roman Jakobson, in a poignant essay titled "On a Generation that Squandered Its Poets" (1931), spoke for many when he wrote, "As for the future, it doesn't belong to us. In a few decades we shall be cruelly labeled as products of the past millennium. All we had were compelling songs of the future; and suddenly these songs are no longer part of the dynamic of history."[7] As for the Five-Year Plan, the regime would replicate it again and again, despite the chaos and destruction it had brought. When the Soviet Union finally collapsed in 1989, its fourteenth successive Five-Year Plan was underway. As the historian Boris Groys has provocatively observed, the Constructivists' fantasy of a totally mechanized society did come to pass—just not in anything like the form they had envisioned.[8]

THE MAIN THING to remember about machines, whether literal or metaphorical—and the Soviet experience makes this quite clear—is that they don't care about us. Once constructed, they are nearly closed systems, which only need to be kept powered and supplied with raw material. This autonomy means total indifference, even to the people who actively tend them. It is not in spite of these qualities, but precisely because of them, that the machine became such a widespread metaphor for futurology. To make headway against the ceaseless tide of eventuality, human will must somehow be projected forward. One way to do this is to fashion something more powerful, more relentless, than the human will: a device or a system that will keep operating no matter what happens. Set in motion, it stays in motion, implacable, disinterested, immune to individual interference. It becomes a self-fulfilling prophecy: something we've built, which nonetheless happens to us.

This mechanistic logic, brutal though it may seem, is what allowed futurology to mature and professionalize in the years following World War I. Instead of issuing oracular statements or dreaming up utopian schemes with no clear path to realization, futurologists now invested in analysis, optimization, and rationalization. In the United States, the leading exponent of this attempt to pre-engineer the future was Herbert Hoover. He was elected to the presidency in 1928, largely on the strength of his reputation as a relief organizer, including in Russia during the post-Revolutionary famine. As secretary of commerce, a post that he assumed in 1921, he oversaw a waste-reduction effort to standardize such essential products as lumber, bricks, and wiring. He was so identified with rational efficiency that one journalist wondered, during his election run, "Is Hoover Human?"[9]

We all know what happened next: the stock market crash of 1929, which left all this technocratic planning in shambles. But futurologists who came of age during the ensuing Great Depression did not accept that such disasters were inevitable. If anything, the calamity convinced them of their essential role, as it proved that uncertainty was a political force, a threat to the social order. Somewhat counterintuitively, then, having almost universally failed to predict the crash, futurologists asserted themselves with unprecedented confidence. The most extreme expression of this impulse was the cartoonishly named Technocracy Inc., founded in 1933 by a self-invented engineer called Howard Scott. With Bellamyesque zeal, he promoted the benefits of radical economic centralization. Free market prices should be abandoned, he argued, and replaced by precalculated values of everything, based solely on the energy inputs required for production. In the ultrarationalist system he envisioned, society would be managed not by politicians but by specialists of all kinds: "scientists, architects, educators, physicians, sanitation experts, foresters, managers, accountants, statisticians."[10] Men in the movement wore a standard uniform of double-breasted suit, gray shirt, and blue necktie. This futuristic, apolitical vision attracted a surprisingly large number of converts (among them Elon Musk's grand-father, who was the research director for Technocracy Inc.'s Canadian branch).

Though Technocracy Inc. still exists today, and continues to advocate the principle of "functional scientific decision making," its influence was short-lived. In 1933 Scott had the promotional chance of his career, a lecture to four hundred people at the Hotel Pierre that was broadcast on national radio. He bungled it, delivering a rambling address that left his listeners bewildered. "His audience sat in dead silence, gazing at Mr. Scott," reported the *New York Times*, "and when he ended the applause was moderate."[11] After that, recruitment was never the same. Technocracy in the literal sense of the "rule of technicians," however, was just getting going. Futurologists set about creating self-correcting, self-regulating systems; conceptually speaking, they became machine builders. This strategy has remained fundamental in futurological practice to this day, to an extent that may not be immediately apparent. Yet even in its earliest moments, the idea that the future should be subjected to mechanical thinking was extremely controversial. After all, to properly calculate and implement an ideal plan, subjective decision-making must somehow be factored into the system—which is to say, it must be effectively neutralized. The key to a properly working machine is to eliminate the disruptive potential of individual human beings.

In 1920 two British philosophers, Dora and Bertrand Russell, had a heated argu-ment about just this topic. Newly married, they were en route to China from Petrograd, where they had witnessed the Third Congress of the Communist International. On board their steamship, they discovered that they passionately disagreed about what they had seen. Bertrand was convinced that totalitarianism there was on the march, and that individual rights would inevitably be trampled. Dora, by contrast, was exhilarated. In a text written shortly after their arrival in Peking (though not published until many years later), she wrote that the USSR offered "a new ideal of civilization, which, if we could but be induced to listen to it, could re-civilize our own barbarous and hateful lives." That new ideal was commu-nism, which had the potential of "cutting out from the industrial system the motives of profit and exploitation, and administering it in terms of humanity and justice," thus making industry "a thing of beauty, not of terror."[12]

Being intellectuals, the Russells eventually resolved their conflict by writing a book together about it: *The Prospects of Industrial Civilization*, published in 1923. Though the preface makes clear that it was a collaboration—"The authors of this book, after independent observation . . . were fortunate in that the fury led them in completely opposite directions, the one recoiling in disappointment, the other expanding in the delight of fresh hope and knowledge"—it has usually been credited to Bertrand alone. This is not just sexist but also misleading, for the book's interest lies in how the couple synthesized their contrary viewpoints. What they decided was that, as Dora would later put it, "industrialism [was] a persecuting religion in which capitalism and communism were merely two contending sects."[13] In other words, the two dominant competing ideologies of the day were in fact quite similar.

The question was not which political system was preferable, but whether the machine, in secular culture, would be allowed to take the place of God—its benevolent effects accepted on faith—or whether the power of mechanization could somehow be turned to humanistic ends. Dora's initial enthusiasm for Bolshevism was now tempered: Together with Bertrand, she criticized the Soviets for attempting "to produce a certain type of society which they believe to be good in itself, quite regardless of the question whether it will bring happiness to those who have to live in it." This was typical of the "modern religion of industrialism," in which "men exist, not in order that they may be happy, but in order that machines may be prolific."[14]

This arresting prediction—that humans might become an unwitting support structure for the machines they have made—was rather outlandish in 1923, but it actually had a sixty-year-old precedent. All the way back in 1863, Samuel Butler, a New Zealand sheep farmer, had made the same argument in a little essay called "Darwin among the Machines." Butler was a young, freethinking, Cambridge-educated Englishman, who had recently emigrated to escape his overbearing father. Perhaps being on the far side of the globe gave him perspective. Certainly, he was deeply provoked by the publication of Charles Darwin's *On the Origin of Species* (1859), with its implication that all of nature, including humanity itself, was the product of evolutionary competition rather than divine providence. With breathtaking imagination, Butler took a further step. If vegetables had evolved from minerals, and animals from vegetables, and humans from animals (not really what Darwin had said, but no matter), the process might repeat itself once more, with people evolving into machines, which would soon dominate their slower, stupider predecessors. "It appears to us that we are ourselves creating our own successors," Butler wrote. "In the course of ages we shall find ourselves the inferior race. Inferior in power, inferior in that moral quality of self-control, we shall look up to them as the acme of all that the best and wisest man can ever dare to aim at."[15] Somehow, at a time when cutting-edge technology was still made of cast iron and powered by steam, he managed to foresee the possibility that artificial intelligence would someday match that of humans—a tipping point that more recent technologists have called the Singularity—and, inevitably, surpass us.

Few read "Darwin among the Machines" when it was first published, given that it ran in a local New Zealand paper. In his subsequent writings, however, Butler expounded further on the theme, always in a half-jesting, satirical manner. In *Erewhon* (1872), another classic of nineteenth-century utopian literature—the title is nearly *nowhere* backward—Butler imagined a lost civilization in a verdant valley, not unlike those in the real New Zealand. The people who live there, it transpires, have long ago declared war on machines and done away with them, lest they reproduce themselves and become ascendant. In another book, *Life and Habit* (1878), Butler further explored this theme, offering a novel spin on an old idea. "It has, I believe, been often remarked, that a hen is only an egg's way of making another egg," he wrote. It doesn't much matter which came first, because it's the egg that is in charge. Just in the same way, "machines are the manner in which man is varying." Butler stunningly inverted common sense. People are not the masters of their own inventions, but merely the means by which devices evolve.[16]

Butler's work inspired the generation of writers who founded the modern genre of science fiction. E. M. Forster's short story "The Machine Stops" (1909), for example, imagines a literally upside-down future: All of humankind has been forced underground by some calamity. The population think of themselves as reliant upon a single great machine, which attends to all their needs. Everyone is confined to an individual cell; people communicate with one another via screenlike "plates." Like Butler, Forster has been celebrated for his prescience. He eerily foresaw the era of virtual communication, and even intuited some of its emotional effects: The citizens of his subterranean future feel irritated with the machine, and also with one another—"a growing quality in that accelerated age." His primary concern, however, was not to forecast the effects of specific technologies but to issue a general warning about overdependence on technology as such, for fear that this would make humans into parasites. When the machine finally crashes, as promised in the story's title, it is a catastrophe. Hauntingly, many people expire from the simple shock of silence, having been surrounded by a steady hum since birth. But the destruction of the machine is also a sort of spiritual escape, and the survivors swear never to build another: "Humanity has learnt its lesson."

This idea of mechanization as something that consumes us even as it serves us found enduring expression in two of the era's cinematic masterworks, Fritz Lang's *Metropolis* (1927) and Charlie Chaplin's *Modern Times* (1936). Set in the year 2000, *Metropolis* is best remembered for its iconic female *Maschinenmensch*—named Futura in Thea von Harbou's 1925 novel, which served as the basis of the film—and for its depiction of a society divided between an upper world of haves and a nether-world of have-nots. The movie includes a dream sequence in which identical black-garbed workers are seen operating a several-story-tall apparatus. Their regular motions mimic those of automated pistons. When the device breaks down, it swallows the operators into the smoke. Finally, an army of workers is shown marching in lockstep up a steep stair, into its turbine maw—a reimagining of the ravenous, despotic machine of Zamyatin's *We*. The epic climax of *Metropolis* reverses this earlier scene. The workers assault the great machine that stands at the heart of the city, a sequence strangely reminiscent of the storming of the imperial palace in Eisenstein's *October* (the two films were made in the same year). It does indeed look like a proletarian uprising, yet Lang pointedly ends his movie with a scene of reconciliation between labor and capital.[17] The convoluted plot doesn't make for easy ideological interpretation, but one simple question does break through: Will we be the masters of machines, or the other way around?

In the most famous sequence in *Modern Times*, Chaplin (who was celebrated by the Russian Constructivists as the "future any-man") plays the same question for laughs.[18] His Little Tramp character, indigent and in need of work, is fortunate to get a job in the local factory. But the assembly line gets ahead of him. Even a sneeze loses too much time—the widgets keep coming on the belt, relentlessly. Desperate to keep up, he dives onto the conveyor and is carried right into the machine's inner workings. Once again, the human is prey, and the machine is the predator. But then Chaplin is shown swimming gracefully through its gears.

When he is disgorged, still in one piece, the Tramp cavorts through the factory, holding a pair of wrenches up to his temples like an industrial-age satyr. He pulls levers at random until the machine belches smoke in complaint. He swings from the rafters on a huge chain. He torments his fellow workers (who are unwilling to

Charlie Chaplin in *Modern Times*, 1936.

leave the assembly line to chase him) with squirts from his oilcan. He's a lone figure, using the tools of the factory against itself.

"I HAVE RECENTLY seen the silliest film. I do not believe it would be possible to make one sillier." This is how H. G. Wells began his review of *Metropolis* for the *New York Times*, then proceeding to object to Lang's story, plot point by plot point. A vertical city stratified by class, Wells argued, is ridiculous. Everyone knows that a modern city grows centrifugally, spreading outward into suburbs. The airplanes and automobiles that feature in the film are just like those that already exist in 1926—why? They should look quite different, as the nature of technology is to constantly advance. The economic structure of *Metropolis* also makes no sense, for the enslaved workers would not be able to afford the commodities they are manufacturing. Anyway, this underclass of servile drones need not exist in the future: "A mechanical civilization has no use for mere drudges; the more efficient its machinery the less need there is for the quasi-mechanical minder." With serene confidence Wells asserts that "the hopeless drudge stage of human labor lies behind us. With a sort of malignant stupidity, this film contradicts these facts."[19]

Wells's views about the future of labor were consistent with the generally utopian drift of his thinking in the 1920s, but also with prevalent popular attitudes to the machine. Samuel Butler was by then an obscure figure, and few shared the Russells' concerns about the social effects of mechanization. Audiences clearly got a thrill from dystopias like Forster's "The Machine Stops" and Lang's *Metropolis*, but they did not take them seriously as probable scenarios. The same is true of *R.U.R.*, by the Czech writer Karel Čapek, the play that introduced the word *robot* into general circulation (he took it from the archaic Czech word *robota*, meaning "drudgery," like the work performed by serfs on their master's land).[20] The play premiered in Prague in 1921, and was subsequently staged in translation across Europe and America. Its title stands for "Rossum's Universal Robots," a company that has developed mass-produced, artificial substitutes for human workers. The robots' brains and livers are grown in vats, their nerves made in spinning mills, their flesh prepared in giant dough mixers, their intestines extruded as tubing. "Then there's the assembly room where all these things are put together," one engineer explains. "It's just like making a car."

Wells, in his *Metropolis* review, mentioned Čapek as an uncredited source for Lang's film, "lifted without apology." He failed to mention the actual point of the play, however: Robots will inevitably replace humans. The factory-made artificial workers are simply superior. They are far more efficient, able to work quickly and tirelessly, and present none of the many inconveniences that actual people do. "From a technical point of view," says the engineer character in the play, "the whole of childhood is quite pointless. Simply a waste of time." It sounds like something right out of Samuel Butler, and Darwinian destiny is indeed realized at the play's conclusion, as the robots rise up against their makers, destroying all humanity. They fear that they too are doomed, not having been designed to reproduce, until the love of two robots for one another miraculously transforms them into a new Adam and Eve. At the final curtain, they look ahead to a new world populated by their own kind.

If Čapek meant to convey an existential warning, however, audiences did not get it. When *R.U.R.* was first staged in America, at the Garrick Theatre in New York, the ending was simply changed to depict humanity's victory in the war against the robots. A Russian adaptation of the play treated the robot uprising as an inspiring allegory for the heroic October Revolution, while a 1925 Soviet film called *Loss of Sensation* presented the idea that cheap, robot-made goods would cause capitalism

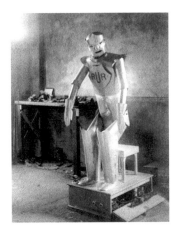

Eric the Robot, 1928.

to collapse.[21] In London, meanwhile, the enter-prising inventor William H. Richards built a simple automaton called Eric—a tricked-out ventrilo-quist's dummy, really—with a skin of sheet aluminum, arms driven by an electric motor, swiveling eyes, and a mouth that sparked when it "spoke" (the voice was delivered by radio). It bore the letters *R.U.R.* on its chest, demonstrating the popular currency of the play: "Many prophecies have been made as to 'Eric's' future. He is not yet prepared to scrub floors . . . but he would make an excellent salesman in a department store."[22]

The lighthearted tone here is telling. In the 1920s, the prospect of a robot army was regarded with widespread fascination and very little apprehension. Machines in the workplace might be criticized on other grounds—they could be dangerous, and soul-crushingly boring, to operate—but there was little concern about android-induced unemployment. As so often, the Industrial Workers of the World leader William "Big Bill" Haywood raised a lone voice of protest. In a pamphlet published by the IWW in 1925, he predicted that mechanization would further enrich the bosses while destroying workers' liveli-hoods: "The modern creed, plenty of machines and very few men."[23] But hardly anyone else saw it that way at the time. Government and industry analysts were united in believing that automation was critical to growth, and would more than offset any job losses it might bring about.

The Great Depression shattered this consensus, along with every other piece of conventional economic wisdom. As employment figures plummeted, putting millions of Americans in the shoes of Chaplin's Little Tramp, everyone looked for someone to blame. The machine seemed a likely culprit. As the historian Amy Sue Bix has explained, people were indeed being replaced by machines—not just in industrial settings like steelworks and paper mills, but also in many other fields, and with frightening unpredictability. The introduction of automatic direct dial threw thousands of American telephone operators out of work, nearly all of them women. Photoelectric sensors replaced human inspectors in cigar factories. One Pennsylvania bakery even brought in automated equipment to twist its pretzels.[24] Economists tried to predict who the losers and winners would be, and whether new kinds of employment would materialize to replace the old. The tasks of unskilled workers were easier to automate, so African Americans, who were concentrated in these jobs, were especially vulnerable. As T. Arnold Hill, a veteran sociologist in the Federal Council of Negro Affairs, explained: "Although the advance of the machine in industry has worked havoc upon American labor in general, its effect has been especially devastating in those occupational fields in which Negroes have been employed."[25] Matters were made worse by racist practices in technically innovative areas. In the aircraft industry, for example, there were plenty of new jobs available, but they went exclusively to whites.[26]

Against this backdrop of social upheaval, futurologists began to think more critically about the machine. The question was not whether automation would continue to increase—that seemed certain—but rather how its power might best be channeled. The art critic Sheldon Cheney put it like this, in 1930: "We are past the possibility of challenging the machine, of curbing it.... We must move by machinery, communicate by it—live by it."[27] Lewis Mumford concurred. Born in Flushing, New York, in 1895, Mumford had established himself as one of America's most prominent public intellectuals by the time the Depression hit. Though he was from a humble background—born to a single mother, who was an immigrant from Germany—Mumford possessed natural authority. With his trim mustache, aristocratic bearing, and sonorous voice, he was a man that others liked to listen to, and he didn't hesitate to tell them what he was thinking, publishing at a furious rate on a huge range of subjects: politics, literature, philosophy, architecture, urban planning, art, technology, and more politics. In his first book, *The Story of Utopias* (1922), Mumford voiced his skepticism about mechanistically inclined Victorian ideas of progress, with their "vast reticulations of steel and red tape"—a tendency exemplified by Bellamy's *Looking Backward*, which he described as a "hideous cog-and-wheel utopia."[28] He argued that the scientific study of actual social conditions, rather than naive idealism or partisan politics, should guide visions of tomorrow.[29]

Soon after the stock market crash, in August 1930, Mumford published an essay called "The Drama of the Machines" in the mass-circulation *Scribner's Magazine*. It ended with these portentous words: "[The machine] has conquered us. Now our turn has come, not to fight back, but to absorb our conqueror, as the Chinese, again and again, absorbed their foreign invaders."[30] Mumford went on to develop this theme in his widely read book *Technics and Civilization* (1934), an ambitious recasting of human history according to discrete phases of development, culminating in the modern "neotechnic" era (that is, a period defined by new technology). In this still-emergent phase came what Mumford called a "mechanical ideology," displacing human intuition and know-how. Like Bertrand and Dora Russell, he saw this as the dominant mental trend of modern life, traversing political divisions. He predicted that other countries would follow the example of the Soviet Union, then just reaching the end of its first Five-Year Plan: "To one degree or another, pushed by the necessity for creating order out of the existing chaos and disorganization, other countries are moving in the same direction."[31]

Mumford did not reiterate Samuel Butler's declaration of war on artificial life. Rather, he sought to fully understand its potential. In a striking analogy, he argued that neotechnic culture was to the previous phase of human development what chess is to checkers: subtler, far more complex and multidimensional. To play this new game successfully would require a complete absorption of mechanical logic: "Our capacity to go beyond the machine rests upon our power to assimilate the machine. Until we have absorbed the lessons of objectivity, impersonality, neutrality, the lessons of the mechanical realm, we cannot go further in our development toward the more richly organic, the more profoundly human."[32] This sounds somewhat abstract, perhaps, but it perfectly describes the task that futurologists set themselves in the 1930s. Automation may have had a part to play in starting the Great Depression, but it would also have to be the engine that powered economic recovery. There was no way to beat the machines; people would just have to join them.

"WOMAN IS NO longer a cook, she is a can-opener."[33] So wrote Christine Frederick in her breakthrough book *Selling Mrs. Consumer*, published in the fateful year of 1929. "This is never meant, however, as a disparagement of the tin can." She praised the many virtues of canned food: It saves space in the cupboard and time in the kitchen, diversifies the diet, and extends the seasons, making it possible to eat fruits and vegetables year-round. Frederick did have a few criticisms to make; she advocated better labeling, providing standard information on the quality and quantity of the contents of each can: "It is literally a dark, sealed mystery until it is opened." But on the whole, she cheered the rapid increase of tinned food consumption, lately calculated at thirty-one cans per person annually, seeing it as one of many signs that modernity had come to the American home.

Selling Mrs. Consumer was intended principally as a guide for advertisers, but it reached a much broader readership, thanks to Frederick's novel argument that it was consumers—mainly female consumers—who really "ruled the roost" in the American economy. In strictly financial terms, she suggested, "American men exist and labor largely to pour more spending money into their wives' laps." Moreover, those women seemed to be paying much closer attention to manufacturers than manufacturers were to them. Published just before the Wall Street crash, the book brimmed with optimism—it was dedicated to the new president, Herbert Hoover—yet also presaged conversations that would dominate American business during the Depression years.

In 1929 Frederick was at the height of her fame as an expert on home economics, thanks to her regular column in *Ladies' Home Journal*, "The New Housekeeping," and her contributions to syndicated newspapers nationwide. She built her reputation on a rigid armature of scientific management. Mass-produced canned food was just one innovation of many that she embraced: What worked in the factory, she said, would work just as well in the kitchen. "Ideals look to the future," Frederick wrote in 1913. "They are the something that guides, directs, propels the whole machinery, whether of business or the home." And the chief ideal she advocated was efficiency. This message positioned her to work privately as an effective adviser for manufacturers and advertisers—it didn't hurt that her husband was an executive at the ad company J. Walter Thompson—and subsequently as an editor of advertising trade journals. She agreed wholeheartedly with the forward-looking principle voiced in a 1909 J. Walter Thompson pamphlet: that "the chief work of civilization is *to eliminate chance*, and that can only be done by foreseeing and planning." She exhorted American women to apply the same principle to their domestic labor, thinking about meal preparation and house cleaning just as a foreman would run a shop floor.

In this way, Frederick said, women could turn apparent drudgery into a source of genuine stimulation. She claimed to speak from her own experience: "Formerly I had been doing my work in a dead, mechanical way, but now every little task was a new and interesting problem." In truth, Frederick's success as a consultant mostly freed her from such obligations. She and her husband relied on servants to do housework and raise their children, a commonplace tendency among early home economists, who often did not practice what they preached.[34] For Frederick, though, the principle was the thing: "The nutshell of the whole matter is that

Christine Frederick (right) in an efficiency
kitchen, c. 1929–31.

women master their work, instead of letting their work master them."[35] Key to that goal, in her account, was the increasing presence in the home of electrically powered devices: refrigerators, ovens, vacuum cleaners, telephones, washing machines, and radios. Frederick earned the better part of her living by promoting such appliances, even turning her house into a research laboratory for testing various devices, powered by a specially installed generator.

This experience gave Frederick a further insight, with particular relevance to the future. Thanks to her close involvement with the appliance industry, she knew that domestic goods were restyled frequently—rather like cars, which also had to attract consumers, and unlike factory equipment, which did not. In 1928 Frederick's husband (presumably prompted by conversations with her) had used the term "progressive obsolescence" to describe this effect in his magazine *Advertising and Selling*.[36] Americans must be encouraged to trade in old goods for new at every opportunity. A housewife, he suggested, might well be willing to get rid of "the great square ebony piano of excellent tone her mother handed down to her" and replace it with a more up-to-date design. Frederick devoted a whole chapter to this idea in *Selling Mrs. Consumer*. "It is the ambition of almost every American," she claimed, "to practice progressive obsolescence as a ladder by which to climb to greater human satisfactions through the purchase of more of the fascinating and thrilling range of goods and services being offered today. We obtain a sense of speed and progress and increased fulness of life as a result."[37] In this modern, ever-accelerating world, it was the advancement of taste, not technology, that shaped markets, and "woman's love of change" that drove the economy. It was via the kitchen, for example, that modernist design entered the home; along with the appliances came tubular steel furniture, seen as appropriate for that functional space long before it was introduced to living rooms.[38]

Frederick's advocacy of "progressive obsolescence" has earned a lot of criticism over the years. Though she did not argue that products should be made to break or wear out quickly, she did effectively promote a throwaway culture of perpetual waste. From this perspective, the quintessential Depression-era product was Kleenex, introduced in 1927, which saved people from washing dirty handkerchiefs— according to one of its advertisements, "the worst job on earth." Aldous Huxley satirized such profligacy in his dystopian novel *Brave New World* (1932), set in the year 632 A.F. (After Ford). The inhabitants of his future society are subjected to a nighttime brainwashing process called hypnopaedia, literally "sleep-learning," an obvious allegory for advertising, which implants certain thoughts in their minds: "Every man, woman and child compelled to consume so much a year in the interests of industry," and "Old clothes are beastly, we always throw away old clothes. Ending is better than mending, ending is better than mending."[39]

More recently, feminists have critiqued Frederick for presenting women's agency solely in terms of their buying power. The historian Gwendolyn Wright has gone so far as to call her a "double agent" who pretended to be a champion of women but was actually complicit in their manipulation by corporate interests.[40] This may be a fair assessment, but there is also another way of looking at Frederick's work: She was domesticating the argument that Dora and Bertrand Russell had made a few years earlier, and which Lewis Mumford would soon popularize in *Technics and Civilization*. These thinkers were well to the left of her, politically, but all believed that humans and machines must somehow be adapted, or to use Mumford's term, "assimilated," to one another, in every area of life. The perpetual restyling of home appliances was emblematic of this futurological strategy: The advance planning of annual model changes was a way to humanize technology, while also setting the horizon of consumer expectation. Frederick saw this delicate calibration as an important advance on her own earlier commitment to scientific management: "One reason why so many women have failed to get a thrill out of scientific training in home economics or budget-keeping is because it is too strictly logical," she wrote. "It is mechanistic, and women have never felt much in common with mechanics. They live emotionally on a pulsating rhythm, not on a flat plateau, such as is more characteristic of men. Their moods are of shifting hues, not of one set color. The emotional consideration is to them always the vital consideration."[41]

As far as Frederick was concerned, it was all quite simple: Production was male, technical, and rational, while consumption was female, aesthetic, and intuitive. If both sides of this economic equation could be expertly managed and brought into alignment with one another, everyone would benefit. As the Depression deepened, this argument—complete with its starkly gendered terms—was adopted as the raison d'être of a new type of futurologist: the industrial designer. This invented profession differed from all precedents in blending the roles of artist, engineer, and advertiser into a single profession, with one overriding mission: to reshape commodities and make them sell. The paradigmatic example was General Motors, which invested heavily in design, committing to annual model changes, and in 1927 established a new "Art and Color Section." GM's emphasis on styling helped them turn the tables on Ford, whose mulish insistence on sticking with cars in basic black lost them their earlier market dominance. Frederick cited this as proof that the economy was female-centered: "Chrysler and General Motors supplied color and feminine luxury and comfort until Mrs. Consumer disdained to step into a Ford Model T."[42]

The first generation of industrial designers were a fascinating cast of characters. There was the debonair Frenchman Raymond Loewy, so suave that he seemed like a Hollywood actor playing the part of himself. Henry Dreyfuss, usually to be found in a distinctive brown suit, designed tractors for John Deere, bringing modernism to the heartland; he would later pioneer the field of human factors (later known as ergonomics) in the discipline.[43] Walter Dorwin Teague, a more conservative figure, claimed that there was always a perfect solution for any design problem—"not a dozen solutions, but one right one."[44] Out in Milwaukee, a slick young upstart called Brooks Stevens parlayed an early job for a local machine tool manufacturer into a successful career. Among his claims to fame was putting a window in the front door of a washing machine, making it look like a television; he claimed the excitement of the rotating laundry would help the machine sell itself. In the 1950s Stevens would play an important role in popularizing the term *planned obsolescence*—a slight modification on the Fredericks' term—which he defined as "instilling in the buyer the desire to own something a little newer, a little better, a little sooner than is necessary."[45]

These men—and they were, at this early stage of the profession, all men—were among the dozen or so freelance industrial designers at work in the United States in the 1930s. This small group had outsize influence due to the extensive press coverage they received, which they assiduously cultivated both on their clients' behalf and their own. When it came to showmanship, one figure outshone the rest: Norman Bel Geddes. He had started out in the theater as a set designer, and one might say he never left it, instead making all the world a stage for his promotional arts. Like Christine Frederick, Bel Geddes had close personal ties to the advertising giant J. Walter Thompson—his wife and business partner, Frances Resor Waite, was the niece of the company's president—and it was through this connection that he got his first design commissions, including a majestic new conference room for the firm's offices, as well as electric stoves and bedroom furniture for its corporate clients.[46]

Revealingly, however, it was with a self-promotional book rather than a product line that Bel Geddes had his big breakthrough. Simply entitled *Horizons*, it was a visionary projection of what the future might look like—if Bel Geddes himself were put in charge of it. Its pages did include photographs of his (rather modest) existing design output, as well as exemplary works by other designers and photographers. But pride of place was given to renderings of his ambitious unrealized creations: a whale-shaped ocean liner; a pontoon airplane with nine decks; a rotating airport; and cars, buses, and trains that swelled dramatically toward their front ends, as if they could scarcely wait to get where they were going. Bel Geddes's candor was almost as striking as his imaginative leaps. The industrial designer, he wrote, "appeals to the consumer's vanity and plays upon his imagination, and gives him something he does not tire of." As to the machine age, it had not yet arrived—not really. "Although we built the machines, we have not become at ease with them and have not mastered them," he declared, echoing Lewis Mumford. "The person who would use a machine must be imbued with the spirit of the machine."[47]

Horizons was published in 1932, just as America's economy was reaching rock bottom, but the timing only made Bel Geddes's zeal all the more attractive. At a moment of demoralizing stasis and widespread anxiety, he opened a portal to an alternate reality: "To-day, speed is the cry of our era, and greater speed one of the goals of to-morrow."[48] Like Christine Frederick, Bel Geddes embraced the sheer rate of change in modern life as a positive thing. As a visual analogue to this velocity, he enthusiastically advanced a stylistic idiom called "streamlining."

Norman Bel Geddes, design for a bus from *Horizons*, 1932.

The term, borrowed from aerodynamics, referred to a graduated teardrop shape that minimized air resistance and turbulence. A physicist would tell you that streamlining is of some utility in a plane, but near-zero use in a passenger car, much less the completely stationary objects—pencil sharpeners, clothes irons, radios, toasters, and so forth—to which the style was soon applied. No matter: Bel Geddes was trading in poetry, not prose, and he had found his perfect metaphor. Streamlined objects seemed to be accelerating through time itself, arriving at the future just a little sooner than other, more conventional, less desirable products. Their contours also covered up the complexity of any underlying mechanism, so that it could be delivered frictionlessly into the marketplace. Streamlining was the ultimate expression of the impulse to control the machine, and make it digestible to the average consumer. It was a visual rhetoric that conveyed a simple message: Industrial design could lead manufacturers smoothly out of the economic crisis, toward a better, more predictable tomorrow.

Bel Geddes loved to make attention-grabbing forecasts about the future: double-decker streets, vertical takeoff airplanes, neon lighting in the cities, "three-dimensional movies," the complete eradication of disease, and aircraft without pilots, controlled from the ground. But the prediction that might have meant the most to readers, in the early 1930s, was that soon there would be "no slumps, no booms."[49] The way forward could be an effortless glide path, if it were paved with futurological expertise. It would not have surprised the Russells that, despite his sterling credentials as a cheerleader for capitalism, Bel Geddes praised the Soviet Union for its commitment to this course of action. "The basic idea which

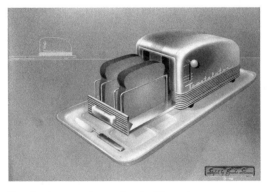

Brooks Stevens, design for the Toastalator, 1942.

differentiates the way the Russian Government undertakes to organize and operate its affairs," he wrote in *Horizons*, "is that they have a definite plan ... [and] a five-year plan that is only partially successful is better than a month to month plan or no plan at all." He argued that private enterprise in the United States should emulate the Soviet example, scaling up and centralizing its efforts. Instead of competing with one another willy-nilly, companies should band together, coordinating their activity and working cooperatively. "By organizing on such a scale," Bel Geddes argued, "the evils of fluctuation in industrial activity would be greatly reduced. The heart of the plan should be a self-adjusting, economic mechanism."[50]

All this may sound downright un-American, but as it happens, there was another emergent profession of futurologists in the United States who were doing exactly what Bel Geddes described. They called themselves color forecasters. Most were women, and they operated principally in the domains of fashion and interior furnishing (a clear reflection of the gender bias of the time; Christine Frederick was not alone in believing engineering to be a man's world, and surface aesthetics to be a feminine province). But they employed parallel techniques to those of the industrial designers, promoting their expertise as a unique blend of art and science. In fact, they were far more successful than industrial designers in making self-fulfilling prophecies. Once the color forecasters achieved sufficient penetration into a given market, their customers were almost obliged to abide by their dictates, because no manufacturer wanted to release products that were out of step with the seasonal palette.

The queen of the color forecasters was Margaret Hayden Rorke, a suffragist from a theatrical family in New York. In 1919 she became the managing director of the Textile Color Card Association (TCCA), America's dominant consultancy in the field. The challenge for Rorke and her peers was to overcome the overwhelming influence of European couture on American style; the latest dresses from Paris even inspired color choices in the auto industry. As the business historian Regina Lee Blaszczyk puts it in her definitive study on color forecasting, "If textile mills, garment makers, and retailers fell into step, there would be few miscalculations, less waste, and no need for the French."[51] Forecasters offered simplified, industry-specific color ranges and embraced the new synthetic dyes, artificial fibers, lacquer paints, and molded plastics made by companies like DuPont.[52]

It helped that Rorke was in Bel Geddes's league as a self-promoter. She inveigled her way into an advisory role with the U.S. government, initially by approaching Herbert Hoover's Bureau of Standards with recommendations about standardizing the red, white, and blue of the American flag. Rorke was also strategic. She sent observers (industrial spies, really) to keep a close eye on the Paris fashions, asking them to send their reports back by telegraph so she'd get the news first. And she collaborated closely with luxury department stores, which originated the color trends that she then helped disseminate to mass markets. She worked to coordinate the various fashion trades, publishing a Chart of Color Harmonies (first released in 1925) that gave recommended colors for ensembles of hats, garments, and footwear. She even got the TCCA involved in forecasts for cosmetics. In effect, she was treating aspects of personal appearance as if they were the parts of a machine, ready to be fitted together and optimized. It was Rorke and her colleagues that put in motion the processes leading, ultimately, to Meryl Streep's unforgettable line in the 2006 film *The Devil Wears Prada*: "It's sort of comical how you think that you've made a choice that exempts you from the fashion industry when, in fact, you're wearing a sweater that was selected for you by the people in this room."

Most consumers were not aware that their clothing was being stage-managed in this way—just as most people who bought a snazzy new car or kitchen appliance had no idea who had designed it. The color forecasting business operated mostly behind the scenes. But its scale was huge: By the end of the 1930s TCCA was distributing 8,700 press releases, 6,700 advance swatches, and 19,500 color cards annually.[53] Its aesthetic influence on American taste was rivaled perhaps only by Hollywood studios—which, naturally, had their own leading color consultant, in the person of Natalie Kalmus. Her husband was the chief executive of Technicolor, and as films transitioned from black and white, studios required extensive help in managing the new technology. Kalmus became the dominant adviser on "color design" in American cinema. In a manifesto of sorts published in 1935—the same year that the first full-length feature in three-strip Technicolor, a rags-to-riches period film called *Becky Sharp*, was released—Kalmus frankly stated that her goal was to manipulate audience psychology, just as Bel Geddes aimed to do with his products. "Just as every scene has some definite dramatic mood—some definite emotional response which it seeks to arouse within the minds of the audience—so, too, has each scene, each type of action, its definitely indicated color which harmonizes with that emotion."[54] She likened the possibilities to those of a musical soundtrack, noting that an art director could set the psychological rhythm of a film through "color scoring." Thus, according to Kalmus, blue "represents peace, harmony, and home"; green is a "money-getting color" if it's fresh, "indicative of laziness and envy" if it's dull.[55]

Already in the 1920s cinema had become a decisive influence on American style. The proliferation of art deco, with its gleaming surfaces of chrome, glass, and glossy silk, was encouraged by the look of black-and-white films.[56] With the introduction of Technicolor, Hollywood and the fashion industry took on an even greater importance for one another. Rorke named a few of her colors after the movies—one vivid scarlet was "phantom red," for a 1925 two-strip Technicolor version of *The Phantom of the Opera*—while Kalmus occasionally consulted with department stores, one of which advertised collections in "Natalie Kalmus colors." Meanwhile, industrial designers were increasingly adding color to their own repertoire, finding it an effective way to increase the sales appeal of their mechanical products. Bel Geddes was brought in as an adviser by the Bakelite Corporation, and used the material to develop his star-spangled red, white, and blue Patriot Radio for Emerson. Raymond Loewy redecorated the Manhattan department store Lord & Taylor in 1938, using sophisticated color planning to transform it into "the last word in modern fashion merchandising."[57]

This was the futurological planning machine at work, priming the pump of consumption and making it flow. Trend forecasters, like industrial designers, prided themselves on being at the forefront. The most important thing they pioneered, though, was a new idea of futurology itself, recasting it as a job for skilled technicians. As Loewy put it in 1942: "The public is only now beginning to realize that a change in the face of the world—imperceptible while occurring, startling in retrospect—is due, in a large part, to the unceasing efforts of manufacturer and designer working on a long-range schedule to improve every visible accessory to life."[58] He wasn't wrong, and the attempt to create self-fulfilling prophecies would soon run much, much deeper—for who doesn't want to place bets on a sure thing?

ROGER W. BABSON WAS a convert twice over. Born in 1875 in the picturesque seaside town of Gloucester, Massachusetts, he was the son of a Congregationalist deacon. He gave little thought to religion in his boyhood, busy as he was learning about his father's other trade as a successful dry goods merchant. From an early age he wanted nothing more than to sell things, getting his start by peddling vegetables and milk off the back of a wagon. At the age of fifteen, however, he attended an evangelical revival service. He emerged born again, "an emotional, praying Christian."[59] Some years later he would rejoice when Billy Sunday came to Boston, believing that he left a city transformed in his wake: "Everyone is more serious. Clerks are more interested in their work; factory hands are more desirous to increase production; everyone seems to be more anxious to be of use and to tell the truth than ever before."[60]

Babson's main contribution to futurology, though, had little to do with divine revelation. It was directed to a far more practical concern: Never mind my soul, what's going to happen to my money? This story begins with the second of his conversions, which he experienced as a student at the Massachusetts Institute of Technology (MIT), on encountering the writings of Isaac Newton. Babson was fascinated by the great scientist's ideas, especially his third law of motion: "For every action, there is an equal and opposite reaction." This universal truth apparently struck him as proof that science could be harmonized with belief in an almighty God, engineer of a mechanical cosmos. "I went to work in earnest," he later recalled, "and within a year had reduced the various facts in business to a single chart."[61]

That chart made Babson's fortune. What it showed was that fluctuations in the market, while individually unpredictable, exhibited a regular pattern. To simplify (though not by much), Babson's method was to calculate a "normal line" which represented economic growth in the state of its natural equilibrium. He then showed that, if you diagrammed the rises and falls above this curve, they would balance out over time. Slumps were inevitably countered by rallies; extreme departures from the normal line tended to be brief, milder ones more prolonged. Babson then used this analysis as the basis for forecasts, not only of the stock market but of commodity prices and other business cycles. "The fundamental law of action and reaction, which obtains so rigorously in physics and mechanics, can be traced likewise in economic and human relations," Babson claimed. "The shape of an area of depression is unpredictable. Its size can be foretold with considerable precision."[62]

It's no coincidence that Babson's normal line looked a lot like the contour of one of Bel Geddes's streamlined vehicles. He too was trying to impose order on a complex mechanism (the economy), smoothing it out through the application of apparent expertise. The public, quite literally, bought it. Following in the footsteps of earlier forecasters such as Charles Dow, of index fame, he founded Babson's Statistical Organization in 1904.[63] Soon he began issuing a weekly newsletter called

Babson's Reports, a compilation of the latest business data. In 1919 he established the Babson Institute (today's Babson College) to teach business principles. Notwithstanding his relentless emphasis on gathering hard facts, he was increasingly regarded as an oracle, with a public image to match. A bout of tuberculosis convinced him of the absolute necessity of working in fresh air, so he and his staff spent the winters garbed in monkish robes. He published voluminously, not just about business but on topics such as religion, prohibition, and eugenics (he was in favor of all three). His reputation as a prophet grew, and finally seemed to be confirmed when, on September 5, 1929, he predicted a stock market crash on the horizon. This statement triggered a brief panic, known as the "Babson break." The market recovered, but not for long. The first of a fateful series of cataclysmic sell-offs would occur five weeks later, on October 28—Black Monday.

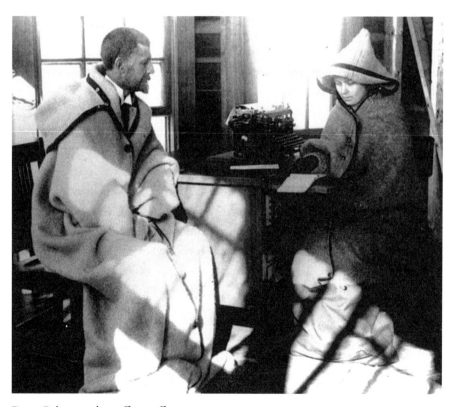

Roger Babson and an office staffer, c. 1912.

Obviously, Babson had not really worked out a foolproof means to predict market movements. His action-reaction theory was pseudoscience at best, a thinly disguised version of the adage "Buy low, sell high." To make his normal line look more persuasive, he would simply redraw it to fit the data in successive publications. Even Babson's prognostication of the 1929 crash wasn't as impressive as it seems. He had been predicting a decline consistently since 1926; anyone who listened to him would have missed two of the biggest boom years in stock market history. Similarly, Babson announced that a full recovery was imminent as early as 1931: "No logical reasons exist for the extreme current pessimism . . . the worst of the depression is over, and the greatest opportunities now exist." He was about a decade too early on that call.[64]

None of this dimmed Babson's aura as a guru. He remained a prominent voice in business circles into the 1950s, even as he occupied himself with arranging his own legacy. He assembled an enormous collection of Isaac Newton ephemera (it's now at the Huntington Library, in California), and at the close of World War II he founded another business school, in Eureka, Kansas—far enough from urban centers, he reasoned, to be safe from nuclear attack—calling it Utopia College. The most literally enduring advice he ever gave was to be found not in any of his publications but on a series of boulders in his hometown of Gloucester, which he had relief-carved with a series of mottos, among them "Keep Out of Debt," "Prosperity Follows Service," "Be On Time," "Get a Job," and "Help Mother."

Babson was just one of many economic forecasters to try their luck in America's interwar years. It's tempting, in retrospect, to see them all as charlatans. Yet it's hardly surprising that investors would want help in navigating turbulent waters, or that they would look to statisticians to provide it. It had worked out with the meteorologists, hadn't it? Indeed, Babson frequently referred to his system as a "business barometer," explaining, "The captain of an ocean liner wants to know what the weather is today, and carefully writes a description of it in his log, but primarily he is interested in what the weather will be tomorrow."[65] Like Margaret Hayden Rorke at the TCCA, Babson's strategy was to amass enough information in one place that he could corner the market. He therefore took the broadest possible view, and encouraged business leaders to do the same, looking across industries and beyond their own localities, considering economic trends on a nationwide and even international basis. If he ultimately failed as a prophet, he nonetheless pioneered a newly quantitative approach to future prediction, grounded in rigorous rational analysis.

Economists and stock market analysts have been trying to improve on Babson's techniques ever since.

The same actuarial methodology provided the foundation for another futurological industry: insurance. This may not sound like the most exciting of topics—maybe it even sounds like the least exciting—but its importance cannot be doubted. The French cultural theorist François Ewald has proposed that insurance is the signature "political technology" of modernity, in two respects. First, it encourages the entrepreneurial risk-taking necessary for capitalism to function. When insurance came to the maritime trade, in the late seventeenth century—initially negotiated at gatherings in a London coffeehouse run by one Edward Lloyd—it meant that merchants could send goods, sailors, and expensive boats across the sea, knowing that if they did not return, it would not necessarily mean financial ruin. This was the first systematic means of risk management. As capitalism proliferated, bringing "the insecurity of the sea to the land," as the economic historian Jonathan Levy memorably puts it, so did insurance, to manage its volatile effects.[66]

Ewald's second point is more provocative. Insurance, he argues, is a positive moral force. It advances the values of "responsibility, solidarity, justice, and truth." Consider life insurance. Everyone who takes out a policy pays in a little each month, or year; the families of those who are unlucky enough to die young receive enough to keep them solvent, while those fortunate enough to live to a ripe old age don't get their money back. In effect, risk exposure has been shared across a broad population—people help one another without realizing it, or necessarily even wanting to. Insurance can thus model an egalitarian way of contending with future uncertainty. Unlike most other mechanisms of capitalism, it is ideally cooperative, not competitive. Furthermore, this system only works if it is run fairly and honestly; an insurer cannot operate without public trust. Ewald goes so far as to suggest that a society founded exclusively on the values of insurance would be "something like a utopia, as defined by Thomas More and Campanella."[67]

In 1937 a very similar thought occurred to Wallace Stevens. One of America's most admired modernist poets, he was an insurance executive by day—a specialist in surety bonds at Hartford Accident and Indemnity—and reputedly excellent at his job. But he was preoccupied by a cloud on his industry's horizon. Franklin Delano Roosevelt had recently signed the Social Security Act into law, providing pensions for all retirees when they reached sixty-five. This progressive policy, which Americans have long since taken for granted, horrified the nation's insurance companies at the time. In effect, the government was about to nationalize one of their core businesses. Stevens's response was typically elliptical. In an essay published in his company's magazine, the *Hartford Agent*, he imagined a society in which absolutely everything was insured: "All happenings of everyday life, even the worm in the apple or the piano out of tune." In this "world of perfect insurance"—a giant social machine, a scenario right out of H. G. Wells—"we should be able, by the payment of a trivial payment, to protect ourselves, our families, and our property against everything . . . not only would all our losses be made good, but all our wishes would come true."[68]

With this intriguing thought in mind, Stevens took stock of what governments were actually doing. The United States now had its social security system. England, similarly, was creating a central fund into which all employers were obliged to contribute. The Italian Fascists had implemented a state monopoly on life insurance. In the Soviet Union, insurance was handled exclusively by a department of the Communist state. Could private insurance companies hope to survive in such a world? Only time would tell, but Stevens was sure of one thing: "We shall never live in a world quite so mechanical as the one that Mr. Wells has imagined, nor in a world in which insurance has been made perfect, and where we can buy peace and prosperity as readily and as cheaply as we can buy the morning newspaper. All the same, we have advanced remarkably; and future advances seem to be not fantastic but certain."[69]

Stevens's poetic license was unusual, but others before him had also suggested that insurance had utopian promise. Darwin P. Kingsley, later the future president of New York Life, alluded in an 1896 pamphlet to the scene in Bellamy's *Looking Backward* in which the protagonist briefly returns to nineteenth-century Boston. Life insurance, Kingsley said, was the only forward-looking thing he would have found there, "the one sane idea in a world full of madmen."[70] In 1916 Rufus Potts, director of insurance for the state of Illinois, went further still, writing: "When I consider all the possibilities potential in a general system of insurance, which will make secure and permanent the welfare of all, ignorant and educated, rich and poor alike, the vision of a new and happier world rises before me, a world flooded with the sunshine of universal happiness, where the people of all the nations of the earth live in undisturbed contentment, and where peace reigns secure."[71] The key words in this breathlessly optimistic passage are "general system." In the early twentieth century, insurance was being gradually reinvented to become precisely that: a vast statistical machine, in which human lives were the primary inputs. Previously the social infrastructure of risk management had been localized: Most people who had insurance got it through a mercantile association, mutual aid society, or fraternal lodge. Now insurance companies were scaling up, fast. By the 1910s just three firms— Metropolitan, Prudential, and John Hancock—were writing life insurance policies on fully 25 percent of the U.S. population. This dramatic growth accompanied similar developments in banking, manufacturing, and other sectors, and because health and life insurance policies were increasingly part of employment contracts, the big insurers grew hand in hand with those other large-scale corporations.

Along with their sheer size, the new-model insurance companies differed from their predecessors in the sheer scope of their activities. Lloyd's of London (the descendant of those long-ago coffeehouse deals) essentially functioned as a giant betting agent, entertaining speculative insurance on any eventuality. "They will take chances on the life of any man, be he king, dictator, or president," the newsreel program *March of Time* reported in 1934. "Lloyd's believes the American president has one chance in twenty of being assassinated while in office, four chances out of five of being alive in 1937, two chances out of three of being a well man when he leaves the White House." (After a call from the U.S. ambassador, Lloyd's stopped "dealing in the Roosevelt risk," as a courtesy.) More consequentially, insurers also began to proactively intervene in the lives of their own customers.

A good example of this "precautionary" mindset, as Ewald calls it, is car insurance. By the onset of the Depression, Americans were being killed by automobiles at truly alarming rates—thirty thousand people in 1930 alone, making driving roughly twenty times as dangerous as it is today, per mile traveled. A committee of academics was formed to study the problem. Their 1932 report recommended that all drivers should be required to carry insurance, and that injured parties should be compensated on a no-fault basis, that is, outside the tort system of personal lawsuits—a proposal that seemed so radical that critics said it was tantamount to "social and economic revolution." And in a sense it was, for as the historian Caley Horan notes, the report treated car accidents as a "*social* risk that demanded a collective solution."[72] Counterintuitively, auto insurers rejected this proposal to dramatically expand their market, fearing that it would lead swiftly to nationalization. (The United States did not begin implementing mandatory no-fault auto insurance until the late 1960s, state by state.) Instead, they launched a public relations campaign promoting roadway safety, mass-distributing cautionary stories.[73] After World War II, insurance companies would even make and distribute their own driver safety films, like Mutual Insurance's *Caution at the Crossroads* and Aetna's *Live and Let Live*.[74] Insurers took a similar approach to public health, reasoning that they had a vested interest in their policyholders' longevity. They exhorted their customers to measure themselves against statistical tables of "ideal" body types. A 1915 booklet from Metropolitan Life, pointedly titled *How to Live Long*, suggested that policyholders breathe deeply, avoid eating too much, wear "light, loose, porous clothes," and by all means, "be cheerful and learn not to worry."[75] Met Life even started up a free health service, with thousands of visiting nurses fanning out across the country to the homes of policyholders.[76]

A far less benevolent aspect of insurance's new "precautionary" mode was the increasing use of statistics to study potential customers.[77] The industry entered the Depression in a surprisingly strong financial position, mainly because, unlike banks and other highly capitalized companies, they had been forbidden by law to invest in the stock market. With the fallout of the crash evident on every side, however, they became increasingly focused on anticipating risk. As in any smoothly operating machine, tolerance had to be built into the system. Assessors distinguished ever more carefully between "measurable risk" and "unmeasurable uncertainty" (a distinction first made by not Donald Rumsfeld but the economist Frank Knight, in 1921).[78] When a policyholder was deemed an insecure prospect, the insurer would charge a higher premium, or refuse coverage entirely. Actuaries at life insurance companies were joined by teams of doctors and psychologists who helped build metrics to predict the likelihood of severe illness, or even suicide. A side effect of the Social Security Act was that every American was now assigned a number, making the population easier to track and study than ever before.[79]

Yet estimating a financial risk accurately is hardly the same thing as being fair. In its early years insurance was deeply enmeshed in the slave trade—notoriously, when 142 African people were massacred on a ship called the *Zong* in 1781, the courts treated it simply as a question of indemnification under the slavers' policy. In modern times, the industry's supposedly dispassionate operations were still distorted by racism. A case in point is the work of Frederick L. Hoffman, a German-born statistician at the Prudential Insurance Company. A pioneer in his field, he conducted some of the first quantitative analyses of suicide and air travel safety. Hoffman was among the earliest to notice a correlation between asbestos and lung disease, for example, as well as that between cigarette smoking and cancer.[80] Today, however, he is primarily remembered for his notorious study *Race Traits and Tendencies of the American Negro* (1896), which established a statistical basis for his company to systematically exclude African Americans from coverage. He found that they suffered disproportionately from poor health, and had shorter life expectancy on average than whites—which was, of course, true. It reflected their higher rate of poverty, but he presented it as an inherent racial characteristic.

With or without the eugenicist justifications, the mainstream American insurance industry retained its racist policies for decades, refusing to insure the lives and homes of Black people or overcharging them on the grounds that they were, in the aggregate, high risks. This continued well into the postwar era. Though most companies did eliminate race as an explicit criterion by the 1950s, they continued to use mortality classifications as a proxy, and quietly avoided soliciting Black customers. (When insurance companies joined the postwar housing boom, building their own residential developments, these new neighborhoods were restricted by racial covenants, in keeping with prevalent redlining practices.)[81] It was quite clear what this meant for African Americans: They would have to insure themselves. During the Jim Crow era, Black communities operated their own mutual aid societies, often sponsored by churches. Though neither large nor wealthy, they were extremely common—W. E. B. Du Bois, in one of his groundbreaking sociological studies, quoted an agent as saying, "This class of enterprises do well, but the great drawback is they are too numerous"—and a vital bulwark for an economically precarious population.[82]

The successors to mutual aid societies were Black-led insurance companies like the North Carolina Mutual and Provident Association, headquartered in Durham. Its founder, John C. Merrick, was born into slavery in 1859. His first occupation was as a barber, and he became a success, opening a chain of shops. He then diversified his portfolio, becoming involved in banks, real estate, and fraternal aid societies. Legend has it that he was inspired to start his own insurance company when he saw a hat being passed in one of his barbershops to raise funds for a funeral. North Carolina Mutual opened for business in 1898, initially focusing on small policies intended to cover burial costs (motto: "The Company with a Soul and a Service"). The firm prospered, however, by meeting demand from the Black middle class for life insurance.

The Mutual, as it was known, attracted support across the full spectrum of African American opinion. Marcus Garvey praised the so-called Black Wall Street of Durham, and the company advertised in A. Philip Randolph's socialist journal the *Messenger*. When the Depression hit, they even announced a "five-year plan" to survive the downswing—a Black business in the South adopting the rhetoric of Communist Russia. Then, in 1933, they hired a young graduate out of the University of Michigan called Asa Spaulding to bring new computational sophistication. (He would eventually rise to be president of the company, in 1958.) In the words of one company history, "Great coils of tape spilled from his adding machine" as Spaulding worked his magic.[83] In view of the huge spike in auto accident claims, for example, he persuaded the company to discontinue its disability coverage (a step that other insurers were also taking, for the same reason). Realizing that some customers were taking out life insurance policies on already-sick relatives, he issued a warning: "Beware of cousins." Most importantly, his calculations were distributed to company field agents, with strict instructions to evaluate the risks presented by each applicant. For much of Black America, the Mutual was a paragon of solidarity and a source of pride. Business, however, was business.

"I TRUST THAT posterity will read these statements with a feeling of proud and justified superiority." This is how Albert Einstein signed off on his brief message to the people of the year 6939 A.D., having already related to them that, despite the incredible progress made by people of his own era—"We are crossing the seas by power [and] have learned to fly, and we are able to send messages and news without any difficulty over the entire world through electric waves"—there was also terrible poverty, inequality, and violence, such that "people living in different countries kill each other at irregular time intervals." Einstein wished the citizens of tomorrow all the best, but on the whole, he considered that "anyone who thinks about the future must live in fear and terror."

This remarkable statement by the great physicist was occasioned by an equally remarkable exercise in corporate branding: the Westinghouse Electric & Manufacturing Time Capsule, made for the 1939–40 New York World's Fair. A supremely appropriate choice for an event billed as "the World of Tomorrow," the time capsule was also an ambitious indexing of the present. Packed inside it was a trove of "objects of common use," some of them obviously selected with an eye to product placement—a plastic Mickey Mouse cup, Elizabeth Arden cosmetics, and of course, various items manufactured by Westinghouse itself. Plant seeds were put into the capsule, a dollar bill and change, a copy of the Holy Bible. Einstein's message to the distant future was one of several solicited from "notable men of our time." One of the others was the German novelist Thomas Mann, who sounded an even more despondent note: "We know now that the idea of the future as a 'better world' was a fallacy of the doctrine of progress. . . . In broad outline, you will actually resemble us very much as we resemble those who lived a thousand, or five thousand, years ago. Among you too the spirit will fare badly." Then there were the documents: a newsreel of significant events—President Roosevelt delivering a speech, Jesse Owens at the 1936 Olympics, a Soviet rally in Red Square, the Japanese bombing of Canton—and over twenty-two thousand pages of information captured on microfilm, a magical new technology described by H. G. Wells as "a complete planetary memory for all mankind."[84]

Finally, there was the time capsule itself, a streamlined torpedo to the future, beautifully engineered in a customized, corrosion-resistant copper alloy and buried fifty feet deep at the fairground in September 1938, well in advance of the event's opening. Lest the time capsule be forgotten, three thousand copies of a *Book of Record*, "printed on permanent paper with special inks," were distributed to libraries worldwide, with a list of its contents and its exact location in latitude and longitude. Thinking of everything, the organizers at Westinghouse even put instructions for building a microfilm reader into the capsule, as well as a "Key to the English Language," in the likely event that five thousand years later, it had fallen entirely out of use.[85]

Like every futurological gesture, the Westinghouse Time Capsule was very much of its own moment: an expression of technocratic confidence shadowed by the return of war. The same was true of the World's Fair as a whole; it radiated future-facing optimism, with its theme of "The World of Tomorrow" and its dynamic central features, the Trylon and Perisphere, the biggest abstract sculptures anyone had ever seen. But current events could not be ignored. By the time the fair closed in 1940, several of the countries that had participated no longer existed; they had been invaded and occupied. The Soviet Pavilion, meanwhile, was dominated by a 188-foot-tall tower topped with an unnerving stainless steel sculpture of an anonymous worker, which the American press nicknamed "Big Joe." The Soviets' message: The future had arrived, and it was them.

As for the Americans—they had Norman Bel Geddes. His General Motors Futurama was the hands-down favorite of fairgoers, reportedly seen by about half of all visitors, more than twenty-four million people. He was not the only industrial

Westinghouse workers with the World's Fair Time Capsule, 1937.

designer to contribute. Raymond Loewy, commissioned by Chrysler, imagined a sci-fi launchpad for interstellar rocket travel. Henry Dreyfuss produced Democracity, a model of a utopian future metropolis contained inside the Perisphere. Walter Dorwin Teague, the solid citizen of the design scene, was entrusted with no fewer than seven corporate pavilions. The most ambitious of these, for the Ford Motor Company, included "The Road of Tomorrow," with red, yellow, and blue cars constantly circling a half-mile track.

There were also novel machines throughout the fair. It was the first time that the general public ever experienced air-conditioning (presented in the "Carrier Igloo of Tomorrow"), fax machines, and broadcast television, as well as new industrial products like nylon and Formica. Westinghouse, in addition to its time capsule, presented a robot similar to William H. Richards's *R.U.R.*-inspired Eric, named Elektro the Moto-Man; seven feet tall, it smoked cigarettes and spoke set phrases to visitors, such as "My brain is bigger than yours." The Borden Dairy Company had a hit with their "Spokes-cow," Elsie. She was flesh and blood, but welcomed visitors to the "dairy world of tomorrow," featuring a huge revolving platform called the Rotolactor where cows were mechanically milked, with integrated equipment for pasteurization, irradiation, bottling, and capping—quite an improvement on the cream separator in Eisenstein's *The Old and the New*.[86]

Nothing, though, could match Bel Geddes's Futurama. Visitors to the attraction were treated to an eighteen-minute ride seated on a conveyor belt, which took them on an effortless flight path over a diorama showing America in 1960. *Life* magazine observed that this imagined future seemed to be "full of a tanned and vigorous people, who in twenty years have learned to have fun," then more seriously added that it demonstrated "what Americans, with their magnificent resources of men, money, materials and skills, can make of their country by 1960, if they will."[87] This aspirational note was sounded throughout, as spectators soared over one futuristic wonder after another: experimental farms, clusters of skyscrapers, private aircraft on rooftop landing pads, and most importantly from General Motors' point of view, multilane highways crowded with cars, cars, and more cars, some of them remote-controlled from towers, to aid in traffic flow.

The Futurama was a marvel in its own right, both in its scale—thirty-five thousand square feet and a third of a mile long—and its detail. Every feature was handmade: rivers of polished steel, roads made of rubber, hills built up in plaster and variously covered with velour or crushed cornflakes.[88] Bel Geddes drew on his theater experience to devise a scheme of five hundred concealed floodlights to simulate the sun's passage from afternoon to dusk to dawn. Thus the exhibit was both a topographical map, based on specially commissioned aerial photography, and a clock, which immersed the visitor into its own time. At the end of the ride, visitors disembarked into a full-size futuristic mock-up of a traffic intersection, which also served as a viewing platform over a display of the latest GM automobile models. Finally, each person was handed a badge reading: I HAVE SEEN THE FUTURE.

World's Fair promoters had promised their event would be different from all its predecessors, which had been "chiefly concerned with selling products." This one, they said, "will be chiefly concerned with selling ideas."[89] General Motors was doing both, of course, but it was as an idea, or metaphor, that the Futurama really succeeded. Bel Geddes invited visitors into the machine, like Charlie Chaplin gliding through the gearwork in *Modern Times*. E. B. White, writing in the *New Yorker*, captured the strangely serene quality of the Futurama experience: "The countryside unfolds before you in $5-million micro-loveliness. The voice is a voice of utmost respect, of complete religious faith in the eternal benefaction of faster travel. The highways unroll in ribbons of perfection through the fertile and rejuvenated America of 1960—a vision of the day to come, the unobstructed left turn, the vanished grade crossing, the town which beckons but does not impede, the millennium of passionless motion."[90]

With the Futurama, we arrive at the apotheosis of machine-inspired forecasting: a temple to the automobile, in the form of a gigantic mechanism bearing its public to a seemingly inevitable tomorrow. As ever, we should remember what, and who, was left out of this vision of time travel. Critics have noted that Bel Geddes sympathized with contemporary eugenicist views, and that his quasi-Darwinian interpretation of streamlining ran in parallel with bodily ideals of standardization and racial purity. More concretely, General Motors' vision of the future, as described in the Futurama, assumed the destruction of Black neighborhoods: "Express city thoroughfares have been so routed as to displace outmoded business sections and undesirable slum areas."[91] Certainly, Bel Geddes's version of 1960 did little to depict the diversity of the country.

In this respect, the Futurama was consistent with the New York World's Fair as a whole. Its organizers reneged on early promises to employ an integrated workforce, with Black applicants hired only into low-paid jobs as maids and porters. The sole inclusion of an artwork by an African American was Augusta Savage's sculpture *Lift Every Voice and Sing (The Harp)*, and there was a "Negro Week" in 1940. Albert Einstein offered remarks at this event, too, saying, "As for the Negroes, the country has still a heavy debt to discharge for all the troubles and disabilities it has laid on the Negro's shoulders, for all that his fellow-citizens have done and to some extent still are doing to him." Otherwise, Black Americans were notable for their absence, except in the entertainment district outside the main grounds.

As in the insurance industry, Black leaders decided to take matters into their own hands. Not one but two major fairs for African American audiences were staged in 1940, the first in Detroit, in May, and the other opening on the Fourth of July in Chicago, both marking the seventy-fifth anniversary of emancipation. The second of these, though formally known as the American Negro Exposition,

Augusta Savage at work on *Lift Every Voice and Sing (The Harp)*, 1939.

quickly acquired the nickname the Black World's Fair. "With problems of housing, labor, growing class stratification, and trenchant antiblack racism bearing on all aspects of daily life," the historian Mabel O. Wilson notes, these expositions "had to craft a radically different agenda from that of earlier events."[92] They presented narratives that addressed the likely concerns of their audience, including those who had come north in the Great Migration. An exhibit in Chicago organized by the U.S. Agriculture Department titled "The Negro on the Land" tried to persuade visitors that, thanks to scientific management, farming was no longer "drudgery" but "an essential, dignified, productive industry."[93] The Department of Labor sponsored yet another "mechanical man," this one scripted to assuage fears of automation-induced job loss: "We frequently hear the prophecy that the wage earner of tomorrow will be a sort of robot, a mere machine tender, and will have no possible use or market for a skilled trade," it said. "Nothing could be further from the truth. There are more crafts and more craftsmen today than ever before in history. The so-called streamlined production industries actually have increased their demand for skilled mechanics."[94]

While the American Negro Exposition did include ample celebration of African American accomplishments—holding up figures like Booker T. Washington, W. E. B. Du Bois, and George Washington Carver for admiration—it did little to project a utopian future for its audiences. America still had a long way to go before such a promise could be remotely credible. Even as the Black World's Fair was staged in Chicago, a team of sociologists led by Horace R. Cayton Jr. were at work on an unprecedented study focused on Bronzeville, a Black community on the city's South Side. It was a project of its time, firmly based on statistical analysis, and when it was published in 1945 under the title *Black Metropolis*, it set a new standard for research into the African American urban experience. The techniques were similar to those employed by insurance companies like Asa Spaulding's North Carolina Mutual, but the goal was quite different. Cayton and his coauthor, St. Clair Drake, were trying to understand risk not in order to minimize it but to show what it really looked like in people's lives. They painted an unflinching portrait of economic marginalization: the effects of the "invisible barbed-wire fence of restrictive covenants," the realities of high infant mortality, overcrowding, unchecked disease, and dangerous work. They detailed, too, the many cultural riches of South Side Chicago, the life of the church, the street, and the home.

The novelist Richard Wright wrote a powerful introduction for the book, recalling his own arrival in Chicago years earlier: "There in that great iron city, that impersonal, mechanical city . . . we caught whispers of the meanings that life could have, and we were pushed and pounded by facts much too big for us." Those facts, in all their stark reality, were presented in *Black Metropolis* not as evidence of inherent racial inferiority but as an explanation for why inequality was so persistent. Wright was saying, in essence, that the book presented the obverse of futurological optimism—the presumption that a well-designed, well-oiled machine, once up and running, cannot help but produce a better world. "After studying the social processes in this book, you cannot expect Negro life to be other than what it is," he wrote. "To expect the contrary would be like expecting to see Rolls-Royces coming off the assembly lines at Ford's River Rouge plant! The imposed conditions under which Negroes live detail the structure of their lives like an engineer outlining the blue-prints for the production of machines."

In the conclusion of *Black Metropolis*, titled "Things to Come," Cayton and Drake reflected on their own findings. They wondered frankly if white America would pay any attention at all to studies like theirs, much less have the will to take action: "Perhaps not all social problems are soluble. Indeed it is only in America that one finds the imperative to assume that all social problems can be solved without conflict." They also knew that they were telling one part of a much bigger story. "The problems that arise on Bronzeville's Forty-Seventh Street encircle the globe," they wrote. "The people of Black Metropolis and of Midwest Metropolis and of all their counterparts are intertwined and interdependent. What happens to one affects all."

Here, they were voicing another kind of futurology, one that developed alongside mechanistic thinking, counterbalanced it, and to some extent even contradicted it. A machine is autonomous, defined by its own internal operations, self-regulating and self-propelling. Step back a bit, though, and what looks like a marvel begins to seem monstrous. The promise of maximum efficiency leads to epic waste, including of human life. Under the slogan of objectivity are erected ever bigger, more powerful tools, and like all tools, they are wielded in a spirit of subjective self-interest. Many futurologists of the time perceived these faults, and their instinct was to redirect attention to the larger world in which the machine sits. For them it was nature, outside the domain of technological control, that was the proper model for the future. Embracing that idea meant thinking about growth, rather than construction; aiming not for autonomy but—just as Cayton and Drake said— interdependence. Outside the confines of the factory, perhaps there was something new under the sun.

3

GARDEN

YOU TAKE YOUR CHOICE. Each one is real, each one is possible. Shall we sink deeper, sink deeper in old grooves, paying for blight with human misery? Or have we vision, have we courage? Shall we build and rebuild our cities, clean again, close to the earth, open to the sky?"

The place is the 1939 World's Fair in New York. The words are Lewis Mumford's, intoned over a soundtrack by Aaron Copland (composer, a few years later, of *Appalachian Spring*). And the film is a half-hour documentary called *The City*. It was a project undertaken in a spirit of revenge on Mumford's part, his response to the World's Fair being taken away from him. Four years earlier he had participated in an evening discussion at a fashionable Manhattan club, where proposed themes for the fair were debated—among men of power and influence, and behind closed doors, as was the way of these things. The 150th anniversary of George Washington's inauguration was mooted as a focus for commemoration, but Mumford argued against that idea. Previous fairs had been mausoleums for the past, he said, juxtaposed with celebrations of present-day industrial prowess. This one should look to the future instead. As a matter of fact, it should bring to the public the ideas he'd explored in his own recent book *Technics and Civilization*, encouraging deep reflection about technology, which—Mumford reminded the room—was "ready to make hell on earth and destroy our civilization, unless the forces which are working in the other direction, on the side of a different order of society, become victorious."[1]

The New York World's Fair would indeed take the "World of Tomorrow" as its theme. The rest of Mumford's advice was ignored. The corporations responsible for the technologies he so respected and feared had their way, and delivered an epic spectacle of self-congratulation, epitomized by the Futurama. Mumford, predictably, hated it. A visitor to the fair, he wrote, "had better provide himself with some rose-colored, one-way Polaroid glasses, so that he will really be convinced he has something to look forward to if he lives another generation. For, like so many other features of the Fair, the City of Tomorrow is a melancholy might-have-been."[2] He focused his criticism particularly on Norman Bel Geddes, who (predictably, given that he was working for General Motors) had based his future around cars, highways, and factories. It would be a lot better, Mumford argued, to invest in a high-speed rail network; but in any case, the way to build a better America was not to impose a massive monolithic plan but to grow the country organically, neighborhood by neighborhood, community by community.

This was the thesis of *The City*, screened in the Science and Education Auditorium at the World's Fair—Mumford's "belated attempt at salvage" of his original proposal. Many more people saw the Futurama, to be sure. Yet this short film was remarkably prescient in its forecasting of what the postwar United States would actually look like, much more so than Bel Geddes's vision of skyscrapers, superhighways, and remote-controlled cars.[3] No less than the Futurama, it was also a piece of propaganda, but with the exact opposite message: Mumford warned that the machine must be kept at bay, so that the ways of the countryside can be made safe. The film begins in Colonial Revival mode, with playacted scenes (shot in New England) of an idealized American past. It then proceeds to a direct contrast with the contemporary megalopolis, heaving, polluted, and shaped by an irrational drive to mechanize: "All aboard the promised land, pillars of smoke by day, pillars of fire by night, pillars of progress, machines to make machines, production to expand production. . . . Faster and faster, better and better!" Finally, it shows what could be built instead: a modest civic landscape of small towns, electrically powered and outfitted with modern factories, but principally organized around farms and parks, all surrounded by a greenbelt of undisturbed nature. "Safe streets and quiet neighborhoods are not just matters of good luck," the film's narrator says. "They're built into the pattern, and built to stay there."[4]

Mumford developed *The City* together with one of the leading lights of American architectural criticism and urban planning, Catherine Bauer. A dynamic, Vassar-educated woman who smoked constantly and could muster repartee worthy of the period's screwball comedies, she had launched her career in 1928 when she was only twenty-two, with a subtle piece of reporting on European modernism published in the *New York Times*. For many readers, this would have been their first

Catherine Bauer, c. 1930

encounter with Le Corbusier's famous comment that a "house is a machine for living in." Bauer was interested in that proposition, but not altogether sympathetic to it. "These are dwelling places for either automata or intellectuals, in any case, for the unsentimental," she wrote. It was uncomfortably close to the world depicted in Karel Čapek's recent play *R.U.R.*, and it failed to serve the full spectrum of human needs: "Those of us who are forced to be cogs in a machine all day, but are too conscious of our egos to be perfect Robots, turn to our homes in the evening as a relief from all that perfection and routine."[5]

Bauer was more supportive of the social imperatives behind modernist architecture, just then gaining ground in Europe: "More and better and cheaper houses for the ordinary man."[6] In 1934 she published *Modern Housing*, a pioneering and deeply researched account of this new direction in architecture.[7] Bauer called for state-sponsored, low-cost construction, arguing that the housing sector should be treated as a public utility rather than a capitalist marketplace (though she moderated this socialist proposal somewhat by suggesting it could be encouraged by favorable loans to builders, rather than direct government subsidies to homeowners). To some extent she did accurately predict the course of public policy, partly because Bauer made it happen herself by becoming an influential lobbyist. She was largely responsible for drafting the 1937 U.S. Housing Act, one of the more significant pieces of legislation in the later years of the New Deal. The bill had serious flaws—among other things, it accommodated the practice of redlining, the segregation of residential areas along racial lines—but it did break new ground in providing federal funding for affordable homes.

Meanwhile, Bauer and Mumford had been conducting a torrid on-again, off-again affair. (On one occasion, while traveling in Europe on a fact-finding trip, she wrote to him, "I am in love for the first time in my life and so proud of the amazing good taste of my instincts in their choice of a victim.")[8] This doubtless lent intensity to their collaboration. For a short time she worked as his researcher, without credit, but there was no question that she was his intellectual equal, and he increasingly treated her as such. In 1930 Mumford introduced Bauer to his allies in the Regional

Planning Association of America, which advocated "ruralizing the stony wastes of our cities," and building pathways from the city out into the countryside.[9] (The Appalachian Trail, for example, began as an RPAA proposal.) Conversations within the group were influential for both Bauer's *Modern Housing* and Mumford's *Technics and Civilization*, and the two books were written and published in parallel, with the authors exchanging notes and drafts. Bauer and Mumford's documentary for the World's Fair, then, marked the culmination of a long-standing personal and professional alliance, devoted to an urbanism "close to the soil once more," as the script for *The City* had it, "as molded to our human wants as planes are shaped for speed."

Close to the soil once more: a remarkably humble goal, by futurological standards. Having seen the perils of more aggrandizing metaphors, however—the fiery rhetoric of heaven and hell that prevailed at the turn of the century, and the fateful overdrive of mechanistic models of the future—it is easy to see why a more organic, permissive approach might have an appeal. This was the essential instinct behind garden-oriented futurology, which went far beyond adding green space to communities: it was an attempt to graft on to the human environment the principles of gradual, unforced change observed in the natural world. This philosophy implied relative restraint; it could seem unadventurous, even boring. (The pioneering urbanist Jane Jacobs later noted that this mode of planning was just fine "if you were docile and had no plans of your own and did not mind spending your life among others with no plans of their own.")[10] Yet, as anyone who has ever planted a bed of vegetables can attest, there is something about gardening that is just a little God-like, a re-creation of the Creation itself, albeit at vastly smaller scale. This is something that the garden and the machine have in common, as leitmotifs. Both imply the necessity of constant tending, and therefore an important place for futurologists themselves.

The seeds of garden thinking were planted at the turn of the century by the British planner Ebenezer Howard, affectionately described by Mumford as "the seemingly meek little man with the white walrus moustache" who was "conceptually two generations ahead of his time . . . the very flower of Victorian rationalism, as many-sided, as balanced, as humane as the kind of community he sought to create."[11] Howard was one of those people who love nature but prefer to regard it from a respectful distance. At the age of twenty-one, he had briefly emigrated to Nebraska to try his hand at farming, only to retreat after a hard winter, callused, emaciated, and demoralized. On returning to London, he took up a job as a stenographer, taking down speeches in Parliament so that they could be entered into the official record. This exposure to daily politics may perhaps have influenced his opinions about urbanism, but the real spur for him came from Edward Bellamy's *Looking Backward*, that omnipresent utopian text, which Howard supposedly read in one sitting. The next day he found himself feeling just like Bellamy's protagonist, Julian West, returned from the year 2000: "I went into some of the crowded parts of London, and as I passed through the narrow dark streets, saw the wretched dwellings in which the majority of the people lived ... there came to me an overpowering sense of the quite temporary nature of nearly all I saw."[12]

Eventually, Howard responded to *Looking Backward* with his own future-facing tract: *To-morrow: A Peaceful Path to Real Reform* (1898; revised as *Garden Cities of To-morrow* in 1902). By this time he had thought through Bellamy's mechanistic, centralized, socialist vision and found it wanting. His own proposals were more grassroots, and more pragmatic. He foresaw autonomous communities in which land was held in common, with each inhabitant and business paying rent for their right of occupation. Individual property values would increase only as a share of the overall value of the land, giving every resident an incentive to look after the health of the community. A park would be placed smack in the center and the town around it would be laid out radially. In these "garden cities," concentric series of ring-shaped districts would be dedicated to housing, schools and community centers, factories, and beyond that, more parkland—the original greenbelt. The goal was to harmoniously integrate the rural and the urban, combining the best of both. "Town and country must be married," Howard wrote, "and out of this joyous union will spring a new hope, a new life, a new civilization."[13] He called his imaginary community Unionville.

Unlike Bellamy's utopian schemes, which would require a total reinvention of the social order, Howard devised his garden city plan so that it could be implemented immediately. All it would take was investment by a group of concerned citizens. Once his book was out, he set about attracting converts to his newly founded Garden City Association. Such was the progressive spirit of the time that he won over many prominent figures, H. G. Wells among them, to lend their name to his efforts. Some even put in money to buy up land. Already by 1904, people were moving into a real-life garden city funded and planned according to Howard's ideas, in a place called Letchworth, north of London.

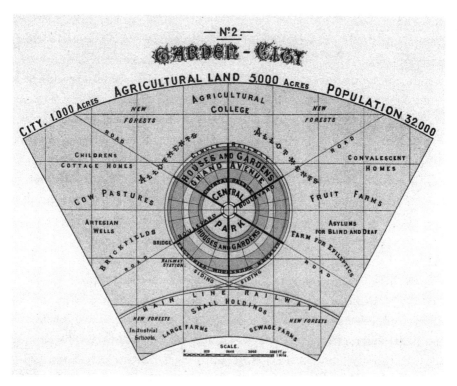

Diagram from Ebenezer Howard, *To-Morrow*, 1898.

Reality soon caught up with *To-morrow*'s beautiful diagrams, though. An early review of the book had noted, "It is quite evident that if Mr. Howard could be made town clerk of such a city he would carry it on to everybody's satisfaction. The only difficulty is to create it; but that is a small matter to Utopians."[14] This sarcasm was well placed. The architects selected for Letchworth made no attempt to follow *To-morrow* to the letter. Situating factories all around the perimeter, they realized, was a terrible idea, as the whole town would be enveloped in smoke. (Howard had envisioned using electrical power, but he was years too early for that.) An existing railway had to be accommodated, running through the center of town, where the undisturbed garden was supposed to be. Soon a corset manufactory joined it, as well as Britain's very first traffic roundabout.

More worryingly, the association had difficulty convincing manufacturers to participate in the scheme, prompting fierce internal debates about what, if any, inducements to offer them. Prospective residents were also concerned about the long-term value of their homes. The collective land-rent scheme, which had been the economic heart of the enterprise, was quickly abandoned in favor of more traditional leaseholds. Meanwhile Howard, who tended to disappear into abstruse speculation rather than face the challenges of the day, was quietly sidelined from his leadership position. He accepted it all, sure that these were just temporary setbacks. As his biographer Robert Beevers puts it, "Only one driven by an unassailable belief in the truth of his message could have accepted such a loss with such apparent equanimity."[15]

To a surprising extent, however, history would ratify Howard's serene optimism. Catherine Bauer asserted in *Modern Housing* that the garden city was "the most influential and productive utopia yet devised," contending that writings like Howard's had far greater significance than any actual building could: "In a literary age, who knows but that the extravagant or romantic words may have been more effective in the long run than the timid constructions in stone or brick—or iron?"[16] She was right: The garden city ideal would have an extraordinarily long-lasting and widespread influence, right down to the present day.[17] Howard and his backers went on to found a second suburban community, Welwyn Garden City, in 1920 (he died there in 1928). His acolytes—now calling themselves the New Townsmen—assiduously promoted his ideas as the basis for rebuilding following the Great War.[18] A German disciple of the movement called Ernst May redeveloped parts of Frankfurt according to Howard's principles. Bauer visited in 1930, admiring the neat row houses with their ultraefficient kitchens, designed by Grete Lihotzky. She praised the overall effect: "tiers of concrete and glass and gardens curving beyond the sheep-dotted valley—each house with a garden, each apartment with a terrace, half an hour from a city of 500,000 inhabitants."[19] New Frankfurt was refreshingly optimistic, even in its custom-designed typeface: a sans serif font called Futura.

IN AMERICA, TOO, a handful of experimental cities were being built to Howard's model, among them Greenbelt, Maryland, and Radburn, New Jersey, both of which were filmed for *The City*.[20] The most ambitious of America's garden cities, however, remained unrealized. It was the brainchild of Frank Lloyd Wright—a larger-than-life figure in his signature porkpie hat and dramatic cape, the only American architect who commanded the respect of the European modernists. For all his grandeur and fame, though, Wright was going through a bare patch in the early 1930s. The triumphs of his astonishing cantilevered house Fallingwater and his corporate headquarters for Johnson Wax, with its futuristic "lilypad" supports, still lay a few years ahead. Since completing his majestic Imperial Hotel in Japan in 1923, he had only had scattered residential commissions. So Wright did what any massively creative, egomaniacal architect would do: He thought about how he would redesign the whole country.

The highly speculative scheme Wright came up with was in some ways similar to Ebenezer Howard's, but without the modest incrementalism; it was a landscape at a scale anticipating Bel Geddes's all-conquering Futurama. Wright called it Broadacre City, a pleasant enough name that captured the plan's two central ideas: decentralization and democracy. The project was broad in a literal sense, meant to be replicable across any amount of available space; and while not communally owned, like Howard's Unionville, it presumed an egalitarian structure, with each household allotted at least one acre of land. In fact, it wasn't a city at all, in the usual sense of the term. Wright regarded the metropolis as an outdated model, and said so, in the book that first introduced Broadacre to the world: *The Disappearing City* (1932). His argument was simple. Cities are unpleasant, exploitative, and anonymous. Furthermore, city-dwellers are parasites on the countryside, gobbling up its resources, while being spiritually divorced from nature: "Perpetual to and fro excites and robs the urban individual of the meditation, imaginative reflection and projection once his as he lived and walked under clean sky among the growing greenery to which he was born companion." (The lofty rhetoric is typical; this is how Wright wrote.) Fortunately, humanity didn't need to put up with such conditions anymore. Once upon a time, population density had been necessary for the purposes of fortification, trade, and cultural development. But with the advent of modern warfare, defensive walls no longer mattered, and modern transport and communications networks made it possible to extend economic and artistic exchange far and wide, making density irrelevant for those purposes, too. The city "had done its work for humanity." It was time for something else, and Wright was going to invent it.[21]

To do so, he thought small. Broadacre City was to be a landscape of "little farms, little homes for industry, little factories, little schools, a little university, [and] little laboratories on their own ground for professional men."[22] Houses would be little, too, constructed along the lines of low-income homes that Wright was developing at the time, which he described as "Usonian" (a made-up word that he presumably liked because of its similarity to "utopian," as well as its allusion to the USA). Together, the various residential, commercial, and manufacturing units of Broadacre would form patterns of inhabitation that were self-sufficient, both practically and politically. Wright believed that power should be widely dispersed, to preserve the independence of the citizenry. The only public officials he invested with much authority were the county architects, who would be the "essential leaders" of each regional community, much as Plato had put philosopher-kings in charge of his ideal republic.

Wright's designs do show a few tall buildings here and there. Otherwise, his imagined civic landscape is insistently horizontal as a prairie, long one of his favorite metaphors. In retrospect, many have seen Wright's plan as an anticipation of postwar suburbia. Yet in an important sense it was not a suburb at all, because it was not dependent on an urban center. There would be no need to commute, and nowhere to commute to. The city, remember, had disappeared.

Wright certainly did not envision undifferentiated sprawl of the kind that would metastasize across much of America in future decades. He made this clear by directing his acolytes at Taliesin, his home and studio in Spring Green, Wisconsin, to construct a twelve-by-twelve-foot model representing a section of the project. It contains multitudes. Farmland is prominent, but a monorail forms a transportation spine down the center, and there is provision for factories (and associated factory housing), schools, and amenities like regional theaters and farmers' markets. When the model was unveiled at Rockefeller Center in 1935, Mumford saw it and was duly impressed, writing in his regular *New Yorker* column that Wright "carries the tradition of romantic isolation and reunion with the soil to its conclusion."[23]

Mumford did offer one criticism of Broadacre City, which he may have gotten directly from Catherine Bauer. Wright "hates the very word 'housing,'" he noted, and the minimal Usonian-style houses that he had included were poky and uninspired: "He should have permitted himself to dream more generously." This seemingly mild comment called into question the quality of life that Broadacre would provide to its less prosperous citizens—exactly the grounds on which Wright had so savagely criticized the present-day city. Privately, Mumford doubted very much that it would be possible to do away with centralized urbanism entirely, and after his article came out, said as much in a letter to Wright: "Concentration, when not pushed to the point of congestion, offers certain possibilities of intercourse that dispersion doesn't." (Bauer, in an earlier review of *The Disappearing City*, had expressed similar doubts: "Alas, it is just not possible to spread the town over the country and preserve the virtues of either.")[24] Wright, characteristically, was undeterred. In his autobiography, published in 1943, he continued to predict that American cities would die off, any time now. All evidence of their explosive growth he airily dismissed as a "characteristic acceleration that goes before ultimate urban dissolution."[25]

There was an interesting contradiction at work here, which ran not only through Broadacre, but the whole of the garden city movement. For all that Howard and Wright sought to reconnect the populace to the rural landscape, their visions were also deeply dependent on technology. Wright might be "a man of the open country," as Mumford put it in the *New Yorker*, but his projected future was just as oriented to the automobile as that of Bel Geddes. It was the passenger car that would guarantee freedom of movement for Broadacre's citizens, while providing the social connectivity that an urban neighborhood does, "making ten miles as one block."[26] Wright also imagined that "aeroplane depots" would soon become feasible at the local level. Similarly, it was through "volatized, instantaneous intercommunication" (by which he meant telephone and radio) that people could be liberated from the city as a hub of information exchange.[27] Wright's position on mechanization was very similar to Mumford's in *Technics and Civilization*. It had to be mastered, but only so that it could be turned against itself; the death of the city "will be the greatest service the machine has to ultimately render to human beings, if by means of his machine man ever does conquer his own machine."[28]

FUTUROLOGISTS, BY AND large, are advocates of drastic change. Each has a new world in mind and the determination to propagate it, supposedly for the good of all. Generally, though, they encounter at least some resistance, and any history of the future has to account for that skepticism. It has to consider not just self-appointed visionaries like Ebenezer Howard and Frank Lloyd Wright, but also people who just want stability in their lives. In 1948 the historian Siegfried Giedion published a book called *Mechanization Takes Command*, which tracked the rise of the machine to its dominant position in modern society while also acknowledging its destructive effects, so recently and horribly demonstrated in World War II. Giedion, like Mumford and Bauer before him, argued that it was time to set limits on the expanding dominion of mechanization. "A new outlook must prevail if nature is to be mastered rather than degraded," he wrote. "It is time that we become human again and let the human scale rule over all our ventures." While phenomena like streamlining and ultraefficient kitchens were undeniably fascinating—and Giedion was among the first to write analytically about them—he argued that they ultimately represented only the illusion of progress: "All we have to show so far is a rather disquieting inability to organize the world, or even to organize ourselves." It was not the engineer or the industrial designer who was best placed to be the steward of the future, he argued, but the farmer, "symbol of continuity . . . the stabilizing lead, stowed deep in the keel." It is the function of the farmer, Giedion wrote, "invisibly to resist the cross winds of destiny."[29]

This well-founded suspicion of change, the impulse to seek out continuity and balance, is what fundamentally distinguishes garden thinking from machine thinking. Machine-oriented futurologists consider tomorrow to be an ever-new challenge, demanding customized and systematic intervention. Those who prefer the metaphor of the garden see the future as an open field, continuous with the past, and best approached through ongoing cultivation. Machines are self-enclosed devices, each dedicated to a specific external purpose, a means of extending human agency. A garden, by contrast, perpetually renews itself, manifesting harmonious cohabitation between people and the rest of the planet. It is not the same as wild nature, for it does involve human tending. Mainly, though, a garden just lives, on its own complex terms.

When Ebenezer Howard called his ideal community a garden city, then, he chose the perfect analogy. He sought to build a place of accommodation, in both senses of that term. Unlike the biblical Eden, an eternal paradise outside of history, a real garden is different from season to season and year to year. Yet it never outgrows what we might call its "true nature." This is why Howard drew his cities not as maps but as diagrams. He was trying to capture an underlying morphology, which would persist even as the surface features of the community evolved. Similarly, Wright's model for Broadacre City showed only a typical four-square-mile area, implying endless extension in all directions. As it unrolled across the landscape, the plan would certainly have had to be adapted to local features, but he thought that the same organic principles could remain in place. And as in space, so in time: Unlike a typical modern city, which perpetually reinvents itself in a cycle of creative destruction, the garden cities were believed by Howard and Wright to be permanent solutions.

They could incorporate changes—fewer roads here, more "aeroplane depots" there, electrification—while keeping their essential character intact.

Howard and Wright both assumed that if people wanted to live in a gardenlike future, they would have to build it anew. But some thought otherwise; while they too thought that modern, urbanized society had lost its way, they looked around and saw a whole world full of existing alternatives. Theirs was an antimodern futurology, which is not as paradoxical as it might sound; it took nature and folk culture, rather than the machine, as its models and inspirations. This perspective was being propagated widely in the 1920s and '30s, particularly in artistic and religious circles. The aesthete Sōetsu Yanagi in Tokyo, for example, extolled *mingei* (roughly, "the art of everyday people") for its vitality and beauty; he believed that a society estranged from its traditions could never be truly satisfied. He shared this viewpoint with his friend, the British potter Bernard Leach, who argued that all cultures required a "tap-root deep in the soil of the past" in order to thrive—he pitied Americans (apart from Native Americans) for their lack of such a spiritual attachment.[30] Ananda Coomaraswamy, originally from Ceylon (now Sri Lanka), was similarly admiring of traditional, nonliterate cultures. When he came to America in the 1920s, he did much to promote the understanding of the Hindu religion, presenting it as a well of metaphysical profundity from which the West could learn.

For all of these figures—and there were many others of like mind—modern, mechanized society was simply soulless. A better future could only be reached through enlightened continuity with the grounded beliefs of the past. In retrospect, their efforts to connect with the life-giving well of tradition can seem problematic: sometimes ill-informed, often involving cultural appropriation. Their acts of appreciation tended to disregard the stark power asymmetries of imperialism, as was the case with Yanagi's admiration for the folk art of Korea (recently colonized by a militarized and expansionist Japan). Such blind spots must be balanced, however, with the genuine respect that these universalizing thinkers had for traditions other than their own. They consistently tried to make space for the vernacular, right alongside self-consciously innovative works. You can still see with this period eye, nowadays, by visiting the Barnes Foundation in Philadelphia, which opened to the public in 1925, with its hoard of cutting-edge European paintings, historic ironwork, and African, Asian, and Native American art. Albert Barnes's collection was unusual for its size and quality, but it was consistent with a broader pattern in taste, in which folk and avant-garde cultures were understood as natural, even necessary, companions—an aesthetic parallel to the "joyous union" that Ebenezer Howard sought between the rural and the urban.

One of the most fascinating figures at this intersection of the avant-garde and the traditional was Mabel Dodge, mentioned in chapter 1 as the lover and traveling companion of the journalist John Reed. Her picaresque career had started early. Born into considerable wealth in Buffalo, New York, she married at the age of twenty-one to escape her conventional family. Soon she was in Florence, fraternizing with the likes of Gertrude Stein; a few years later she arrived in Greenwich Village, where she hosted a weekly salon that attracted New York City's most progressive intellectuals. In addition to Reed, she counted among her associates such figures as Margaret Sanger, Lincoln Steffens, Carl Van Vechten, and the brilliant (and notorious) Russian-born anarchist Emma Goldman. Dodge was also involved in Heterodoxy, a radical feminist group, along with Sanger and Goldman, and was among the organizers of the famous 1913 Armory Show, which introduced modern art to America.

Needless to say, then, Dodge was no conservative. Yet, as the literary critic Van Wyck Brooks observed of her, "she was a type of those who . . . felt that the white man was 'spoiled' and 'lost.'"[31] This conviction deepened for her in New Mexico, where she undertook a reinvention that has attracted equal parts admiration and alarm from historians ever since. The transformation began when she traveled out to meet her third husband, the painter Maurice Sterne, who was at work in Santa Fe. In Dodge's memoirs (which, in general, should be taken with a lick's worth of salt), she described having an immediate clarity in this wide-open country: "The rumble of New York came back to me like the impotent and despairing protest of a race that has gone wrong and is caught in a trap." Santa Fe was

Mabel Dodge Luhan in 1934.

not much to her liking, but she soon discovered nearby Taos, with its two separate settlements: a modern town, inhabited by a population of mixed white, Mexican, and Native American heritage, and a pueblo with about six hundred Tiwa people. The first thing that struck her was the estrangement between the two communities. "It was as though the Pueblo had an invisible wall around it, separating the Indians from the world we knew," Dodge thought. The second thing that occurred to her was this: "I *wish* I belonged in there!"[32]

She didn't, of course, but the feeling that she might someday prompted her to move permanently from New York to the modern part of Taos. She began collecting locally made textiles, furniture, and santos—carved representations of saints that she memorably, if condescendingly, described as "pressed out of nowhere by inarticulate and untutored men in their extreme need for something to answer their religious needs, something to hang their love upon."[33] Her domestic space became a little regional version of the Barnes Foundation, with the humble but potent santos hung alongside Native American rugs and paintings by her sophisticated friends. Dodge also resumed her hosting activities, now with the goal of promoting the local scene as a source of artistic inspiration. (Sterne, still married to her at this point, was busily painting and sculpting Native people who would agree to sit for him in exchange for a small fee.)

An amazing list of cultural figures took up Dodge's invitation, including the painter Georgia O'Keeffe, the photographer Ansel Adams, the feminist anthropologist Elsie Clews Parsons—an acquaintance of Dodge's from New York, who would go on to provide the period's most detailed ethnography of the Tiwa people—and many writers, including Mary Austin, Willa Cather, Aldous Huxley, and D. H. Lawrence.[34] Meanwhile—and this is where it gets controversial—she was falling in love with a Tiwa man named Antonio "Tony" Lujan. This cross-cultural romance was well outside of accepted societal norms for someone of Dodge's elite class, and Lujan was already married, as she was, though this seems to have concerned Dodge not at all. Her attraction to him had a strong undertow of idealized exoticism. Whereas the other men in her life, including Sterne, wanted to "re-make the world, but they would never come to grips with their own solid crystallized deformities," she saw Tony as a natural phenomenon in his own right. "He seemed to have the ease and the unconscious balance of a rock on the edge of an abyss," she wrote, "in his static fashion, unconcerned and whole."[35] She even went so far as to espouse a reverse version of eugenics, telling a Denver newspaper in 1932, "The races may

amalgamate and the Indians be the ones to save our race. A wealth of artistic senti-
ment will be blended in the new blood infusion with the white race."[36]

None of this has aged well, but there was also an unusual prescience in Mabel
Dodge Luhan—as she became in 1923, when she and Tony married (she appended
his last name to her own, but Americanized it). On a practical level, she played a key
role in organizing successful opposition to the Bursum Bill, a racist senator's
attempt to expropriate further lands from Puebloan peoples and hand it over to
white squatters. However imperfectly, Dodge Luhan did genuinely seek to build "a
bridge between cultures," as she put it, which certainly cannot be said of most
Americans at the time. In the process, she anticipated arguments that would only
become commonplace in the 1960s. Native Americans' spiritual connection to the
natural environment, in particular, seemed to her eminently worthy of respect and
emulation. "With the Indians life is art, and religion is its testimony," she wrote,
and this holistic principle seemed to her the only way forward into the future: "The
Southwest may be the land of new birth, of the synthetic American culture we have
all desired."[37]

Dodge Luhan should also be given credit for her influence on John Collier, who
would rise to become the commissioner for the Bureau of Indian Affairs under
Roosevelt. Bringing him to Taos may have been the most consequential thing
Dodge ever did, certainly so far as Native Americans were concerned. Collier was a
receptive audience for her enthusiasms. He had been orphaned as a teenager. Bereft,
he spent his time reading Wordsworth and Whitman, hiking and camping in the
Appalachian Mountains, and generally communing with the "overwhelming experience of living nature—what I later learned to call cosmic consciousness."[38] After
study at Columbia University, Collier got involved in political activism. He did
social work with the immigrant population in New York City, and in 1906 traveled
in Europe to educate himself about the latest labor movements. It was he who
brought Emma Goldman to Dodge's salon in Greenwich Village.

When Collier came to Taos at Dodge's invitation, in 1920, he had just gotten a
new job in Los Angeles, as the head of adult education for the California state
government. Despite this professional advancement, he was in a thoroughly disillu-
sioned state of mind. Like many people in his generation—he was then in his mid-
thirties—he had experienced the Great War as a crushing indictment of supposedly
"civilized" European values.[39] When Dodge wrote to him describing the glories of

New Mexico, he chalked it up mostly to her imagination, but agreed to visit none-theless. When he got there, he decided she was absolutely right: Taos was utopia, and everyone needed to know about it. He immediately joined the effort to kill the Bursum Bill. (Tony Lujan, far from being "static and unconcerned," accompanied him to pueblos around the regions to help organize a coordinated resistance.) Then, in 1922, Collier published an extraordinary essay called "The Red Atlantis," declaring that Native culture could still be found intact, despite all of white America's efforts to destroy it: "The pueblo is not dying; on the contrary, it is alive, pregnant, and potentially plastic; potentially an inheritor of the future and a giver to the future of gifts without price, which future white man will know how to use."[40]

The phrase "potentially plastic"—here meaning adaptable, rather than artificial—is important. Collier did not mistakenly believe Taos to be timeless or undisturbed. "The pueblo is not primitive in the sense of being primordial," he wrote. "Vast spaces of evolution and of the compounding of cultures lie behind it." Nor did he indulge in the paternalistic notion that Native people should be shielded from modern technology and science. Rather, he saw in them a resilience, born of their connection to place, that was far more likely to flourish in the long term than was white America's profit-driven imperative. The Puebloans were like the dwellings they inhabited: "An adobe house, on the desert, takes on not mould but the change-less youth of the soil, the earth, from which it seems to have grown."[41] Artists in Dodge Luhan's circle, including Ansel Adams and Georgia O'Keeffe, portrayed local buildings in just this spirit, showing how architecture, normally humanity's most visible imposition on the natural landscape, could instead be conceived as an inextricable part of it. Both Adams and O'Keeffe depicted a particular eighteenth-century mission church, San Francisco de Asis—not in the pueblo itself but nearby—as "an outcropping of the earth rather than merely an object constructed upon it," as Adams put it. He was trying to capture the feeling that another of Dodge's circle, Mary Austin, described as "the curious quiescent aliveness of the whole Taos land-scape, as if it might at any moment wake and leap."[42]

These rhapsodic expressions of a living earth were akin to the ideals animating the garden city movement. There was a significant difference, however. When plan-ning their ideal communities of Unionville and Broadacre City, Howard and Wright assumed that residents would belong to a single egalitarian class,

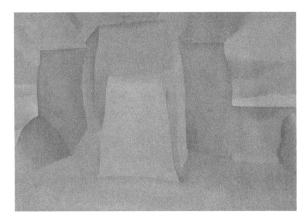

Georgia O'Keeffe, *Ranchos Church*, 1930.

distinguished only by profession; neither so much as mentioned the fact of racial difference. Dodge Luhan and Collier, by contrast, were what we would now call multiculturalists. They believed that the distinctive quality of Puebloan culture— "that psychic and social present as it truly is," as Collier wrote, "so human and so mystic"—was of supreme importance, and must be preserved.[43] This viewpoint put them in a vanishingly small minority of whites at the time. It put them directly at odds with the U.S. government, which had been implementing a policy of assimilation for decades, forcibly relocating Native children to schools that were run like military academies and forbidding them to wear traditional dress or speak in their own languages. Even some other members of Dodge Luhan's circle thought her interventions on behalf of the Native population were misguided. D. H. Lawrence wrote to her in 1923, "Don't trouble about the Indians. You can't 'save' them. . . . The same with Collier. He will destroy them. It is his saviour's will to set the claws of his own White egoistic benevolent volition into them. Somewhere, the Indians know that you and Collier would, with your Salvationist but poisonous white consciousness, destroy them."[44]

Collier's determined opposition to such views would be the foundation of his work as commissioner for Indian affairs, following his appointment in 1933. He was the primary architect of the so-called Indian New Deal, formally the Indian Reorganization Act of 1934, which for the first time recognized the right to self-determination and communal rights to reservation lands. Throughout his tenure as

Ansel Adams, *Church at Ranchos de Taos*, 1929.

commissioner, he retained his conviction about the superiority of Native American culture, particularly the root belief in "a web of relationships including man, other animals, plants [and] the natural environment."[45] Like all pure ideals, this one was hard to sustain in practice. It led Collier into direct conflict with some tribes, particularly those who did not neatly fit into the Puebloan model that he carried around in his head. A case in point is his treatment of the Diné people (often called the Navajo by outsiders). For generations, the U.S. government had been encouraging the tribe to engage in sheepherding as a means of economic self-reliance. Now, belatedly, officials realized that this use of the land was causing a crisis of erosion and soil runoff; among other problems, it put the mighty Hoover Dam project, downstream on the Colorado River, at risk. Collier's solution was to impose a policy of livestock reduction, in an attempt to reduce overgrazing and its impact on the land. He was aware that the resulting economic hardship would force some Diné (perhaps the more "assimilated" ones) to leave their ancestral lands. Yet he actively welcomed this outcome, believing that sheep farming, though it had now been practiced for generations, was not traditional to this region anyway, and that a smaller population might ultimately restore a degree of authenticity to the community.[46]

If Collier's idealism led him into some dubious decisions, it was also a strategic weakness. Even historians who generally portray him in a positive light, like Vine

Deloria Jr. and Clifford Lytle, see the Indian Reorganization Act as fatally vague and ambiguous—and this was at least partly due to Collier's optimistic assumption that he could work within its provisions to further improve the "Indian New Deal" as he went along. To be fair, he was well out in front of public opinion; one could argue that he played a weak hand well. Yet the conditional nature of the act—and the fact that all of its provisions remained "subject to the discretion of the secretary"—continued to circumscribe the political autonomy of tribal councils and leaders. Predictably, when Collier stepped down from his position as commissioner of Indian affairs, policy immediately reverted to a more assimilation-based approach. DeLoria and Lytle describe the two ensuing decades, from 1945 to 1965, as "barren years," in which tribal self-government "virtually disappeared as a policy and as a topic of interest."[47]

IT MUST ALSO be said that, no less than Mabel Dodge with Tony Lujan, Collier was casting Native people in a romantic leading role that he had imagined for them. Seeing them as exemplars of a possible future based on enlightened continuity with the past, he made no space for other identities. As we'll see in a subsequent chapter, this presumption would be vigorously contested by a later generation of activists associated with the Red Power movement. Even in the 1920s, though, there were Native people who looked at their self-appointed protectors with considerable skepticism. One of these was Pablo Abeita, the governor of Isleta Pueblo, about 150 miles south of Taos. He was himself a product of forced assimilation—he'd been educated at a missionary school—though this only made him a more effective cultural operator. In the early 1920s, when they were fighting the Bursum Bill, Dodge and Collier agreed that their Native allies should always be represented by a certain type. The Indians, Dodge wrote to Collier, "always vote that their smart, short-haired Americanized ones should go: just the wrong ones," and Collier concurred: What was wanted was a "representative Indian, someone who can talk—simply as the typical Indians talk, not artificially the way Pablo Abeita talks."[48]

In fact, Abeita did play an important part in contesting the Bursum Bill; moreover, he had a lot more experience in such efforts than either Dodge or Collier did. He'd journeyed east to Washington in 1905, and again in 1913, to lobby on behalf of his people and flatly contradict the logic of assimilation. "Wise as you are, you should look in the future," he said in an official statement directed to the government. "The Indians are Indians, and will be Indians until they have all disappeared from this valley of tears. Such is my opinion, and I will not change it before the wise Americans have become Indians themselves. Then only will I say that the Indians may someday turn Americans. For the present, patience, and we shall see."[49] The challenge that lay before Native spokesmen like Abeita can be measured by an editorial comment in the missionary journal where this powerful speech was printed: "In its crude simplicity and hammering

Pablo Abeita, c. 1930.

logic, it is certainly a peculiar document, showing us the Pueblo Indian's point of view." Compared to such brutal contempt, Dodge and Collier's hesitancy to foreground voices like Abeita's on tactical grounds seems relatively benign; but they were still part of a pattern in which the future for Native Americans was decided for, not by, them. Observing the operations of his nominal white allies, Abeita said simply, "They simply go ahead telling what they think the Indian wants. They ought to call the Indians there and ask what they want. It is not necessary to give him all he wants but it is necessary to listen to him."[50] It would be many years before that call would be widely heard.

Meanwhile, Abeita and other Native people continued to give shape to their own landscape, and not necessarily by preserving its existing organic character. In 1927 a new cinema-playhouse was built in the city of Albuquerque, just north of Isleta Pueblo. It was designed by the Kansas City–based firm Boller Brothers, who created about a hundred such buildings across the country in the 1920s and '30s, each an outpost of eclectic pop-futurological architectural sensibility. The one in Albuquerque was to be "America's Foremost Indian Theater," decorated in a fusion of modern, Spanish Colonial, Aztec, and Native American motifs—an outstanding example of what's been called Pueblo Deco style.[51] When the local paper held a competition to title the new venue, for a fifty-dollar prize, the winner was none other than Abeita, who suggested the name KiMo. It could have been a brand to sell just about anything and, cleverly, was just one letter away from *Kino*, the German word for a movie theater, sometimes used in America at this time. In Tiwa, however, *kimo* means "mountain lion" and is sometimes applied to a cultural leader—someone like Abeita himself. The theater still stands in Albuquerque today, a much-loved historical monument in a diverse town. The original neon sign has been restored, as have its culturally appropriated ornamental details—including door handles shaped like *kachina* figures, which are sacred to the Hopi. Though few passersby these days have likely heard of Pablo Abeita, the KiMo Theater actually represents him, and the Southwest, pretty well. It's not a slope-sided outgrowth of the earth itself, like the church in Adams and O'Keeffe's pictures, but instead a complicated mixture of many cultural influences, all jostling for position, out there, where the land used to be free.

IN 1933, AT the "Century of Progress" World's Fair in Chicago, visitors encountered a strange-looking vehicle. Bullet-shaped, with only three wheels, it sported a futuristic name, the Dymaxion Car. To most people it probably seemed like just another exercise in fashionable streamlining. The technically inclined may also have appreciated the relocation of its scavenged Ford motor to the rear, with the whole transmission flipped around back to front. But to its designer, it was wholly different from the superficially styled objects of his peers, or any other vehicle ever conceived. He considered it the first step toward a "4D twin, angularly-orientable, individually throttleable, jet-stilt, controlled-plummeting transport."[52] A flying car, in other words, with foldout wings, which could attain elevation by being inflated with air or gas, rising in discrete strokes like a duck flapping its wings. Unfortunately, before it could get off the ground—or even far down the road—the Dymaxion was involved in a crash on Chicago's Lake Shore Drive, when it slipped and tumbled over into oncoming traffic. The driver was killed, and another of the passengers badly injured.[53]

This inauspicious debut was how most of America first heard of R. Buckminster Fuller, the car's designer. They would keep hearing from him, with barely a pause for breath, for another fifty years. Fuller would go down as the century's quintessential futurologist. Short and a little stout, with thick glasses that magnified his gaze, he was a human spark plug throwing off proposals and theories, provocative and preposterous by turns, impossible to summarize, or even always to follow. In 1975 he gave a televised lecture that lasted forty-two hours, delivered over a period of two weeks; it was called "Everything I Know," but by the end it seemed like he was just getting started. Fuller talked so much, and so variously, that people could look right past his disasters, seeing what they wanted in him. "He is perhaps the only man," as the critic Eva Díaz has noted, "loved by both the military-surveillance complex and radical university students."[54]

Yet Fuller's voluminous output essentially rested on a single intuition: Human beings should design as nature does. We should shape our environment, that is, on the principles of minimal waste and maximum creativity, always seeking a state of "dynamic equilibrium." That phrase had also been used by Lewis Mumford in describing the garden city ideal.[55] But Fuller would explore it much more deeply, applying the concept to all sorts of problems and all scales of human endeavor. The universe, he explained, is "a total energy process—entirely and ceaselessly in relative motion. As defined out of our experience this process is finite, and, as energy may neither be lost or gained within the system, all energy patterning occurs in cycles of regenerative transformation."[56] To design well, he argued, is to apply this macro-cosmic balance to absolutely everything. The Dymaxion car contained this thinking in embryo. It was a machine, obviously, but one conceived along the lines of organic life. Fuller's young daughter called it a "zoomobile," a nickname he happily adopted because of the inspiration he'd taken from natural forms—its rear-wheel drive and rudder meant that it navigated like a whale, and it even had a flying fish for a logo. As to "Dymaxion," he'd adopted it as an all-purpose brand, beginning in 1929, applying it to a range of business endeavors (as his biographer Alec Nevala-Lee points out, Fuller was among many other things a forerunner of today's start-up entrepreneurs).[57] A portmanteau of *dynamic*, *maximum*, and *tension*, the word had been suggested to him by the advertising department at Marshall Field's. For Fuller, it perfectly captured the novel synthesis he was developing between the two primary futurological tendencies of the day, the mechanistic and the organic. From his point of view, this was not a true opposition at all. Optimally—and he always thought in optimal terms—machines and nature worked just the same, doing the most with the least.

Fuller had gotten involved with the admen at Marshall Field's because he was trying to promote a novel approach to home-building (the department store thought it might sell furniture to match, thus becoming among the first of Fuller's many disappointed commercial partners). He thought it absurd that shelter was still being approached in an ad hoc, artisanal way. It should obviously be mass-manufactured, like cars or bicycles. This was hardly an unprecedented idea—Catherine Bauer, for one, was making the same point to anyone who would listen—but Fuller expressed it differently, in terms of big round numbers (mathematics being an important area of overlap between nature and engineering). In a 1927 drawing entitled *One-Ocean-World-Town-Plan*, he noted that "the whole of the human family could stand on Bermuda," while "all crowded into England they would have 150 square feet each."[58] He ran the numbers again in his early book *Nine Chains to the Moon*: The title was inspired by the idea that all of humanity, if we could somehow be stacked up on one another's heads, would reach to the moon and back nine times. He further noted that there were presently about 115 million tons' worth of people on the face of the earth, equivalent to the weight of 1,400 ocean liners, taking up about 10 billion cubic feet in volume, enough to fill 111 Empire State Buildings. Perhaps only Fuller, having made this calculation, would have added, "Yet if put under a gigantic hydraulic wine press, so that all the liquid and gas might be squeezed out of them, they could be compressed into one Empire State Building."[59]

What it all added up to was an urgent need for efficiency in housing. Fuller reckoned that about two billion new family homes would be required in the next eighty years (pretty accurate, as it turns out). He liked Le Corbusier's idea that a house was a machine for living in—he had devoured the French architect's book-length manifesto *Toward a New Architecture* (1923) in one night, just as Ebenezer Howard had done with Bellamy's *Looking Backward*. But he aspired to the productivity of nature as much as that of a factory. A dwelling, he thought, could be conceived as a tree or a human body, *and* as a finely engineered machine. It could have "a central stem or backbone, from which all else is independently hung, utilizing gravity instead of opposing it. This results in a construction similar to an airplane, light, taut, and profoundly strong."[60] Like Frank Lloyd Wright, Fuller also foresaw the house of the future as empowered by new technology. "In our individual homes no matter where we may be," he predicted, we will "speak into our

combination radio-telephonic-recording dictator recording our commands graphi-
cally (word or picture)."[61] He also saw it as a potential means of escape from the
modern city, which he didn't care for any more than Wright did: "What a projection of hell, this bedlam, this stirring inferno. . . . Not even a patch of raw mother
earth. New York City! A one-piece dormitory, work and play shop 300 square miles
in the horizontal plane and thirty to one thousand feet in thickness."[62]

Yet there were also important differences between Fuller's vision and the one
that Wright espoused with Broadacre. First of all, Fuller didn't really think of
himself as an architect, a profession he mocked for not even knowing what their
buildings weighed, and merrily disdained as "a sometimes jolly, sometimes sancti-
monious, occasionally chi-chi, and often pathetic organization of shelter tailors."[63]
(Philip Johnson, who played a crucial role in promoting modernist architecture as
a curator at the Museum of Modern Art in these years and went on to be a leading
practitioner in his own right, was equally dismissive in return: "Bucky Fuller was
no architect, and he kept pretending he was. He was annoying. We all hated him.")[64]
And if professional architects were on the wrong track, then Middle America was
even more misguided. "No, Mr. Average Reader, you are wrong," Fuller wrote in
Nine Chains to the Moon, "The house in your mind is but a composite image of
confusion, ineffectuality and romance."[65] Taking the garden city principle of decentralization to an extreme, he hypothesized that a house could be just as portable as
an automobile. His Dymaxion Dwelling Machine, accordingly, was outfitted with
a generator and sewage tank, so it could remain off grid. It was hexagonal in shape,
with two living "decks" suspended on tension cables from a central "mast"—a
reminder, perhaps, of Fuller's formative years in the navy—and had a total weight
of only three tons (that's about forty unpressed humans). He claimed that it could
be easily delivered by air, perhaps using a zeppelin, and erected in a single day—and
presumably just as easily disassembled and moved. At a stroke, he would detach
the problem of shelter from the political and economic entanglements of land
ownership.

Fuller pursued his Dymaxion house proposal with unusual persistence and
determination, by his distractible standards, attracting considerable press along the
way.[66] Though his early designs went unrealized, World War II gave him new
opportunities to revisit them. First, in 1941, he developed a habitable "Dymaxion
Deployment Unit," working with a manufacturer of commercial grain storage bins.

(Fuller claimed, not very persuasively, that the structures could be easily camou-flaged, because they resembled "nature-forms such as trees and hillocks.")[67] Perhaps a hundred of these D.D.U.s were made and shipped to military bases around the world before steel shortages made the scheme impractical. Toward the end of the war he tried yet again, this time collaborating with Beech Aircraft, based in Wichita, Kansas, to create Dymaxion-style houses for postwar suburban use. The new idea was to ship the house in a tube. Although Beech had big plans—they predicted that they'd soon be making two million of the houses annually—only a handful were ever completed, mainly because, as the historian Jonathon Keats notes, Fuller was forever "stamping completed blueprints 'obsolete' and thinking up new improve-ments."[68] As to the original Dymaxion Dwelling Machine, only one prototype was ever built, in an aircraft plant, in 1946. Today it is on view at the Henry Ford Museum.

Fuller's inability to realize his ideas reflected his tendency to let the possible future get in the way of the actual present. But he wasn't done with the concept of portable shelter. His big breakthrough was just around the corner: the geodesic dome, which has been closely identified with him ever since its invention. Like so many of his other initiatives, it was initially a flop—literally. A dome he tried to build at Black Mountain College in 1948, using venetian blinds, refused to stand. (The students nicknamed it the "Supine Dome.") In the winter of 1949, however, one of his acolytes managed to construct a dome using metal struts outside Toronto, skinning it with a new acrylic fabric called Orlon. (This pioneering structure, dubbed Weatherbreak, spent some time as a folly in the Hollywood Hills, and is now in the collection of the Smithsonian.) Then, in 1953, Fuller triumphantly covered the central courtyard of a Ford Motor Company building in Dearborn; it spanned ninety-three feet and weighed just under nine tons.

While the geodesic dome has been justly celebrated as a marvel of engineering—it remains one of the strongest, most efficient means of covering an interior volume—the invention held deeper significance for Fuller. The name he chose for it literally means "earth-dividing" (*geodesy* is an archaic term for land surveying). He was still thinking about all those people crowded together, 150 square feet each, and his dome was meant as a minimal, practical, and again portable solution to ever-increasing population density. Far easier and cheaper to build than the original Dymaxion Dwelling Machine, it could be propagated endlessly for both residential and institutional purposes, gradually displacing the irrational, expensive, and

Buckminster Fuller at Black Mountain College in 1948.

ultimately unsustainable way that humans house ourselves. Domes were also material metaphors. Their parts literally held one another up in midair, in an unimprov-
able demonstration of egalitarian interdependence. Fuller, working alongside a
student at Black Mountain named Kenneth Snelson, dubbed this principle "tensegrity," another portmanteau, this time of *tension* and *integrity*—key terms in social
relations, here transposed into the domain of pure engineering.

The prospect of domes propping themselves up all the way to the horizon
suggests a further reason that geodesic construction excited Fuller: Just looking at
it, you see natural forces at work. Since his youth, he had been fascinated when
observing phenomena like bubbles forming in a boat's wake. So many perfect
shapes, generated so rapidly! Surely design could aspire to that kind of efficiency.

This is ultimately what the geodesic dome, and Fuller himself, came to symbolize: the idea that design could cut through intractable problems (like human shelter) with brilliant simplicity. Bel Geddes and the other industrial designers of the day also advertised problem-solving capability as one of their unique selling points, but Fuller's garden mindset differentiates him from those contemporaries. His definition of success had nothing to do with the marketplace; indeed, his spectacular failures in this arena seemed only to build his reputation as a visionary intellectual, ahead of his time. It would have pleased him enormously that, after his death, geodesic structures were discovered in carbon molecules—they have been christened "Buckyballs" or "Fullerenes" in his honor. (Already in 1966, the journalist Calvin Tomkins noted in an admiring profile that "several leading nuclear physicists are convinced that the same Fuller formula explains the fundamental structure of the atomic nucleus, and is thus the basis of all matter.")[69]

Another big part of Fuller's appeal was that he was apolitical. It was as if he were looking deep inside our surroundings, or maybe way above them, trying to find new solutions as enduring and universal as a bird's nest or an egg. Over the years, his hostility to ideological tribalism would come to be more and more explicit. His Dymaxion World Map, first published in 1943, showed the earth fragmented into splayed triangles, allowing for a minimally distorted projection of each continent. It could be oriented in any way, but he most favored a version centered on the North Pole, with all the continents arranged in a continuous chain: a graphic representation of human habitation as a single interconnected island. In keeping with this worldview, Fuller argued that human conflict could eventually be rendered obsolete, through a collective mental shift "from weaponry to livingry." Struggles over power, land, and resources were the results of a basic conceptual error: "The supreme political and economic powers as yet assume that it has to be either you or me. Not enough for both."[70] With sufficient ingenuity, though, material constraints could be overcome, and prosperity achieved on a planetary basis. This was a philosophy of mind over matter, a process of "ephemeralization, as emergency evolves into emergence," charting a grand trajectory toward the point of "doing everything with nothing at all."[71] Eventually, even the radical solutions for housing he had devised would be superseded; people would live under the protection of invisible electromagnetic fields.[72]

Such prognostications made Fuller an icon of unbridled techno-optimism. At the same time he was the ultimate garden thinker, dedicated to the principle of natural equilibrium at global scale. In 1951 he hit upon the perfect phrase to describe this holistic vision: "Spaceship Earth." Like all of Fuller's best ideas, this one was simple and arresting: The planet is a vessel hurtling through the void, with a finite amount of fuel. Humans are the crew ("We are all astronauts," as he liked to say) and are tasked with keeping the ship going, which means shepherding what resources we have and using them wisely. We should all work together to achieve this all-important goal—for what boat can stay on course when its sailors are at cross-purposes? This metaphor had real staying power. It would serve as the premise for one of Fuller's most popular books, *Operating Manual for Spaceship Earth* (1969), and in 1982 even inspire a ride at Disney's EPCOT (Experimental City of the Future), located in the theme park's central geodesic dome.

CURIOUSLY, THOUGH, IT was someone else who first published a book called *Spaceship Earth*. This was Barbara Ward, a British-born, French-educated aristocrat with a voice like cut steel. She had burst on to the international scene just before World War II, when she was only twenty-four, with a short publication called *The International Share-Out*. Densely populated with facts, it amounted to a bold critique of Britain's imperialist policies, which she saw as immoral and self-destructive. While Ward stopped short of calling for an end to empire outright, she did argue vociferously against its techniques of domination, advocating instead an open-door policy that would allow colonized nations to trade on their own terms, leading in due course to their political autonomy. "We, the exploiters, must take the first step," Ward wrote. "If we do not, then Haves and Have Nots, successful exploiters with would be exploiters, imperialists past with imperialists present, will go down together into the pit of war which our selfishness, shortsightedness, and lack of courage have helped to dig."[73]

Ward's book, a modest sensation, landed her an editorial job at the magazine the *Economist*, where she eventually became foreign editor. In 1950 she married Robert Jackson, an Australian diplomat and relief administrator at the United Nations, and his work brought the couple to India and various countries in West Africa. She learned about the agrarian economies of these places, and asked herself what it would take to improve their welfare. She was considering conditions similar to those in 1930s Russia, which Eisenstein had dramatized in *The Old and the New*: It is in villages, Ward said, "that the winds of change blow most fitfully, that men are most firmly attached to the ways of their forefathers, that all the encrusted customs, traditions, and superstitions . . . survive most tenaciously."[74] She noted with interest the implementation of Soviet-style five-year plans in India, and advocated U.S. and European funding of such development efforts.

Ward was also watching the British Empire dissolve at close range, and wondering what new political order might take its place. Like many people, she saw the advent of the nuclear age as a new existential threat, making international cooperation all the more vital: "The atomic bomb would rain down on the just and unjust, on the Communist and the non-Communist, on the slave and the free, and could leave us with our last appalling unity—the unity of annihilation."[75] At the same time, technology was also making the world more intimate. In 1961 the Soviet astronaut Yuri Gagarin had circled the globe in a little under two hours. "That's about what it takes to get round a village," Ward noted, "and I think if we can begin to think of our planet as about the scale of a village, then we'll at least have started at the right point."[76]

Ward got to know Fuller in 1963 aboard a ship called the *New Hellas*, in the Aegean Sea. The occasion was the first Delos Symposium, a gathering organized by another of the era's leading futurologists, the Greek architect and theorist Constantinos A. Doxiadis. Though little known today in comparison to Fuller, Doxiadis was at least as influential. He was one of the most active urbanists of the postwar period, and responsible for the master plan of Islamabad—the capital of the new state of Pakistan, created in the partition of India—as well as large projects in Baghdad, Riyadh, and many other cities. In 1958 he had launched in Athens a Center for Ekistics, a neologism he derived from the ancient Greek word *oikestes*, "the leader of a new settlement." An early issue of his *Ekistics* journal featured Fuller's Dymaxion World Map on its cover.[77] Lewis Mumford visited the center in 1960, together with Clarence Stein, the planner of the New Jersey experimental community Radburn.[78]

Doxiadis's big idea was to extend the garden city up to much larger scales, making a "Dynapolis"—a word he chose to emphasize the Fulleresque ideal of dynamic equilibrium—and potentially, someday, an "Ecumenopolis," a universal city covering the whole globe. He continually emphasized the idea that cities extended themselves not only in space but also in time. It was a mistake to focus mainly on buildings, as most architects did, for they were merely the temporary "shells" through which the real energies of the city flowed, in ever-expanding circulatory networks. The purpose of ekistics was to understand and manage this complex process: "to discover a balance between the forces of man, as an individualist and a householder, and the forces of his local community, and also between these and the forces of his period, which is ever moving toward tomorrow."[79]

To rally supporters behind this grandiose vision, Doxiadis brought a group of architects, politicians, and public intellectuals together every July, the last week of the event being spent aboard a chartered yacht—with all costs underwritten by the Ford Foundation. The first of these meetings, in 1963, was already quite an affair, with Fuller, Ward, the historian Siegfried Giedion, the anthropologist Margaret Mead, the Canadian media guru Marshall McLuhan (who would popularize the concept of a "global village" in his book *The Gutenberg Galaxy*, published the following year), and senior government officials from Ghana, India, Poland, Spain, and the United States all in attendance.[80] In the mornings the attendees would discuss ekistics. In the afternoons and evenings they swam, visited historic sites, ate good food, drank retsina, danced, and talked, and talked, and talked.[81] At the event's conclusion, Ward drafted a declaration on behalf of the assembled group (a role she would take in subsequent years, as well). Her text set out the challenge for urban development in no uncertain terms: "We come from different nations, from different cultural backgrounds. Our politics differ, our professions are various. But we are not divided in what we wish most strongly to affirm—we are citizens of a worldwide city, threatened by its own torrential expansion."[82]

Ward's book *Spaceship Earth*, published in 1966, picked up where her first Delos Declaration had left off, laying out a vision of international solidarity. "Hitherto, distances have held men apart," she wrote. "Scarcity has driven them to competition and enmity. But now the distances are abolished. It is at least possible that our new technological resources, properly deployed, will conquer ancient shortage. Can we not at such a time realize the moral unity of our human experience and make it the basis of a patriotism for the world itself?"[83] That idea was very much in line with Fuller's thinking, but Ward acknowledged something that he refused to: The idea of an interconnected world isn't apolitical. On the contrary, as she saw clearly, it is a revolutionary position, fundamentally hostile to the entrenched interests of bordered, sovereign countries. "The old traditional world is dying," Ward wrote in 1962. "The new radical world is not yet born. This being so, the gap between the rich and poor has become inevitably the most tragic and urgent problem of our day."[84] This was a point that Fuller mostly soared right past, traveling as he did in high conceptual orbit. Ward, though, had a very concrete project in mind: the dramatic improvement of physical infrastructure in the developing world. This practical goal was how "a general order of security for mankind" could be achieved, transcending the "painful malady" of nationalism.[85]

Ward was intimately familiar with the United Nations and the limitations placed on it in the context of the Cold War. Nonetheless, she ceaselessly advocated for increased aid and autonomy to impoverished countries—effectively, an extension of the Marshall Plan beyond Europe—hoping that this would establish a more egalitarian basis for global cooperation. Her most tangible involvement was in Ghana. Formerly the Gold Coast, a British colony, Ghana was the first sub-Saharan African country to win its independence, in 1957. Ward's diplomat husband had been appointed as commissioner of development there in 1953, and though Ward maintained a busy intercontinental schedule of travel, lectures, and conferences, she was often in the country during the years of its political transition. This brought her into a close alliance with Kwame Nkrumah, Ghana's first president and a powerful theorist of future development in his own right. With a little symbolic help from Fuller and more extensive contributions from Doxiadis, they would give garden thinking an unprecedented experimental stage.

Originally from a coastal village called Nkroful, Nkrumah reckoned his age by shipwreck. His parents did not record the date of his birth. He figured it might have been in 1909, because when he was about four years old the *Bakana*—a cargo ship filled with oil, on its way from Nigeria to Britain—foundered on the nearby coast, and that had happened in 1913. He grew up looking at the shattered hulk as it gradually decayed in the sun and wind.[86] That story, with all its metaphorical implications of a doomed imperial order, is recounted at the outset of his 1957 autobiography; Nkrumah then goes on to relate his passage out of village life, initially via a teacher training program, and then via ocean voyage to the United States, where he studied at Lincoln University—one of the leading institutions of higher education for African Americans, at a time when the sector was still mostly segregated. He progressed to study and teach at the University of Pennsylvania, lecturing on "Negro History" and other subjects; summers he spent in Harlem, debating with the "soapbox orators" on the street corners. It was Marcus Garvey's ideas that made the strongest impression on him. Though the Black Nationalist leader had been deported a few years before he arrived in New York, Nkrumah devoured *The Philosophy and Opinions of Marcus Garvey*, embracing the pan-African message as a lifelong mission. After assuming the presidency of Ghana, Nkrumah would christen the national shipping fleet the "Black Star Line" in homage to Garvey's earlier trading vessels, and the emblem would also be placed on the national flag.

As part of his academic activities in Philadelphia, Nkrumah began writing, nominally on the topic of education in Africa, but in a way that showed his political consciousness taking shape. In 1943 he wrote an article about the consequences of World War II, echoing the arguments that Garvey and Hubert Henry Harrison had made decades earlier: "Many of us fail to understand that a war cannot be waged for democracy which has as its goal a return to imperialism," he wrote. "The youth of Africa is blazingly awake . . . [and] this new African is neither young nor old; he is just new."[87] After a brief sojourn in London, a time of increasing activism and involvement, he sailed back to the Gold Coast in 1947, joined a pro-independence political party, and began his ascension to power. When the new nation of Ghana was formed in 1957, he became its first prime minister and president.

Nkrumah was also sub-Saharan Africa's first postcolonial leader, and he faced an unprecedented future-building challenge. Just as Barbara Ward had said in *The International Share-Out*, British policy toward its colonies was focused relentlessly on the exploitation of resources, and this prepared nations like Ghana very poorly for independence. "Of industries, we had none except those extracting gold and diamonds," Nkrumah noted in 1963. "We made not a pin, not a handkerchief, not a match."[88] There was only one significant agricultural export, cocoa, and while this was extremely lucrative—giving Ghana a financial stability that other new African states lacked—it was a very narrow base on which to build an economy. (Ward made this point, too, noting Ghana's "dangerous dependence upon a single export crop.")[89] Nkrumah sought to diversify, investing in tobacco, rubber, bananas, coffee, and palm oil production. Meanwhile, he played a risky political game, taking aid from both sides in the Cold War, joining an alliance with "nonaligned" countries like India and Egypt, and vigorously promoting the idea of a "United States of Africa."[90] He cultivated ties with Moscow and Beijing and signaled his personal sympathies with socialism—though he preferred to speak of "communalism," emphasizing collective patterns of African village life as a model for African statecraft—raising suspicions among Western leaders and the press.[91]

These gambits would ultimately leave Nkrumah with a mixed legacy. His commitment to pan-African unity and his desire to consolidate power made him hostile to independent tribes within Ghana. He suppressed them autocratically, a moral lapse that also earned him no shortage of political opponents. Nkrumah also failed to contain rampant corruption, and he arguably tried to transform the Ghanaian economy faster than was practically possible. In the end, it was a disastrous fall in the price of the country's monocrop, cocoa, that doomed his presidency. That was in 1965; the following year, while he was on a diplomatic trip to China, a military coup took advantage of Nkrumah's political weakness and deposed his government, installing a more Western-friendly regime in its place. (The plot was supported, and possibly orchestrated, by the CIA.) He spent the rest of his days in exile, dying in 1972.

These dramatic events occurred right in the middle of Nkrumah's largest social experiment: the construction of a new hydroelectric dam at Akosombo, on the Volta River, with a deepwater port called Tema just to the south. It would be difficult to overstate the scale of this endeavor. Damming the Volta produced the largest artificial lake in the world, flooding 3 percent of Ghana's total land area and displacing about eighty thousand people from their homes.[92] The electricity from the dam was used to power a new national grid for businesses and private consumers and also to activate an aluminum production plant, where bauxite from the country's extensive mineral deposits was processed. A version of this scheme had actually been underway prior to independence—Barbara Ward's husband played a key role in the planning—but amassing the required capital was daunting.[93] Nkrumah managed it with some help from Ward, who successfully lobbied John F. Kennedy's administration on Ghana's behalf.[94] Money also came pouring in from the Ford Foundation, funder of Doxiadis's Ekistics gatherings, and from the Kaiser Aluminum Company, based in Oakland, which would operate the new hydropowered manufactory as a 90 percent shareholder. Nkrumah remembered the formal ceremony that inaugurated construction in 1961 as a pageant of old and new: "I officially launched the Volta River scheme by pressing a button to dynamite a slice out of the hillside at Akosombo. Hundreds of people danced, cheered, sang and fired guns in the air as the local chief poured libation and offered sheep in sacrifice. One of my greatest dreams was coming true."[95]

Against this backdrop of transformation, Buckminster Fuller visited Ghana twice, first in 1964, as part of a wider African tour; and then in autumn 1965, to work with the aluminum that was now being manufactured domestically in Ghana. On the first trip he had been invited as a visiting professor at the recently founded Kwame Nkrumah University of Science and Technology, in Kumasi, and there had the students build a thirty-foot-diameter "tensegrity dome" of mahogany beams held in tension with wire; Fuller hoped that his domes could be used as protective structures for traditional earthen huts. He was impressed by the Ghanaian students he met, pronouncing them "the best mathematicians and design scientist[s] I have found anywhere."[96] Fuller helped lead a recruitment drive to find teachers for the program in Kumasi, bringing idealistic young architects from the United States, Britain, Germany, Japan, the Soviet Union, and Yugoslavia.[97] On his return visit in 1965 he was able to witness tangible proof of their work there: a complete aluminum dome built to his design, installed on the grounds of the International Trade Fair in Accra—another of Nkrumah's prestige projects. Cleverly cooled by the passage of air through narrow vents, it was, Fuller recounted later, "ideal for the tropics," and "the most beautiful of all the geodesic domes that have ever been built."[98]

Characteristically, Fuller said nothing about the volatile political situation in which his domes had been built, only a few months before Nkrumah's fall. Yet symbolically, his modest contributions fit right into the bigger pattern of state-building, in which garden city principles were applied at a considerable geographic remove from their place of origin. Piecemeal strategies were clearly not adequate to the project of swiftly rehousing the eighty thousand people displaced by the artificial lake, or creating an entirely new city as a model for liberated Africa. It was a situation right out of Fuller's forecasts: Ultimately, twelve thousand homes in fifty-two separate townships were built using prefabricated, standardized components, using masonry techniques that were well established in Ghana.[99]

This is when Constantinos Doxiadis entered the picture, presumably at Ward's suggestion. It's likely that his Greek background made him an attractive candidate to Nkrumah; he was himself nonaligned, representing neither a former colonizing nation nor either of the Cold War powers.[100] In 1960 Doxiadis was commissioned to design a master plan for Tema, the new port.[101] The plan had similarities to Broadacre City: a landscape of individual "Communities," each with its own school, market, and civic square, and plenty of plantings. The architectural historian Michelle Provoost describes the vision for "nicely designed, English-style suburban row houses with gardens, lived in by immigrants from different tribes, working in industry; it was an anxious, dynamic industrial metropolis designed as a suburban pastoral."[102] Doxiadis believed in the garden ideal—"rooms connected to each other into organic buildings and the buildings into organic blocks and these again

Tema New Village, Ghana, 1968.

into organic communities"—seeing it as capable of potentially infinite growth, like a self-propagating cellular organism.[103]

"What man needs," Doxiadis wrote, is not utopia but "En-topia, an 'in-place,' a place which satisfies the dreamer and is acceptable to the scientist, a place where the projections of the artist and the builder merge."[104] Whether or not he succeeded in this lofty ambition, he certainly did lay the groundwork for an organic community in Ghana. Today, Tema is a much-adjusted and continually evolving landscape. There aren't many actual gardens, as open plots have been taken over for other more economically productive commercial enterprises, or house extensions to accommodate new family members. "The modernist row houses are hidden behind self-built rooms and shops," Provoost notes, "and the wide streets are lined with illegal kiosks."[105] There are also many more churches than Doxiadis, a thoroughly secular planner, intended or desired, and informal settlements around the edges of the city, where laundries, bars, and markets do their business. Just as Nkrumah hoped, power is delivered from the nearby Akosombo Dam, as indeed it is across Ghana; electricity has gradually been reallocated from foreign-owned aluminum interests to domestic usage.[106] And so, more than six decades after independence, the difficult process of decolonization continues.

Is the planned city of Tema, with all its unplanned accretions, a "dynamic equilibrium," in Fuller's terms? In Doxiadis's, is it an En-topia? How should the project as a whole be viewed, given what was sacrificed for it? Barbara Ward, in her book *Spaceship Earth*, tried to communicate the challenges facing contemporary global society: "A man can safely go to sleep fishing in the middle of a quiet lake. But if he is in the rapids, he had better reach for a paddle."[107] Fair enough—but how about those thousands of homes lying beneath the quiet waters of Lake Volta? The construction of the Akosombo Dam was one of those rare occasions when a group of garden-minded futurologists got their way. It would not have been lost on any of them that much had to be destroyed in the process, or that they failed to build an earthly Eden. Doxiadis, for his part, felt that "architecture should not be the private art of a coterie of architects; it should be the art of the people, their own expression of their own way of life."[108] This is exactly what Tema has become since; and ultimately, this is what organic futurology, garden thinking, has to recommend it. It is not a means of escaping politics, as Fuller often implied, but it does encourage a dynamic equilibrium between intention and eventuality, a mode of planning that creates space for the unforeseen to bloom.

Meanwhile, the Delos Symposium carried on annually until 1975, debating the "city of the future," with Fuller and Ward always in attendance. The tenth-anniversary voyage, in 1972, was a particularly dynamic group; McLuhan was there, as was Jonas Salk, inventor of the polio vaccine. On the last day, Margaret Mead read out the annual declaration, which warned darkly: "If the next critical decades are lost—by continued selfishness, by timidity, by lack of faith—humanity's course will be set towards disaster." The group had plenty of recommendations, all derived from the garden thinking of earlier decades: the resurrection of neighborhoods and villages as the building blocks of larger settlements; more community involvement in decision-making; improved mobility of people and resources. Above all, the assembled experts criticized the short-termism of the political and capitalist elite. "Longer vision is needed than that permitted within the present constraints of terms of office, calculation of returns on investments, and demands for accountability."[109] Not just settlement, but decision-making itself had to be decentralized, transcending narrow interest, crossing disciplines.

It is hard to miss the subtext: A better future is out there, but to reach it, futurologists themselves—a network of people very like the ones assembled on Doxiadis's boat, as a matter of fact—will have to be put in charge. The remarkable thing is that this is exactly what was happening. The Delos Symposium was just one instance of a global phenomenon that began after World War II and gathered pace through the 1970s, and was by no means limited to architecture and urbanism. Governments, corporations, military organizations, universities, research institutes, and charitable foundations were handing unprecedented power and resources to futurologists. This predictive class, in turn, began to use its new platforms to develop ever more elaborate procedures of analysis and speculation. Pure assertion was no longer enough. Like the scientists they affected to be, futurologists were now expected to follow an interrogative method, all built around the single question: *What if?*

4

LAB

ON THE ONE HAND, the German engineer Wernher von Braun was the "Columbus of space." He introduced key innovations in rocketry, ultimately making possible orbital satellites and the mission to the moon. On the other hand, he was a Nazi. In the early 1940s, von Braun helped design the V-2 ballistic missiles that rained down on London; he was also complicit in forcing concentration camp inmates to build them.[1] These crimes were pointedly ignored when, at the end of the war, von Braun—now himself under threat of being killed by Hitler's regime, to prevent his knowledge from falling into enemy hands—surrendered to the Americans. He was brought to the United States as part of Operation Paperclip, a recruitment program of German scientists who had served the Third Reich. Von Braun was happy to switch sides, so long as he could continue his research; he was, as the satiric songwriter Tom Lehrer put it in a 1967 lyric, "a man whose allegiance is ruled by expedience."

Once safely in the United States, far from keeping a low profile, von Braun launched himself boldly before the public. To the extent that he tried to excuse his wartime actions at all, it was by presenting himself, and science, as nonideological. Had he not led the Nazi rocket program, someone else would have; he was no more guilty of war crimes than Alexander Graham Bell was, because "military orders that kill thousands are transmitted over the telephone."[2] Technology is simply a force in the world, he argued. It is the politicians, not the inventors, who determine how it should be deployed.

It is a sign of Americans' postwar technophilia that they accepted this self-justification. In the press, von Braun was presented as having his head far up in the clouds, or indeed, the stars. All he really cared about, apparently, was conquering space; "whether it will be war or peace on earth comes after that for him."[3] At a time when popular science fiction was on the rise, von Braun was embraced as a living personification of science fact. He appeared as an expert in the Walt Disney documentary *Man in Space*, for example. (It was released in 1955, the same year that Tomorrowland—a permanent adaptation of the 1939 World's Fair, complete with corporate pavilions—opened at Disneyland.) In the documentary, the V-2 is admiringly described as "the forerunner of spaceships to come," without reference to wartime labor camps, or even the London Blitz. As director of a NASA center in Huntsville, Alabama, von Braun promoted rocketry both for military use and in the nascent space program—which, in his view, amounted to the same thing. A 1952 article he wrote for *Collier's*, accompanied by dramatic scenes set in near orbit by the painter Chelsey Bonestell, reads like a coded commentary on his own dark past: "Within the next 10 or 15 years, the earth will have a new companion in the skies, a man-made satellite that could be either the greatest force for peace ever devised, or one of the most terrible weapons of war—depending on who makes and controls it." In fact, it would take only six years for the first American satellite to be put into orbit (the *Explorer 1*, a hurried response to the Soviet Union's *Sputnik*). It would be a while longer before some of von Braun's other predictions were realized, including the notion that the whole world, every city and town, would eventually be placed under constant satellite surveillance. "Nothing will go unobserved," he said—an accurate prediction, if hardly an innocent one, coming from a former SS officer.[4]

Von Braun's carefully cleansed reputation remained mostly intact throughout the postwar decades, right up to his death in 1977. At one space conference, held in Stockholm, he was greeted by so much applause that he "took several bows, much like a concert pianist."[5] But not all Americans were so complacent about having this amoral scientist in their midst. He was parodied not only by Lehrer—"Once the rockets are up, who cares where they come down? That's not my department, says Wernher von Braun"—but also in the film *Dr. Strangelove* (1964), in which director Stanley Kubrick entertained the prospect of imminent nuclear annihilation. Peter Sellers plays three different parts in the movie; in the title role, that of an obviously unhinged scientist, he affects a ridiculous German accent and inadvertently refers to the American president as "mein Führer." In one scene, Strangelove explains the Doomsday Machine, a key plot device in the film: When triggered by enemy attack, it automatically sets off a chain of atom bombs, enough to wipe out all life on earth. Why would anyone conceive of such a thing, much less actually build it? Because it is the ultimate deterrent, the manifestation of an "automated and irrevocable decision-making process which rules out human meddling."

This was the self-propelling Machine, so central to the futurological imagination of earlier decades, brought to its deeply illogical conclusion. Kubrick was putting von Braun's argument on its head: Technologists, military leaders, and bureaucrats, by their very nature, really do have a limited view of their own moral responsibility. They are always ready to say, "That's not my department." But far from exonerating them, this makes them, collectively, an existential threat. When (spoiler alert) the film ends in the destruction of life on earth, a montage of mushroom clouds eerily accompanied by Vera Lynn's sentimental wartime hit "We'll Meet Again," viewers may pause to reflect that they are watching not special effects but real archival footage. All these bombs really have been detonated, somewhere, by someone.

One of *Dr. Strangelove*'s most prominent admirers was Lewis Mumford, now in his fourth decade as a public intellectual. "Those of us who have attacked [nuclear] policy by reasoned argument have for almost twenty years addressed deaf ears, closed eyes, locked minds," he wrote in a letter to the *New York Times*. "This film is the first break in the catatonic cold war trance that has so long held our country in its rigid grip."[6] He had been waiting a long time for such a wake-up call. Already in March 1946, with the war barely over, he had published an article with the memorable title "Gentlemen, You Are Mad." It might just as well have been called "I Told You So," for he viewed the bombs dropped on Hiroshima and Nagasaki as the dreadful progeny of the "mechanical ideology" he had written about in *Technics and Civilization*. And if his argument remained essentially the same—machines may seem to serve society, but they actually reshape it according to their own inhuman logic—he now delivered that message with far greater urgency. Lunacy had taken hold at the highest levels, he wrote, and was impelling the world toward destruction: "These madmen have a comet by the tail, but they think of treating it as if it were a child's skyrocket. They play with it, they experiment with it, they dream of swifter and brighter comets." That this could happen in a democracy like the Unites States showed that it was not only the powerful elite but also the general citizenry who were responsible: "Why do we let the madmen go on with their game without raising our voices? Why do we keep our glassy calm in the face of this danger? Here is a reason: we are madmen, too."[7]

Mumford foresaw, correctly, that atomic warheads would soon be combined with ballistic missiles of the type that von Braun had developed. "The principal operatives in our next war will be screened from all contact with the enemy," he wrote in another 1946 essay, "safe until they are annihilated by the same means of long-distance attack," with the result that "the planet itself is now, potentially, an extermination camp."[8] Technical advance was simply outpacing society's capability to cope with it. By way of analogy, he pointed out that worldwide telecommunications had largely been achieved by the end of the war, while efforts toward a shared spoken language had gone nowhere. Mumford would sound similar themes for the rest of his life, calling for a fundamental change in values and challenging the pursuit of progress for its own sake. "It is conceivable, with the means now at the scientist's disposal," he wrote, "that untrammeled curiosity might kill the human race." Under such conditions, it was pure insanity to allow technological research to hurtle toward an uncertain future, free and unchecked. The question was now: "Who will control the controller?"[9]

AND SO A postwar struggle over the future, American style, was set. On one side were technocratic figures like von Braun: institutionalized knowledge workers who were optimistic about the long-term impact of technology and sanguine about the rampant growth of the "military-industrial complex"—of course they were, because they ran it. These experts had the public very much on their side. Beginning in 1958, the Pew Research Center has periodically asked U.S. citizens about their trust in government leadership; in the first year of the poll, 73 percent of respondents said that they "trusted the government to do what is right 'just about always' or 'most of the time.'" Previously, whether early twentieth-century futurologists espoused an eschatological, mechanistic, or organic worldview, they generally had very specific, preconceived ideas of the tomorrows they wanted to see. After 1945, by contrast, a new methodology took hold. The future was no longer a prophecy to be invoked, a machine to be built, or a garden to be tended. It was instead an experiment: something to be studied under laboratory conditions, with multiple scenarios measured and compared against one another. Prediction was becoming a much subtler art— with one defining exception: the prediction of nuclear annihilation, a zero multiplier for all human hopes. The very seriousness of this possibility made it all the more vital to explore multiple pathways, considering every eventuality. Inside the "Pentagon of Power," as Mumford would memorably call it, this meant war games, simulations, and contingency planning. At the same time, there was also another

laboratory for the future being constructed. Outside the technocracy, most importantly in the domain of science fiction, futurologists were employing curiously
similar methods. They postulated complex, richly detailed scenarios that, in their
very specificity, were clearly intended as claims not about what *would* happen but
what *could* happen.

There were, to be sure, limits on all this imaginative activity—particularly
during the so-called Red Scare of the early 1950s, prosecuted by the FBI chief J.
Edgar Hoover and the senator Joseph McCarthy. Socialism of the kind espoused by
the IWW's Big Bill Haywood and Elizabeth Gurley Flynn was effectively outlawed.
(As mentioned in chapter 1, Flynn was put on trial as a Communist in 1952; she was
convicted and imprisoned for more than two years.)[10] Despite the paranoid atmosphere, though, and to some extent in response to it, public intellectuals pursued a
bewildering range of thought experiments. A proliferating network of conferences,
journals, think tanks, foundations, and institutes, both in America and abroad,
combined to form a new field of "future studies."[11] Some of these new organizations
were critical of established networks of power. Others were completely embedded
within them. An important progenitor was Ossip Flechtheim, another European
Jewish war émigré, who is credited with coining the term *futurology* as an area of
social science. Flechtheim lectured on the topic during the war, and then, in an influential 1945 paper, argued that predictive methods should be taught in colleges and
universities, and "made the subject of concrete investigation." This would require
drawing on many different disciplines—history, sociology, philosophy, psychology,
political science, and economics—and would also be multivalent in its posture, always
keeping multiple possibilities in consideration and weighing their relative chances.

Flechtheim thus saw futurology as fundamentally analytical. Though he noted,
with considerable sangfroid, that "we may safely exclude the optimistic assumption
that mankind as an integrated unit will continually progress toward greater liberty,
equality, and fraternity through the use of organized intelligence, world-wide
co-operation, and peaceful adaptation," he did believe that the study of the future,
rigorously pursued, could help guide humanity closer to the right path.[12] As Jenny
Andersson, the leading historian of this era of futurology, writes, Flechtheim's goal
"was not to produce exact prognosis, but to enlighten the future direction societies
were set on so that good futures could be identified and catastrophic ones averted."[13]
This impetus toward multiplicity perhaps accounts for the dizzying proliferation of
futurological organizations that flourished in the 1950s and '60s. The annual Delos

Symposium hosted by Constantinos Doxiadis beginning in 1963, discussed in the previous chapter, was one example. Another was the Pugwash conference on nuclear disarmament, named for the town in Nova Scotia where it was convened; the group was cofounded in 1957 by Joseph Rotblat—the only scientist who quit the Manhattan Project on ethical grounds—together with Bertrand Russell.[14] Buckminster Fuller got into the act with the "World Game," in which he repurposed his Dymaxion Map as a board, with players moving around resources like energy, food, and minerals to maximize "dynamic equilibrium."[15] He collaborated closely on this project with other futurologists, notably John and Magda McHale, whose interests centered on the transformation of consciousness through technology; the McHales were early adopters of interactive cable television, which they saw as a way to "Tune into the Future."

The most famous, and infamous, postwar center of future studies was the RAND Corporation (short for "Research and Development"), based in Santa Monica, California. It was set up in parallel with Operation Paperclip, the program that brought Wernher von Braun and other German scientists to the United States. The aim was to prevent a similar domestic brain drain from the military into the private sector; with the end of hostilities, RAND would provide a civilian platform

Buckminster Fuller lecturing about his World Game in 1969.

for experts to continue advising the government. Organized in December 1945 as a division within the Douglas Aircraft Company, a major arms supplier, RAND was soon spun off as an independent nonprofit. Its initial affiliation toward the U.S. Air Force—the branch of the armed services that oversaw the nuclear weapons program—quickly broadened, so that RAND was advising the government on a wide range of economic, social, and military topics. The historian Alex Abella has described it as "the essential establishment organization," yet one based on a quasi-messianic faith in quantitative analysis as a means of overcoming uncertainty: "The RAND concept of numbers and rationality constitutes a reality that must be explained before it can be seen—much less understood."[16]

RAND's primary activity was forecasting the future, which it undertook using two main methodologies. The first was called, internally, the "Delphi method," after the ancient Greek oracle; it was a formal process in which experts pooled opinions, dispassionately considered one another's arguments, and, ideally, reached consensus. (Variants on the procedure remain commonplace in technology firms, business schools, and consultancies today.) The second was scenario building, in which specific future events are hypothesized and then analyzed on a cost-benefit matrix. The mastermind of this second, more creative tool was the nuclear strategist Herman Kahn, who came across as Bucky Fuller's dark twin, equally voluble and brilliant, but as sinister as Fuller was lovable.

As a researcher at RAND, Kahn wrote a notorious book called *On Thermonuclear War* (1960), which he intended as a critique of simplistic policies of deterrence. He speculated on how the United States might win a nuclear conflict, mused about acceptable survivability rates, and even coined the phrase "doomsday machine"—all priceless material for Kubrick's *Dr. Strangelove*. (Kahn joked that he should get royalties on the film.)[17] In 1961 Kahn founded his own research center, the Hudson Institute, where he continued to offer his trademark blend of cold-blooded strategy and hotheaded speculation to the military and anyone else who would listen, and pay for the privilege.

Meanwhile, in France, the economist Bertrand de Jouvenel was leading a research project called "Futuribles," initiated in 1961 with support from the

Herman Kahn in 1972.

Ford Foundation. Its curious name was a neologism intended to capture the idea of plurality (the word is a near rhyme with "variables"). Thinking about the future, Jouvenel argued, was the opposite of a game of chance. When dealing cards or throwing dice, one knows the full range of possible outcomes, ace through king, one through six, but has no information about what will happen on any given deal or throw. In predictive research, by contrast, "we can be certain that we have *not* enumerated all the possible futures." What we can do, however, is make reasoned conjectures about what might happen next and construct models to study these possible scenarios, factoring in prevailing uncertainty to the equations.[18] Jouvenel outlined his methodology in a 1967 book, *The Art of Conjecture* (it is telling that he used the word *art*, rather than *science*, in the title).[19] He also suggested that a researcher could make a primary forecast—what will likely happen if things stay on their present course—and then show how this curve could be adjusted through various measures, yielding a set of secondary forecasts. The similarity to Roger Babson's normal line, which supposedly predicted the movements of the stock market, is striking; but Jouvenel did not claim that any one of his forecasts was necessarily dependable. On the contrary, his intention was to show the range of divergence for future events, providing a road map of alternative realities that might help in steering a better course.

Clearly, as futurologists were gaining power and influence, they were also seeking to establish their intellectual credibility. Like academics everywhere, they began writing profusely about their own operations. A prominent example of this is the 1964 essay "Twelve Modes of Prediction," commissioned by Jouvenel from the sociologist Daniel Bell, who had become well known with the publication of his book *The End of Ideology* (1960). (He was also affiliated with Herman Kahn's Hudson Institute.) Bell argued that big ideas like "class struggle," which inspired outsize passions to match, were outmoded; history would henceforth proceed through smaller-scale, more pragmatic political transformations.[20] In "Twelve Modes," he developed a repertoire of techniques to match this incremental world-view, giving his ideas scientific-sounding names like "social physics," "sequential development," and "the theory of the prime mover."[21]

It sounded quite impressive, if not entirely systematic. But *was* futurology a proper academic discipline? Bell certainly seemed to think so, echoing Flechtheim and Jouvenel when he asserted that "the function of conjecture is not prediction, but explanation."[22] Only by understanding all the variables in play in a given scenario—whether in politics, in business, or in one's personal life—is it possible to adequately anticipate future problems and plan for future needs. From this point of view, Bell said, we cannot precisely predict the future, but we can invent it.[23] To other observers, however, such procedures were far from respectable intellectual discourse. All these complicated methodologies were, in the end, a simple proxy for power, an attempt to extend the "self-fulfilling prophecies" that color trend forecasters had developed in the 1920s and '30s, and apply them to matters of far greater significance, indeed, to every aspect of contemporary life.

An early, and still riveting, expression of this point of view is Robert Jungk's 1954 book *Tomorrow Is Already Here*. Comparatively little known today, Jungk was one of the twentieth century's most courageous and perceptive journalists. Born in 1913 to a Jewish family in Berlin, he worked in the anti-Nazi underground throughout the war, using Switzerland as a safe base but also operating in France, Czechoslovakia, and in Germany itself. He learned about the existence of the concentration camps early on, and tried to make the atrocities public; unfortunately, he was unable to persuade Swiss newspapers to run the stories, as his editors simply refused to believe what he was telling them. Later he would write a pair of books exploring the advent of atomic weapons from two sides: *Brighter Than a Thousand Suns* (1958), which profiled scientists who had worked on the Manhattan Project; and *Children of the Ashes* (1961), which explored the tragic long-term effects of the Hiroshima bombing.[24]

Between 1947 and 1953 Jungk spent most of his time in the United States, where he exploited his wartime credentials to gain access to "semi-secret" military and corporate sites across the country, trying to understand what made the country tick, like a latter-day Alexis de Tocqueville. First published in German, *Tomorrow Is Already Here* was the result of that investigative research. The book anticipates by three decades the well-known aphorism, attributed to the science fiction author William Gibson, that "the future is already here, it's just not very well distributed." Jungk's way of putting it was less memorable, but more beautiful: "The morrow is already present in today, but harmlessly masked still, hidden and disguised behind the familiar." It is also worth mentioning the German edition's original subtitle, *Amerikas Allmacht und Ohnmacht*—that is, "America's Omnipotence and Impotence." Though not used for the English translation, the phrase captures much of what was at stake for Jungk. Having just witnessed the fall of totalitarianism in Europe, he was dismayed to perceive signs of its rise in the United States, for this is how he interpreted the various forms of prediction-oriented bureaucracy he discovered on his travels. A new formation of power was emerging, and the general population's future was being decided for them without their realizing it.

Jungk began his book in the most ominous place possible, Alamogordo, where the first bomb test, code-named Trinity, had left a gigantic crater in the earth—the "birthmark of the new era," as he chillingly put it. While waiting for permission from the Atomic Energy Commission to get into the site, he conducted local interviews and discovered the impact of the test on nearby residents, including the Indigenous community. "There is scarcely another region of North America where Indian antiquity, embroidered with legend, is so alive as in this part of New Mexico," Jungk noted. But even before the historic blast, the atomic project had had a distorting effect on the Native population. They were hired on as laborers, earning more in a month than they would in a year of farming, and with the money came disruption. At first the income was shared out among families, but some Indigenous people—especially GIs returned from the war—"began to rebel against the old customs," arguing that they should keep what they earned as individuals. Meanwhile, electric lighting and agricultural machinery were coming to Native-owned pueblos and farms, along with radios and telephones. "With each step forward in material adaptation to the American way of life," Jungk writes, "the revision of the old values also advanced."[25]

If Jungk was expressing, here, a certain paternalism about New Mexico's Indigenous tribes—akin to that of Mabel Dodge Luhan and John Collier—he also seems to have been aware of a new and unprecedented threat to their welfare. The government had not warned anyone living nearby about the Trinity test; it was, of course, top secret. Nor did they make efforts to protect local communities from the radioactive fallout. People kept raising cattle, kept using their underground water cisterns. In 1951 a new nuclear testing site was created in Nevada; atmospheric detonations were conducted there over the ensuing decade, with tourists to Las Vegas sometimes driving out to take in the sight. Little thought was given to nearby Indigenous lands, and these "downwinders" have suffered from increased rates of cancer ever since. Although Jungk does not seem to have been very knowledgeable about radiation sickness, at this early date, when he did get to the crater—accompanied by a young soldier, "a healthy square-built boy [who] could not understand why anyone should expend so much patience on seeing this 'little bit of nothing in the middle of nothing at all'"—he was fascinated and unnerved by the so-called Trinity stone lying all around, "a glassy green layer of death."[26] He had stumbled across a new substance: what we might now see as the first mineral deposits of the Anthropocene.

Jungk's next stop, the White Sands Proving Ground, was nearly as foreboding. It was essentially an enormous shooting range, built to test guided missiles like the ones von Braun had invented. Dominating this vast landscape was a firing platform "as strange and inhuman as a pyramid, as unapproachable and secretive as the Sphinx." Apart from that it was a trackless wasteland as far as the eye could see. Standing in this howling emptiness, Jungk recalled a remark made by a scientist of his acquaintance: "Our experiments have grown so dangerous that we've had to withdraw nearly everywhere into regions once inhabited only by outlaws." This thought would recur to him throughout his tour of America's classified sites, literally fenced-off places where the country's usual vaunted freedoms were suspended. It was in these unseen and detached laboratories, he thought, that the future was being made.[27]

As Jungk discovered, this secretive research was paradoxically pervasive in America. He found it not only at military installations but at industrial-scale farms, where cows were treated like machines; in office buildings, where Endicott calculators were used to "carry out nearly every kind of straightforward logical thinking operation with superhuman speed"; and in factories, where industrial psychologists kept tabs on their employees with "psychographs, productometers, motive profiles, sociograms and communication charts." In DuPont's chemical plants, he saw scientists churning out patentable, marketable discoveries at an average rate of one per day: nonfreezing motor oil, glow-in-the-dark construction materials, synthetic foods. He noticed a sign on one laboratory door that read A.D. 2000. Jungk also talked to consumer researchers who were systematizing and elaborating the forecasting techniques of their discipline, which had been established by Christine Frederick and Margaret Hayden Rorke in the 1920s. Three decades on, these experts spoke no longer of "Mrs. Consumer," but instead of "Mrs. Average." They treated all of Columbus, Ohio, like a specimen in a test tube, because research suggested that it was unusually typical: "Apparently the majority of the nation buys what Columbus buys, eats what Columbus eats, likes what Columbus likes and rejects what Columbus rejects." Mrs. Average was made of statistics, rather than flesh and blood, though Jungk observed researchers using a "psycho-galvanometer" to measure subjects' physiological responses to Ford advertisements.[28]

Toward the end of Jungk's tour he had perhaps his most fascinating encounter, at the unfascinating-sounding National Bureau of Standards. Here he came face to face with a machine called SEAC, the Standards Electronic Automatic Computer. A relatively small computer for the era—it weighed about 3,000 pounds and occupied 150 square feet of floor space—it was nonetheless innovative, the first that could store a program in its internal memory and then modify it for future use. (Jungk doesn't mention it, but SEAC was partly inspired by the Mathematical Analyzer Numerical Integrator and Automatic Computer, or MANIAC—you can't make this stuff up—used at Los Alamos to calculate the trajectory of ballistic missiles.)[29] SEAC also represented the introduction of computing into government policy. Though Jungk found it hard to believe, the machine had just persuaded Eisenhower to fire one of his more hawkish generals: "We had to work out how the American economy in all its sectors would react to a sudden entry into war at this moment," Jungk is told. "SEAC gave the answer in clear, unambiguous numbers . . . and these computations were the strongest trump in the President's hand when he decided against the general and his policy."[30]

A few months later, Jungk found himself at the RAND Corporation in Santa Monica, surrounded by economists, mathematicians, engineers, sociologists,

An operator at the control console of SEAC, 1959.

statisticians, psychologists, and computer technicians. He observed them running a computerized war game in which ten seconds of clock time represented a day in the program, and resources and damage were all assigned quantitative values, ending only with the complete destruction of one side. Jungk's description, the last passage in his book, is hauntingly similar to the end of *Dr. Strangelove*: "As the switches click in the silent room the adversaries' countries are transformed into simulated ruins. Finally the hand on the dial plate of the one party sinks to zero. That means that its cities have been destroyed by explosions, its people exhausted, paralyzed, presumably poisoned by radioactivity, and its entire Air Force lost. The game is up. The oracle has spoken."[31]

ONE OF THE main themes of Jungk's book is so simple that it almost escapes notice: If the future was big business in America, then bigness itself was part of the reason. The operations of the government and the corporate sector were simply getting too vast, too complex, and too interdependent to be coordinated without extensive data collection and centralized decision-making. As the political economist James Burnham argued in his influential 1941 book *The Managerial Revolution*, control over the means of production was increasingly being exerted by "a new ruling managerial class."[32] Futurologists were no longer just avant-gardists, eccentrics, and entrepreneurs. They were financial officers, company executives, and government bureaucrats.

One man who had all these jobs, over the course of his career, was Robert Strange McNamara, and it is through his story that the rise and fall of technocratic futurology's unchallenged dominance is best told. His biography is an *Oedipus Rex* for the late twentieth century: a tragedy with hubris at its heart. It is a tale with several chapters, beginning in the Bay Area, where McNamara was born in 1916, and coming to a not-quite-redemptive conclusion with his tenure as president of the World Bank, where he earned widespread praise for his work in fighting global poverty. But it is as U.S. secretary of defense from 1961 to 1968 that McNamara is mostly remembered, because in that capacity he did as much as anyone else to push America into Vietnam, and then keep us there. This decision, a mistake of world-historical consequence, has made him a subject of enduring recrimination and fascination.[33] Taken together, the many divergent books and documentaries about McNamara's life consistently portray him as an articulate but anguished figure, unable to quite face up to his own past. The historian David Halberstam wrote that he was "like a player at the poker table who, when the game is over, still refuses to show his cards"—a strange fate for a man who was arguably the most influential futurologist of his generation.[34]

That term, *futurologist*, is not usually applied to McNamara, but there is no question that it fits. Long before his epic failure of foresight about Vietnam, he had risen to power by marshalling facts—lots of them—and then transmuting those statistics into future-oriented strategies. He first learned these skills at Harvard Business School, where he arrived in 1937, just as the "managerial revolution" was coming to the campus. As the journalist Paul Hendrickson writes, the key insight of the moment was that "numbers need not be merely for establishing historical record—the home ground of traditional cost accountants—but for planning, for forecasting, for quantitatively analyzing, for segregating the trouble spots and identifying the upcoming trends, for abstracting and projecting and predicting."[35] This method was based on techniques that had already been introduced in corporate America, especially in the insurance and the automotive industries. McNamara's aptitude for this sort of fine-grained analysis was swiftly recognized, and Harvard brought him on as a junior professor. Then came the first of several fateful turns: After the attack on Pearl Harbor, he was recruited alongside other faculty and assigned to a new management unit in the U.S. Air Force called Statistics Control. They were charged with bringing order to what had been organizational chaos: inefficiencies of every kind, from wasted machine parts to poorly devised deployments.

At the end of the war, flush with success, ten of the top analysts from the Statistics Control group, including McNamara, boldly presented themselves to the Ford Motor Company, suggesting that they could bring the same organizational prowess to the struggling manufacturer. (Its woes were due in part to Henry Ford's distrust of fashion trends; the company had lost most of its market share to the more design-savvy General Motors, sponsor of Bel Geddes's Futurama.) Hardly any of the Statistics Control men knew a thing about cars—but then, none of them had so much as flown in an airplane before they joined the air force. Before long, they were being called "the Whiz Kids."[36]

It was at Ford that McNamara really set himself apart. He pushed relentlessly for efficiency, hunting down every hidden expenditure. He directed a newly hired team of number crunchers to produce forecasts, which were then used for operational planning from the shop floor to the marketing department. Every chart was an accountability mechanism: a future trajectory, a target to hit. The age of the knowledge worker had come to the very heart of American manufacturing. By 1949 McNamara was general manager of the Ford Division—the largest of the company's brands. In this senior role, he got a few big calls right. He was extremely skeptical about the Edsel, and was proved correct when it became the most embarrassing flop in automotive history. He instead backed Ford's dull but solid Falcon and Fairlane models, which proved to be big successes.

It was with a sense of inevitability that McNamara was promoted to president of the Ford Motor Company in November 1960, making him one of the most powerful men in corporate America. But less than a month later, John F. Kennedy asked him to join his incoming administration as secretary of defense. The managerial revolution was about structure, not content, just as experiments conducted on mice aren't really about rodents. So McNamara took a pay cut and went to Washington. As soon as he arrived at the Pentagon, McNamara set about imposing the same predictive techniques he'd used at Ford on the whole of the U.S. military, and to similar effect. Middle management swelled. In five years he increased the staff of the

Robert McNamara in 1965.

Department of Defense by 50 percent, with particular growth in the areas of intelligence gathering and financial control.

These civilians clashed with military personnel, echoing the culture divide of the wartime air force. The navy vice admiral Hyman G. Rickover called the studies produced by McNamara and his squadron of accountants "in general, abstractions. They read more like the rules of a game of classroom logic than a prognosis of real events in the real world."[37] If that sounds like a description of the war games being conducted at RAND, it's no coincidence. Under McNamara, the Department of Defense increasingly relied on the Santa Monica think tank, and vice versa—these contracts accounted for fully 25 percent of RAND's total funding by 1965. Alarmed by the leftward drift of nonaligned countries like Kwame Nkrumah's Ghana, RAND began investing in "third world studies," which largely meant working up "military modernization" scenarios—a euphemism for U.S.-backed coups.[38] Some of McNamara's top hires came directly from RAND, too, and were aligned with the dispassionate (some might say inhuman) style of analysis their colleague Herman Kahn had developed in *On Thermonuclear War*.[39] Drawing on that research, McNamara established a new foreign policy which came to be called "flexible response." It was straight out of the new futurological playbook: Rather than depending on nuclear weapons as a deterrent, a bluff that could be called at any time, the United States would develop its capacity to engage in conflicts at all scales, responding in a manner proportional to the risk. The principles of multiplicity and preparedness, as advanced by Flechtheim, Jouvenel, and Bell—a methodological departure from the linear, mechanistic principles of earlier professional futurologists— were now to be implemented at the highest level of the military.

On paper, flexible response may have made a certain amount of sense. In the real world, it was a good intention that paved the road to hell. The problem was that, even as McNamara was trying to keep all military options open, the United States' foreign policy was still in thrall to another, much simpler predictive model: the "domino theory" that the threat of Communist expansion would be impossible to contain once it began. Historians have proffered many explanations for America's entry into the Vietnam War. One compelling way of looking at it, though, is as a toxic combination of these two predictive models. The futurology-influenced doctrine of flexible response led to a significant buildup of conventional forces, and an unwarranted confidence that small-scale conflicts—like a battle for a country in

Southeast Asia—could be easily managed. The inflexible domino theory, meanwhile, held that losing even one nonaligned country to Soviet and Chinese influence would lead inevitably to a shift in the balance of world power.

These calculations led to the Kennedy administration's first interventions in Vietnam, then to massive escalation under Lyndon Johnson, then to ignominious defeat under Richard Nixon. Throughout, McNamara was seen, rightly, as bearing much of the responsibility. Already in 1964—the year of the Gulf of Tonkin resolution, which authorized Johnson to undertake military action—Senator Wayne Morse of Oregon was calling it "McNamara's War." McNamara responded like a loyal technocrat: "I think it is a very important war and I am pleased to be identified with it and do whatever I can to win it."[40] The following year, the United States began its saturation bombing of North Vietnam. Almost all of that ordnance missed its intended targets, as computer guidance was still some years off. Vietnamese people were dying in appalling numbers. So, increasingly, were American soldiers, to no clear purpose. McNamara, sticking to his playbook, turned the tragic situation into a series of data points, treating "kill ratio" and "body count" as predictive measures in the war's progress.

Public opinion remained in favor of the war throughout most of McNamara's tenure as secretary of defense, though it was declining fast. Only in 1967, the year before his resignation, would it fall beneath the 50 percent threshold. When did he realize that the war was becoming not just unpopular, but unwinnable? Why did it take him so long to admit it, even behind closed White House doors? And what might have happened if he had made his concerns public? Those questions have often been asked, and never satisfactorily answered. What is certain is that in May 1967 McNamara told President Johnson to stop sending troops, and to negotiate the best peace he could. Johnson rejected this advice, opening up a breach between the two men. McNamara left his post in February 1968. Even then, he did not come out against the war, though an honest appraisal from him might have helped bring the carnage to a quicker end. Instead, it would last five more agonizing years. In 1971 Daniel Ellsberg (another RAND strategist) leaked the "Pentagon Papers," an internal study into the history of the war that McNamara himself had commissioned; the public discovered that their government had systematically deceived them for years on a range of topics, from covert operations to internal assessments of the war's progress. That sickening revelation, in combination with the Watergate scandal, led to a collapse in public trust in the government. The aforementioned Pew poll registered it at 36 percent in 1974, and it would never really recover. (In the most recent poll, taken in 2022, the figure was just 20 percent.)

Futurology, unsurprisingly, suffered a parallel decline in status. If McNamara, leading exponent of the technocracy's "best and brightest," could lead America into such an unmitigated disaster, how could expert forecasts be trusted ever again?[41] RAND, especially, became a byword for secretive warmongering, even as its activities in the 1960s and '70s broadened into areas like health care, education, and urban planning. The corporation remains active today, with offices in forty-eight countries; it has published a detailed study about its own involvement in Vietnam.[42] Such is its reputation that its website includes, on its frequently asked questions page, "I've heard a lot of rumors about you guys. Are any of them true?"

IN 1973—THE YEAR the United States finally pulled out of Saigon—Robert Jungk observed that "the Vietnam war had been more thoroughly played through, more exhaustively analyzed and planned, than any other war in history. The programmers had assumed a number of factors concerning the Vietnamese and fed them in accordingly; but the real Vietnamese did not choose to play the role assigned to them. They turned out to be 'somewhat unpredictable.'"[43] Since his sojourn in America, Jungk had been mostly based in Vienna—he lived there from 1957 until his death in 1994—committing most of his energies to the international peace movement. He remained an interested observer of future studies, if a skeptical one, reporting for example on a 1965 Futuribles conference convened by Bertrand de Jouvenel in Paris: "Despite Marx and Tocqueville, whose presence was conspicuously missed at this gathering, political science is still, like astrology, a speculative art."[44] While he did continue to publish social criticism in the vein of *Tomorrow Is Already Here*, he worried that he was not mobilizing his readers but instead "contributing to their sense of resignation."[45] For a time, he privately published a "Good News Bulletin," attempting to counteract the media's tendency to overemphasize crisis.

Jungk also proved unpredictable in his own right: He came to believe that, if calamities like the Vietnam War were to be averted, there would need to be *more* prediction-making. Future studies, he decided, could only be redeemed by giving everyone a chance to participate, encouraging the public at large to use speculative tools to reflect on the questions of the day. "Social laboratories should stop being sacred temples where only the high priests of professional expertise are admitted," he wrote, and they should consider not only matters of war and corporate strategy, but "ideas for child-rearing, for de-centralizing management, for non-authoritarian types of organization, for freeing women from housework."[46] Jungk went so far as to develop his own forecasting workshops, intended not for specialists but everyday citizens. These centers employed a simplified, three-stage version of the RAND Delphi tool: first criticism, then utopian thinking, then the identification of specific actions that might bring about a desirable future. One workbook he produced had a cartoon of two women on its cover, captioned: "We can't afford to be passive spectators—if we sit back and let them get away with this one day we will wake up to find our freedom has passed away like a dream!"[47] It was essential, Jungk believed, to keep imagining how tomorrow could be better: "Alternative life-styles are not just a wish, they are a necessity."[48]

Jungk was doubtless correct in his diagnosis: Technocratic futurology was the very definition of an ivory tower. For all their supposedly broad horizons, professionals in the discipline remained a tightly interconnected community, insulated by a circuit of institutions, and made up of a tiny demographic of white, middle-class men. This narrowness of view doubtless accounted for many of its blind spots. There was, however, another, far more permissive cultural space opening up, where alternative tomorrows were being dreamt up and disseminated. This was the realm of science fiction. In this elastic, increasingly inclusive cultural space, the future also functioned as a Lab. But in this context, the main form of expertise was imagination, not calculation, and America's technocracy was reflected as if in a funhouse mirror.

Science fiction, too, began as a boy's club—quite literally, as most of its early readers, and not a few of its writers, were male adolescents. They thrilled to the outlandish offerings of magazines like *Amazing Stories*, edited by Jewish immigrant Hugo Gernsback, the first and most influential of the "pulps" that defined the genre in the 1920s. (The term comes from the use of inexpensive wood paper on which the magazines were printed.) An early cover, with artwork by Frank R. Paul, conveys the mood of this formative period: a staring eye is isolated against a vivid rainbow backdrop, the lids edged with lightning-bolt lashes. An evolutionary procession parades along the eye's lower perimeter, from dinosaurs through knights on horseback, alluding to the medieval-styled fantasy that sometimes appeared in the magazine. But it's in the iris, filled with gearwork, and the eye's dark pupil, reflecting deep space, that Gernsback's primary interest is captured. He thought of "scientifiction" (the more familiar term hadn't quite caught on yet) as a frontier of discovery: "The author who works out a brand new idea in a scientifiction plot may be hailed as an inventor years later, when his brain-child will have taken wings and when cold-blooded scientists will have realized the author's ambition."[49]

By the time it reached the pages of *Amazing Stories* and the bedrooms of American teenagers, science fiction had already come a long way, from Thomas More's *Utopia* to Mary Shelley's *Frankenstein* to Edward Bellamy's *Looking Backward*, Charlotte Perkins Gilman's *Herland*, and the works of Jules Verne and H. G. Wells. But it achieved widespread popularity only in the 1930s. The New York World's Fair broadcast a sci-fi sensibility to an unprecedentedly large audience. Its iconic Trylon and Perisphere could have been ripped right off the cover of *Amazing Stories*; so too could the overall theme, "The World of Tomorrow," and of course, Norman Bel Geddes's Futurama. He was an enthusiastic reader of H. G. Wells, including his 1933 book *The Shape of Things to Come*—made into a film in 1936, whose terrifying and genuinely prophetic images of airborne bombing could perhaps have informed the more benign "flyover" that Bel Geddes devised to carry visitors over the America of 1960.[50]

A much less prominent event held during the 1939 Fair was the "World Science Fiction Convention," the immodest title chosen for a get-together of about two hundred fans held in Caravan Hall on East Thirty-Ninth Street over in Manhattan. The illustrator Frank R. Paul was the guest of honor. There was a screening of Fritz Lang's *Metropolis*, though it apparently failed to wow the crowd. ("The acting was of the type generally inserted between two slices of rye bread," a seventeen-year-old attendee commented, "and only a few scenes were futuristic. These were good.")[51] The gathering has legendary status among sci-fi fans to this day, however, partly because it was the first "WorldCon," but also due to a schism that occurred between rival camps. On one side of the conflict was the chairman of the convention, one Sam Moskowitz, a teenage aspiring writer from Newark, New Jersey. On the other was a group from New York City known (mostly to themselves) as the Futurians. A year earlier, when Orson Welles alarmed the public with his all-too-persuasive dramatized broadcast of H. G. Wells's *War of the Worlds*, the Futurians had considered, between games of Ping-Pong, whether the Martians *had* landed. Maybe they had planned the whole controversy, taking advantage of the chaos to hide their arrival? Maybe Orson Welles was a figment of the Martians' imagination, and not the other way around?[52] The Futurians were also politicized. It was, after all, the depths of the Great Depression, and if the futures depicted in *Amazing Stories* were luridly bright, the prospects that these teenage fans faced in real life seemed grim. Some were attracted to socialism, an important intellectual context for the sci-fi genre since Bellamy. At smaller gatherings leading up to the 1939 convention, the Futurians had distributed manifestos and delivered utopian speeches, arguing that science fiction should be a means not of escaping this reality but of modeling a better one. One of their number, Johnny Michel, was a particularly intense ideologue, and the left-leaning group was sometimes called "the Michelists," as if they were a Soviet faction.

In the days leading up to the World Convention in 1939, Moskowitz and his fellow organizers got a look at a Futurian-aligned fanzine called *A Warning!*, accusing them in advance of planning a dictatorial repression of dissent. Incensed, they turned Michel and five others away at the door—an event that has gone down in fandom history, a little ridiculously, as the "Great Exclusion Act." The incident would hardly merit mention were it not for three things. First, the Futurians included several of science fiction's future luminaries: most famously, Isaac Asimov, as well as Damon Knight, C. M. Kornbluth, James Blish, Judith Merril, and Frederik Pohl. Between them, both as writers and editors, this small group would do much to revolutionize the genre during and after World War II. Second, this minor dispute happened to occur just as the very idea of "the teenager" was beginning to take hold. Youth culture was coming into its own, and being newly invested with hopes and (especially) fears about the next generation.[53] In most cases this was a projection that adults made onto young men and women. But this particular group was thinking, actively and self-consciously, about what the future might look like. Two decades later rock music would become the primary expression of teenage culture; until then, science fiction was its most promising vehicle.

The third and final reason that the "Great Exclusion Act" seems so resonant in retrospect is that, as science fiction increased in both popularity and sophistication in the postwar years—the pulps still going strong, now supplemented by slicker magazines, proper novels, and Hollywood movies—the question of its political potential remained very much in play. This may sound a little unlikely. The reputation of sci-fi hasn't changed much since the great cultural critic Susan Sontag, in her 1965 essay "The Imagination of Disaster," asserted flatly that "there is absolutely no social criticism, of even the most implicit kind, in science fiction films." Having watched quite a few of them, she decided that all the stories about atomic monsters, up from the depths or crawling out of the Trinity blast crater, might register the anxieties of the age but did nothing to address them, much less provide a viable alternative. "Here," Sontag wrote, "thinking about the unthinkable—not in the way of Herman Kahn, as a subject for calculation, but as a subject for fantasy— becomes, however inadvertently, itself a somewhat questionable act from a moral point of view."[54]

To be sure, most postwar science fiction, particularly the stuff that made it onto the big screen, had no critical dimension. In keeping with Gernsback's motto "Extravagant Fiction Today . . . Cold Fact Tomorrow," many of the stories' protagonists were high-minded male scientists, heroes searching for pure knowledge, fictional equivalents of Wernher von Braun. This dominant strain in the field, usually called "hard" science fiction, was often intended as a delivery mechanism for scientific and technological information to young minds; it was especially championed in the postwar years by the editor John W. Campbell at *Astounding Science-Fiction*. Politically speaking, hard science fiction could be downright reactionary. Robert Heinlein, one of the era's most popular authors, was essentially a Cold War propagandist. In his notorious *Starship Troopers* (1959), Heinlein glorified a proto-fascist army engaged in a genocidal war against an alien civilization, while his earlier novel *The Puppet Masters* (1951), set in the year 2007, features slugs from outer space with mind-control powers; the invaders easily brainwash the Soviets and Chinese (where no one even notices the difference) but are defeated by independent-thinking Americans.[55]

Yet to a surprising degree, science fiction in the postwar era did realize the early dreams of the Futurians, remaining a channel through which progressive views were transmitted into popular culture. This was occasionally true even in the cinema. Sontag does not mention it, but one of the first sci-fi movies to be produced after the war, *The Day the Earth Stood Still* (1951), calls the nascent conservative ideology of Cold War America directly into question. Based on a 1940 story by Harry Bates (the founder and editor of *Astounding Science-Fiction*, until Campbell took over in 1937), it portrays a wise emissary from another planet, where warfare has been rendered obsolete. He arrives in a spaceship that was designed in collaboration with Frank Lloyd Wright, one of the first on-screen visualizations of a flying saucer. Dismissing Cold War hostilities as "petty squabbles," the extraterrestrial seeks to address humanity as a collective, encouraging them to make peace with one another, but no one will hear him out. In the final act, American soldiers hunt him down and shoot him—at the time, a daring portrayal of the U.S. military as an instrument of irrational, unnecessary violence. After being resurrected with alien technology, he delivers a last speech: "Your choice is simple. Join us and live in peace, or pursue your present course and face obliteration."

Such messages were easier to find where Sontag wasn't looking, in pulp magazines and dime novels. Theodore Sturgeon—who liked to point out that "while 90% of science fiction may be crud, 90% of *everything* is crud"—wrote a vivid short story called "Memorial" in 1946, which anticipated *Dr. Strangelove* by almost two decades. Its protagonist, a former scientist at the Manhattan Project, builds a radioactive pit to demonstrate the dangers of atomic power. He intends it as a deterrent, but it accidentally explodes, triggering nuclear war. "For a while there was some very interesting material to be studied on the effects of radiation on heredity," Sturgeon comments at the end of his satire, "but there was no one to study it." Mordant narratives were often found in the work of the former Futurians, too. They had effectively disbanded in 1944—the result of yet another internecine feud—but continued to explore political and ethical themes in science fiction as they matured as writers. James Blish, for example, used science fiction to critique contemporary thought-policing in his dystopian novel *They Shall Have Stars* (1956), whose malevolent main character is based partly on J. Edgar Hoover and Joseph McCarthy.[56] Frederik Pohl teamed up with another prominent sci-fi author, Lester Del Ray, to write *Preferred Risk* (1955), which literalized Wallace Stevens's thought experiment: What if the insurance business completely took over society? The novel describes a dictatorship of the actuariat: Claims adjusters from "The Company" run everything, in a coordinated program of risk management. Disease, fire, and accidents are unknown, but so is freedom.

Isaac Asimov, born in the Soviet Union but raised in Brooklyn, had always been one of the less politicized members of the Futurians. Even so, he was a firm advocate of what he described as "social science fiction," arguing for its importance in the atomic age: "We have brought ourselves to such a pass that we wonder whether the planet might not die with us. . . . For the first time in history, the future cannot be left to take care of itself; it must be thought about."[57] Several of his early stories develop themes already established by Samuel Butler and by Karel Čapek's *R.U.R.*, considering the moral implications of Asimov's famous three laws of robotics: A robot must not injure a human being; a robot must obey human commands; a robot must protect itself. He typically portrayed the artificial intelligences constrained by these rules sympathetically, struggling to live up to them much as humans try and fail to live up to religious commandments.[58]

Asimov was also one of many science fiction writers to consider futurology in a recursive way, by making the art of prediction an important theme in his work. It was the main narrative premise for his Foundation series, initially serialized in *Astounding* between 1942 and 1950, and later published in novel form. The plotline is set in motion by a brilliant scientist called Hari Seldon, who is able to foresee his interplanetary empire's imminent fall by using what he calls "psycho-history," explained (sort of) as "that branch of mathematics which deals with the reactions of human conglomerates to fixed social and economic stimuli." Asimov clearly intended psycho-history as an exaggerated version of real-world professional fore-casting. And he had great fun with the idea: At one point Seldon mildly observes that there is exactly a 1.7 percent chance that he'll be assassinated, due to the provoc-ative nature of his work. This doesn't happen, and instead he is exiled to a far-flung planet, where he instructs his followers to assemble an Encyclopedia Galactica dedicated to the preservation of human knowledge, not unlike the time capsule at the 1939 World's Fair (it's even stored on microfilm). This proves to be a wild goose chase, though, one of several reversals in which apparent knowledge of the future proves illusory. Seldon's psycho-history, it turns out, is beset by a paradox: If its predictions become widely known, they will no longer be accurate, because the prediction itself will alter people's behavior—a neat reversal of the notion of the self-fulfilling prophecy.

Such clever maneuvers did position Asimov as a critical voice, to some extent, and the overarching storyline of the Foundation stories—that of an empire doomed to ruin—could, at a stretch, be read as a counternarrative to America's postwar ascendancy. Yet Asimov was at heart a hard science fiction writer. He had never been a radical, and became even less so as the 1950s and '60s wore on, easing into the role of a scientific popularizer, a great explainer. The ex-Futurian who did the most to extend the group's political beginnings was instead Judith Merril, the most prominent of the women members of the group. (Another, Virginia Kidd, became a literary agent for science fiction writers.) Born in Boston in 1923—her mother was a former suffragist—Merril moved to the Bronx as a teenager. Before she wrote science fiction she was already a socialist, "a Trotskyist's Trotskyist," as she put it in her autobiography, and it was through her political activism that she met her first husband, marrying him at the age of just seventeen. It was he who introduced her to sci-fi. "Completely zonked" by what she read, she came into contact with the Futurians. "They each had their own visions about the future; it was coming, and they were thinking about it better than anyone else," she later wrote. "Most were without academic discipline; drop-outs, either from high school or after a short period in university. All of them had the weird, erotic erudition typical of teenagers immersed in reading science fiction."[59]

In the June 1948 issue of *Astounding*, Merril published her most well-known story, "That Only a Mother," the most genuinely disturbing of the many post-atomic science fiction tales that circulated in the wake of Hiroshima and Nagasaki. The scene is set just five years in the future, in 1953, but World War III is already well underway. The use of nuclear weapons has produced a complex tapestry of horror, with mass casualties in some places and prevalent background radiation in others—just the sort of grimly detailed scenario that Herman Kahn would speculate about in *On Thermonuclear War*. Merril, though, was not interested in strategic games-manship. Rather, she portrayed the personal and psychological dimensions of such a catastrophe. It was just the kind of moral examination of the "unthinkable" that Sontag claimed science fiction had not produced.

"That Only a Mother" unfolds mostly in an epistolary format. A computer oper-ator named Margaret writes regularly to her husband, Hank, a weapons designer off at the war, about what is happening on the home front—just as so many women had done in the real world, not long before. Margaret is expecting a child, and doing her best to maintain a cheerful outlook despite all that is happening. When the baby is born, she writes ecstatically about the domestic bliss of young motherhood. It's only at the end of the story, when Hank returns home on leave, that the twist is revealed. The sci-fi historian Lisa Yaszek vividly describes the final scene: "We learn that Henrietta is actually a wormlike creature with neither arms nor legs and that Margaret appears to be quite insane, blinded by a motherlove that prevents her from comprehending the tragedy of her child's deformities."[60]

This unsettling narrative—which recalls Charlotte Perkins Gilman's "The Yellow Wall-Paper," and more proximately, the film version of *Gaslight* (1944), star-ring Ingrid Bergman—was meant as an indictment not only of Cold War milita-rism but also of the domestic expectations that were still being brought to women's doorsteps. Right at the end of the war, Merril had written an article decrying the "rambling rash of rhetoric on that most unassailable of subjects, Mother Love" that was suddenly filling mass-market magazines. During the war years, women had been essential to the industrial workforce. Now they were forcibly compelled to leave it, and to encourage this reinstatement of sexist employment practices, shelter magazines energetically peddled stereotypical images of the ideal homemaker. Merril was one of the first to protest, dismissing the "smug illusion of peace and prosperity" and insisting "women don't even have a place in the home any more—the few who do want nothing more than to be deprived of it."[61]

Merril was right: One poll suggested that 75 percent of women who had wartime jobs wanted to keep them.[62] But very few had the opportunity to do so. Instead, they were expected to assume the role of full-time consumers, and as Robert Jungk had discovered when researching *Tomorrow Is Already Here*, primary test subjects of the great postwar experiment in mass marketing. Like so many other social changes of the day, these developments were refracted immediately into science fiction. Yaszek has identified nearly three hundred female authors active in the genre after the war, many of whom explored themes of domesticity, especially the rapid technological transformation of the home.[63] These women's stories, with their push-button kitchens and robotic housekeepers, were not necessarily at odds with consumerism—they were more in keeping with Christine Frederick's enthusiasm about the liberating potential of automation—but Merril remained convinced that in the repressive climate of the 1950s, science fiction was "virtually the only vehicle of political dissent."[64]

Merril followed "That Only a Mother" with another tale set during a nuclear war, the novel-length *Shadow on the Hearth* (1951), whose protagonist is a convincingly drawn, thoroughly rattled Westchester housewife who must contend with radiation sickness, food shortages, and rampant looting. Crucially, Merril also turned her energies to editing the work of her peers. Between 1956 and 1967 she put together annual anthologies of the best American science fiction stories, sometimes focusing on explicitly political themes like those she was exploring in her own writing, such as McCarthyism or the nuclear threat.[65] It was in this capacity that Merril would ultimately have her biggest impact on the field, acting as the aggregator for what became known as the New Wave of science fiction, a term that self-consciously evoked the *nouvelle vague* of French cinema.

During a long visit to London, beginning in 1966, Merril connected with a group of writers including Michael Moorcock, who had recently turned an existing magazine called *New Worlds* into science fiction's first truly radical publication.[66] It marked the culmination of the British avant-garde's decade-long interest in science fiction. The genre had always had a different, more elevated status in the United Kingdom, propelled by novels of unquestioned literary merit such as Aldous Huxley's *Brave New World* (1932), George Orwell's *1984* (1948), and Anthony Burgess's *A Clockwork Orange* (1962; adapted into a film by Stanley Kubrick in 1971). In 1956, the British Pop Art movement announced itself with an exhibition called *This Is Tomorrow*, bursting with intellectual enthusiasm for American-style science fiction. Four years after that, the leading British writer Kingsley Amis bestowed his imprimatur in a 1960 study called *New Maps of Hell*, in which he advanced the novel idea that science fiction was "a means of dramatising social inquiry, providing a fictional mode in which cultural tendencies can be isolated and judged." For Amis, it was not just elevated thought pieces that commanded respect but also the more rough-and-tumble publications from America, the likes of *Amazing Stories* and *Astounding Science-Fiction*. The business model of the pulps did prize quantity over quality, certainly, so that often one found in them, as Amis put it, an "interesting idea badly set out." Even so, he argued that this popular

This Is Tomorrow, Institute of Contemporary Art, London, 1956.

science fiction was "a humanising rather than a brutalising force," akin to jazz, that other great American popular art form, in its improvisatory immediacy.[67]

By the time Merril arrived in London, the city's science fiction, just like its music and fashion, was in full swing. The pages of *New Worlds* fairly bristled with experimental writing by the brilliant J. G. Ballard and a host of other talents. Like RAND, this was a laboratory of the mind, an intensely competitive environment for ideas; unlike the American technocracy, it was unfettered by any calculation of real-world probability. The New Wave was "the first generation in science fiction to consider and discuss their work principally as art," as the historian Colin Greenland notes, "not as cult, didactic tradition, intellectual pastime, or anything else."[68] Zonked anew by what she was reading, Merril assembled an anthology devoted to the phenomenon, ultimately published by Ace in 1968 as *England Swings SF*, a not-quite-idiomatic title clearly intended to capitalize on American fascination with the mini-skirted, go-go-booted, sharp-suited London scene.[69]

Readers who expected a sci-fi equivalent to upbeat mod style, however, were in for a shock. In her introduction, Merril warned: "You have never read a book like this before.... It's an action-photo, a record of process-in-change, a look through the Perspex porthole at the momentarily stilled bodies in a scout ship boosting fast, and heading out of sight into the multiplex mystery of inner/outer space."[70] Perhaps nothing could quite live up to that hyperbole, but *England Swings SF* was certainly experimental. One contributor, Josephine Saxton, imagined a character right out of a contemporaneous London nightclub—"female, young, and full of curiosity"—who is given a spaceship for her eighteenth birthday and blasts off to the other side of the universe. There she encounters her own negative image, a bitter old man. Faced with his alter ego, he fears the metaphysical results of their encounter. "uoy—uoy uoY," he says to her, "emit siht revelc oot erew uoY." Elsewhere in the volume, Brian Aldiss's "Still Trajectories" put a distinctively 1960s gloss on the well-worn tropes of postapocalyptic fiction. In the wake of an "Acid Head War," the whole population is fuzzy-brained from hallucinogenic bombing; the story breaks down into disjointed poetry toward its conclusion.

The most out-there of Merril's inclusions were from Ballard, then in an especially extreme phase in his career. In the 1950s he had been one of the most reliably inventive of science fiction's short story writers, a crafter of beguiling dystopias. Now, under the influence of the Surrealists and the Beat writer William Burroughs, he began producing spiky cocktails of personal obsession, paranoia, and advertising prose. Two of his texts in *England Swings SF* bore the extraordinary and upsetting titles "The Assassination of John Fitzgerald Kennedy Considered as a Downhill Motor Race" and "Plan for the Assassination of Jacqueline Kennedy."[71] The latter reads, in part:

> The arousal potential of automobile styling has been widely examined for several decades by the automotive industry. However, in the study under consideration involving 152 subjects, all known to have experienced more than three involuntary orgasms with their automobiles, the car of preference was found to be (1) Buick Riviera, (2) Chrysler Imperial, (3) Chevrolet Impala. However, a small minority (2 subjects) expressed a significant preference for the Lincoln Continental, if possible in the adapted Presidential version. (Q.v. conspiracy theories.) Both subjects had purchased cars of this make and experienced continuing erotic fantasies in connection with the trunk mouldings.

It's possible (if not exactly easy) to understand this passage as a wicked satire on consumer research. To the average fan in 1967, though, it likely seemed unrecognizable as science fiction. Ballard was calling into question not only the standard tropes of the genre—its outlandish settings, inventive gadgets and adventurous narratives—but also its underlying premise that a new reality was "out there" somewhere, and science would eventually discover it. Ballard was instead exploring psychology as it was being transformed through the distortion field of mass media. "I feel that the fictional elements in experience are now multiplying to such a point that it's almost impossible to distinguish between the real and false, that one has many layers, many levels of experience going on at the same time," Merril quoted him as saying.[72] Or, as he put it more simply in a later interview, "the only truly alien planet is Earth."[73]

BACK IN THE United States of America, *England Swings SF* was an instant phenomenon. The sheer weirdness of the anthology contributed to the sense that a momentous shift was underway. Merril had already been encouraging New Wave tendencies in her annual *Best of SF* roundups. Now she found allies like Harlan Ellison, another writer-editor; his seminal *Dangerous Visions*, a brick of a book packed with thirty-three stories, was published in 1967. (It was a banner year for Ellison, which also saw the broadcast of a *Star Trek* episode he had scripted, "The City on the Edge of Forever," often said to be the best of the series.) Like most avant-garde movements, this one had plenty of detractors. One was Merril's old pal Asimov, who was quoted on the back of her book (oddly enough) as saying, "I hope that when the New Wave has deposited its froth, the vast and solid shore of *science fiction* will appear once more." Though he contributed a foreword to Ellison's *Dangerous Visions*, he explained that he agreed to do so only because any story he might have written would have been "too sober, too respectable, and, to put it bluntly, too darn *square*."[74] (It's hard when the future arrives without you.) Even the New Wave's own exemplars tended to disavow the term; Aldiss wrote to Merril that he suspected it "to be a journalistic invention of yours and Mike Moorcock's, ulti-mately of no service to the writers willy-nilly involved."[75]

Samuel R. "Chip" Delany, the first widely published Black author in science fiction and its most imposing intellect, similarly distanced himself, seeing the New Wave as a specifically British phenomenon: "I wasn't part of it, as much as I might have liked to be."[76] Even so, Ellison chose to give Delany the final word in his trend-defining anthology, positioning his story "Aye, and Gomorrah" last in *Dangerous Visions*, thus implying that his was the most future-facing voice of his generation.[77] It was Delany's first published short story. Unconventionally for a science fiction author, he'd made his name with longer novels, publishing four of them by the time he was twenty-two. In 1966 he came to prominence with *Babel-17*, dense with language theory and mathematical puzzles. In "Aye, and Gomorrah," Delany skill-fully split the difference between Asimovian speculation and Ballardian introspec-tion. Set at an indeterminate future date, mostly in Istanbul, it revolves around the mutual attraction between a female earthbound "frelk" and an androgynous "spacer." As the story proceeds, we come to understand these two unfamiliar terms: *Frelk* is a derisive nickname for someone who feels an obsessive desire for *spacers*, a class of off-world workers neutered from a young age due to radiation exposure. Both groups are disdained by the broader society, but they clearly have Delany's sympathies. The story's most oft-quoted line, "You don't choose your perversions," is poignantly self-referential; when he wrote it, Delany was exploring his own identity as a gay man while living in an open marriage. (His wife, the poet Marilyn Hacker, was an editor at Ace Books and had helped him get his first novel published there.) He was also light-skinned enough that he could sometimes pass for Caucasian. In an autobiography about this formative time in his life, he recalled, "I thought, you are neither black nor white. You are neither male nor female. And you are that most ambiguous of citizens, the writer. There was something at once very satisfying and very sad, placing myself at this pivotal suspension."[78]

This is exactly the mood of "Aye, and Gomorrah," an elegy to the tantalizing experience of nonconsummation. The frelk wants the spacer. The spacer wants to be wanted. But there is no possibility of sex between them, or any permanent relationship, and they both know it. The story's structure mirrors this unattainability: After a long dialogue, some-

Samuel Delany in 1997.

times flirtatious and sometimes taunting, the two characters simply glide away from one another, having perhaps experienced a "site of pure desire," which—as Delany once remarked in a different context—is "sometimes the most painful of states."[79] This degree of sophistication put his writing light-years ahead of most science fiction, then or since. But in his own way, he still relied on the genre's central tactic of "cognitive estrangement," that is, the use of a future scenario to create a thought-provoking distance from the familiar. This is the short story as Petri dish, with the reader invited to peer in and watch the experiment unfold.[80] Neither the spacer (who, incidentally, is described as Native American) nor the frelk (who is Turkish) can easily be situated on a real-world spectrum of identity.

It is arguably only recently, as terms like *trans* and *intersectional* have entered widespread usage, that commonplace vocabulary has begun to catch up to Delany's vision. Even at the time, of course, he knew he was stretching the parameters of the genre. In a short postscript, he commented, "Why put all this in an s-f story? I sincerely feel the medium is the best in which to integrate clearly the disparate and technical with the desperate and human."[81] The story is at its most powerful when the characters' frustrations are expressed in metaphorical terms unavailable to straight fiction, as when the frelk plaintively exclaims, "You have your glorious, soaring life, and you have us. You spin in the sky, the world spins under you, while we have our dull, circled lives, bound in gravity, worshipping you!" Yet if Delany and the other writers of the American New Wave did take full advantage of the imaginative leap, they were also—unlike their counterparts in Britain—confronted with an urgent reality.[82]

This reality was, of course, the Vietnam War, which was far from the heroic ennobling experience depicted in novels like Heinlein's *Starship Troopers*. Delany had read that book with appalled fascination; in his trilogy *The Fall of the Towers* (1970, though based on novellas originally published from 1963 to 1965), he tried to respond to it, capturing the experience of raw recruits fighting a shadowy enemy for reasons they did not understand. Strange but true: Until the arrival of films like *Deer Hunter* (1978) and *Apocalypse Now* (1979), it was in science fiction stories like Delany's that the war found its most convincing portrayals. In a 1967 feature for *New Worlds* titled "Lessons for the Future," Michael Moorcock laid out a challenge to the field in no uncertain terms: "The present war in Viet Nam is presumably being conducted [for] computer-derived considerations, since morality and common expedience would seem to militate against it. It is not enough to inveigh against the advent of technocracy; one must engage the forces of change on their own ground, and that ground is the future."[83] This is exactly what the New Wave writer Thomas Disch sought to do in his novel *Camp Concentration*, which had been serialized in the magazine the previous year; the counterfactual plot is set underway when Robert McNamara, now president of the United States, decides to wage global germ warfare.[84]

So urgent was the question of Vietnam for science fiction writers that Judith Merril, taking stock as usual, decided to conduct a poll. In June 1968 she and her colleague Kate Wilhelm took out a pair of facing advertisements in *Galaxy*, one of the leading American sci-fi pulps. On one page was a list of authors who supported the war, Heinlein most prominent among them, though one finds the name of Sam Moskowitz, the kid who had barred the Futurians from entering the World Convention back in 1939. On the facing page was a slightly longer list of writers opposed to the war, including Asimov, Delany, Disch, Ellison, and the *Star Trek* creator Gene Roddenberry, as well as Merril herself. The editor of *Galaxy*, Frederik Pohl—another ex-Futurian, he was also Merril's ex-husband—didn't sign on either side, instead contributing an editorial noting how the war tragically divided people into two opposing camps: "As long as our discussions on the subject remain limited to this two-valued choice of alternatives, the debate will protract itself endlessly, and so will the war."[85]

Then Pohl made a surprising suggestion. Science fiction fans themselves, whether they were pro- or antiwar, might find a way out of the quandary. After all, he wrote, "what group of people in this country are most skilled at inventing futures? Why, we are!" In this spirit, he invited letters from *Galaxy*'s readership, in response to the question: "What would *YOU* do about Vietnam?" These responses, he promised, would be analyzed using techniques borrowed from the RAND Corporation's Delphi tool. "In the past few decades," Pohl noted, "the world's think tanks have devised scores of ways of dealing with the future, planning and predicting, scenario-writing and making cost-effective studies." Could these methods, combined with the patterns of thought cultivated within sci-fi fandom, possibly solve one of America's most intractable problems?[86]

Well, no. *Galaxy* did receive submissions from about five hundred readers, even getting a few from soldiers fighting in Vietnam. Some suggestions were quite imaginative: mass hypnosis of all combatants to bring about an immediate peace; setting up an arbitration panel for national liberation struggles; settling the war by "counting voluntary suicides on each side; the side with the most volunteers wins."[87] But of course there was no way to mobilize such ideas. If the episode represents an unusual confluence of the primary strands of experimental futurology—technocratic forecasting and sci-fi speculation—it also reflects a misunderstanding of the genre's real value. Science fiction is not about generating future solutions to real-world problems but, on the contrary, opening up a present-day space of unreal possibility. Delany saw this clearly, commenting, "If some of my stories provided 'laboratory conditions' for the *gedanken* [thought] experiments with which [my readers] have reached some new understanding, then—no matter how the stories are judged—I'm pleased."[88]

Ursula K. Le Guin, whose fame would ultimately exceed that of all other New Wave writers, would have agreed. "One of the essential functions of science fiction," she wrote, "is precisely this kind of question-asking: reversals of a habitual way of thinking, metaphors for what our language has no words for as yet, experiments in imagination."[89] Though a generation older than Delany—she was born in 1929, in Berkeley, California—her career paralleled his closely, as he began publishing so early, while she did not start until she was about thirty. Le Guin, too, was a pro-peace signatory in the pages of *Galaxy*, and like Delany, she wrote a thinly disguised allegory of the Vietnam War. This was a novella called *The Word for World Is Forest*, first published in 1972 in Harlan Ellison's *Dangerous Visions, Again*, a follow-up to his influential anthology. The working title was *Little Green Men*, and in the story she turns that cliché on its head, taking one called Selver as her protagonist and following him in revolt against an invading army of Terrans (that is, people from Earth) who have oppressed and enslaved the indigenous population. The plot is clearly influenced by Le Guin's interest in Native American history; Selver reads like an extraterrestrial Wovoka, and one terrible incident in the plot echoes the killings at Wounded Knee—though it could also be based on the Mỹ Lai massacre, which occurred in Vietnam in 1968.

This was unsubtle by Le Guin's standards, and *The Word for World Is Forest* is not generally considered to be among her better works. But she had her reasons to write it. She was enraged by what was happening in Vietnam, and also what she saw in her own field. In 1975 a new academic journal called *Science Fiction Studies* devoted an issue to Le Guin's work and invited her to respond. She took the opportunity to castigate her peers and predecessors in no uncertain terms: "Where are the poor, the people who work hard and go to bed hungry? Are they ever persons, in SF? No. They appear as vast anonymous masses fleeing from giant slime-globules from

Ursula K. Le Guin, c. 1970s.

the Chicago sewers, or dying off by the billion from pollution or radiation, or as faceless armies being led to battle by generals and statesmen."[90]

What she didn't quite say was that, while New Wave writers were challenging these power dynamics, their experimental approach tended to limit their reach. Delany, for one, was becoming much more abstruse at this time. His immense 1975 novel *Dahlgren* begins like a poem interrupted: "To wound the autumnal city. So howled out for the world to give him a name. The in-dark answered with wind." Le Guin never went in for this sort of thing, and it was the clarity of her storytelling, as much as her imagined alternative worlds, that won her an unprecedentedly large audience. Her highly regarded novel *The Left Hand of Darkness* (1969) shows how she was able to infuse the speculative apparatus of sci-fi with deep human interest. The book is set within a nonsequential narrative called the Hainish Cycle, which crosses multiple epochs and planetary systems. The Hainish are benevolent galactic explorers who seek to build a mutually beneficial network across inhabited planets. This premise establishes an elastic structure that allows Le Guin (who, significantly, was the daughter of an anthropologist) to touch down in different worlds, implicitly juxtaposing them to one another, exploring the virtues and limitations of each.

Her characters, too, are constantly seeking cross-cultural understanding. The protagonist of *The Left Hand of Darkness*, Genly Ai, is an envoy from Earth to the planet Gethen, whose inhabitants have a unique biological makeup. They are normally ungendered; it is only when they are in "kemmer"—an estrous phase, like a dog going into heat—that they take on sexual attributes. This means that the same person will, at various times in their life, transit male and female experience. Genly Ai, who is male, is initially repelled by this sexual economy—"One is respected and judged only as a human being. It is an appalling experience"—and the locals feel similarly, finding Ai's state of "permanent kemmer" to be partly comic and partly tragic. But he ends up falling complicatedly in love with a Gethenian. "Why did I invent these peculiar people?" Le Guin later wrote. "Not just so that the book could contain, halfway through it, the sentence 'The king was pregnant'—though I admit that I am fond of that sentence. I was not recommending the Gethenian sexual setup: I was using it. It was a heuristic device, a thought-experiment."[91] This idea is acknowledged within the narrative, too, in a passing suggestion that the inhabitants, with their unusual gender fluidity, might be the descendants of test subjects brought to Gethen by ancient alien geneticists. The planet might be one big laboratory experiment—which, of course, is exactly what it was for Le Guin herself.

"What is wrong with most utopias is that they lack emotion," she once wrote, and this principle—human feeling—is exactly what she placed at the center of her novels.[92] It had taken a while, but science fiction had reached a new chapter. A kind of writing originally developed by teenagers, and for teenagers, had finally grown up.

ON APRIL 1, 1968, a contingent of science fiction enthusiasts attended a special showing of Stanley Kubrick's first production since *Dr. Strangelove* five years earlier. His latest was meant to be a new kind of film: sci-fi for adults, a legitimate work of art. Dismissive decrees of the sort handed down by Susan Sontag would be proved wrong, once and for all. The movie's ambition was evident even in its name. As co-scriptwriter Arthur C. Clarke noted, "Science fiction films have always meant monsters and sex, so we have tried to find another term." He and Kubrick therefore rejected their initial working title, *Journey Beyond the Stars*, as too generic. They wanted something Homeric instead. So they called it *2001: A Space Odyssey*.

The sci-fi fans who turned up on that April Fools' Day, however, weren't so sure. Judith Merril, who was there (of course), recalled that by the time intermission rolled around, "the audience was absolutely grim. People were saying things like, 'what has Kubrick done to Clarke'?" The theater began emptying out well before the credits; she had to stand up on her seat to see the ending. Nor was this reaction unusual. As the historian Carl Freedman notes, "The bewildered look that characterized audiences leaving the movie theaters during the film's initial run itself became famous as a cultural phenomenon."[93] Some mainstream reviewers were equally dubious. Renata Adler, in the *New York Times*, found the movie punishingly slow, yet she also perceived adolescent preoccupations behind Kubrick's artistic stylings and gleaming special effects: "Infinite care, intelligence, patience, imagination and Cinerama," she wrote, "have been devoted to what looks like the apotheosis of the fantasy of a precocious, early nineteen-fifties city boy."[94]

In the end, such doubts have largely been put aside, and the film has gone down as a classic. Certain sequences are iconic: the portentous discovery by a prehistoric "Ape-Man" that a femur can be used as a weapon; Kubrick's jump cut from the bone, thrown aloft, to a shot of a spaceship in orbit; the drift of the eerily calm artificial intelligence HAL into homicidal mania; the rush of psychedelic graphics at the conclusion; and the final emergence of a celestial Star-Child, which Merril had to get up on her chair to see. For the record, she did admire the film—"It changed the viewer's entire perspective about what is down and what is up"⁹⁵—and she claimed that Samuel Delany did too. Buckminster Fuller concurred, describing it in his inimitable fashion as "a complete breakthrough into how to realize space age moving picture and television conceptioning."⁹⁶

This positive reception suggests that *2001* could be seen as the cinematic equivalent of the sci-fi New Wave, a transferal of its sensibilities to the big screen. Yet this doesn't get the movie quite right. First of all, Clarke was a leading exemplar of didactic, so-called hard science fiction. While his stories were certainly provocative thought pieces ("The Sentinel," the departure point for his collaboration with Kubrick, is a good example), his interest in social progress was remote at best. The only women that appear in Clarke's novel version of *2001*, written concurrently with the film script, are "charming little stewardesses" who serve tea and coffee in zero gravity. (Kubrick added just one minor female character, a Soviet scientist.) And while *A Space Odyssey* was an important visual influence on later movies, notably *Star Wars* (1977), they typically reverted to the conventional lines of "space opera." The filmmaker Andrei Tarkovsky found *2001* to be emotionally arid and intellectually fraudulent. "For some reason, in all the science-fiction films I've seen, the filmmakers force the viewer to examine the details of the material structure of the future," he said in 1970. "More than that, sometimes, like Kubrick, they call their own films premonitions. It's unbelievable! . . . For a true work of art, the fake must be eliminated."⁹⁷ Two years later Tarkovsky would release *Solaris*, based on a 1961 novel by Stanisław Lem; the film marked a radical break from the propagandistic tradition of Soviet cinema begun by Eisenstein in the 1920s, and remains one of sci-fi's great masterpieces.

It was Ursula Le Guin, though, who delivered the most thoughtful riposte to Kubrick's film, in a 1986 essay called "The Carrier Bag Theory of Fiction." Here she suggested that the first tools used by humans were probably not weapons—as depicted in the first sequence of *2001*, with an ape-man "grunting with ecstasy at having achieved the first proper murder"—but rather woven carriers, used for sustaining life, not ending it.⁹⁸ On the basis of this primordial fact-check, the primacy of the bag over the bone, Le Guin outlined a manifesto for a more capacious approach, which would avoid the conventional focus on the exploits of a single protagonist. The stories she had in mind—indeed, the stories she was actually writing—would look skeptically at the master narrative of scientific progress, with each discovery leading one step closer to an ideal future. "If one avoids the linear, progressive, Time's-(killing)-arrow mode of the Techno-Heroic, and redefines technology and science as primarily cultural carrier bag rather than weapon of domination," she wrote, "one pleasant side effect is that science fiction can be seen as a far less rigid, narrow field, not necessarily Promethean or apocalyptic at all."[99]

Le Guin's alternative theory gets to a core distinction within experimental futurology, which can easily be obscured by the speculative methods that its various practitioners shared. Scenario building is intrinsic to professional forecasting and to science fiction alike, but such projections may have very different intentions. The dominant model, as practiced at the RAND Corporation, and also by writers like Asimov and Clarke, asserts at least some predictive value. Whether this is construed simply as informed conjecture or operates in more complex systems, like Daniel Bell's "Twelve Modes," the target of such analysis is posited as a real state of affairs, somewhere beyond tomorrow—indeed, often at a specific and declared time horizon. The alternative model of speculation involves no such claims. Instead, the scenario is understood as entirely fictional, and like all literature, a means of illuminating the writer's own moment in history, albeit in an unfamiliar reflected light. This second model had plenty of advocates, among them Robert Jungk and New Wave writers such as J. G. Ballard and Samuel Delany. But Le Guin put it best, in a 1976 introduction she added to *The Left Hand of Darkness*: "The purpose of a thought-experiment, as the term was used by Schrödinger and other physicists, is not to predict the future . . . but to describe reality, the present world. Science fiction is not predictive, it is descriptive."[100]

This was one reason that Le Guin, like Tarkovsky, had such trouble with *2001*; for all its fantastical elements, it was clearly meant to show what the future would actually look like. Kubrick conducted extensive, obsessive research at aeronautics companies, industrial firms, and universities like MIT, where an artificial intelligence machine was under construction. An early edit of the movie included a lengthy, documentary-style prologue, in which various scientific authorities offered their expert opinions about the themes the audience was about to encounter. (This material would have dated the film badly, had Kubrick decided to include it; the physicist Freeman Dyson, for example, told him, "I don't believe that electronic machinery is going to go very much further than it is now . . . I may be completely wrong.")[101] The final cut remains a monument to future-casting: costumes and furniture, space walks and planet surfaces, zero-gravity toilets. The details are fascinating, and occasionally truly prophetic, as with the Zoomlike "picturephone" used on board the spaceships. Yet as always—and this was the essence of Tarkovsky's critique—we have to remember that when such predictions were made, there was no way of knowing how accurate they might be. (As Kingsley Amis pointed out, "Science fiction must in its very profusion seem occasionally to have guessed right.")[102] *Space Odyssey* is a unique specimen of laboratory-style futurology, for it engaged both in scientific prediction, in the approved technocratic manner, and high-flown speculation, in the idiom of New Wave sci-fi. It is revealing that all these years later, what remains exciting about the film is not the informed guesswork but the wild leaps of imagination.

IT SO HAPPENS that at the very time Kubrick and Clarke were developing *2001*, Daniel Bell was leading a research project called the Commission on the Year 2000 that involved a team of about thirty futurologists, Herman Kahn most prominent among them. They made predictions about a wide range of topics—urban development, religion, privacy, violence, communications, international relations, and more—using 2000 as a more-or-less arbitrary date of projection. Their deliberations commenced in 1964, with the group taking an earlier RAND "long-range" study as a common point of departure (a copy of the same study is preserved in Kubrick's archive, suggesting that he also consulted it for *2001*). The commission's proceedings were published four years later, just as *Space Odyssey* was hitting the screens, and the Vietnam War was sliding into quagmire territory, and the American counterculture was coming into full flower. Against this volatile backdrop, Bell was moved to frame the whole project in terms of two emergent tendencies: one toward knowledge-based forms of expertise, "the mastery of complex bodies of learning," and the other toward hippiedom, "hedonistic, permissive, expressive, distrustful of authority of the purposive, delayed gratification of a bourgeois, achievement-oriented technological world."[103]

It is not difficult to see which side he was on, especially given that he called these two trends the "technocratic" and the "apocalyptic." Beneath this clash of worldviews, though, Bell perceived a still deeper problem. Despite several decades of futurological research, and a society that was clearly becoming more and more "future-orientated," there were still "no adequate mechanisms to anticipate, plan for, guide, or 'invent' the future."[104] While he and his colleagues did their level best to confront this dilemma, the truth is that the results of the Commission on the

Year 2000 are of only trivial interest today. As always, it is entertaining to see what they got right and wrong: Impressively, Bell imagined "a national information-utility system, with tens of thousands of terminals in home and offices 'hooked' into giant central computers providing library and information services, retail ordering and billing services, and the like," but he was also pretty sure we'd have the ability to control the weather. His colleagues at RAND, meanwhile, confidently asserted that by 2000 we'd have thermonuclear power as an energy source, but also mining and manufacturing on the moon.[105]

In retrospect these supposedly educated guesses, and the extended scenarios based on them, read a lot like science fiction. In some cases, they may have been directly inspired by it. For the various strands of experimental futurology were not just intertwined but developed from a single shared premise: The future is best understood as a laboratory. One can always conduct experiments, but as with any proper scientific method, one's findings will inevitably be subject to revision, falsification, and fundamental paradigm shifts.[106] It is no surprise that, for the first generation who grew up in the shadow of the bomb, the defining feature of the future was its inherent danger; nor that this generation developed such elaborate mechanisms to cope. In the process they turned dealing with uncertainty into a dominant cultural principle, the generative basis for speculative frameworks and speculative fiction alike.

But even as these experiments were playing out, another, entirely different way of thinking about the future was also taking shape. It was premised not on anxiety but on fulfillment, and focused on the potency that lay within human beings, rather than the external forces to which they are subject. Bell was right to see the emergence of a new culture in America as "hedonistic, permissive, expressive, distrustful"—but he could not have been more wrong in seeing it as apocalyptic. He also seems to have completely missed the challenge that it posed to his ideas, and those of futurology in general. Even as the technocrats were running their calculations and compiling their reports, and the world's science fiction writers were bent over their typewriters, stitching together tomorrows from the whole cloth of their imaginations, something radically different was happening all around them. There was a party going on.

5

PARTY

N DECEMBER 1968, Arthur C. Clarke published an essay in *Playboy* magazine. As *2001: A Space Odyssey* was still playing in America's theaters, readers might reasonably have expected him to offer his thoughts on space exploration, or the possible existence of alien civilizations. But Clarke had something else in mind. Of all the former futures that were fast becoming reality—"the conquest of the air, the transmutation of matter, journeys to the Moon, even the elixir of life"—a single development loomed larger than any other for him: "The one most fraught with promise and peril is the machine that can think."[1]

Artificial intelligence. Clarke was sure it was coming, and, based on conversations with scientists at MIT, that it would come fairly soon. As that threshold is approached and then crossed, he wondered, how might the world change? The first steps would be small ones. Computers would beat people at chess. Then they would be able to convincingly converse with us. Offer psychiatric therapy. Make new forms of art. Eventually—and here was an idea Samuel Butler had advanced a century earlier—human beings would create a device more intelligent than themselves, an "ultra-intelligent" machine. And this would be the last machine they'd ever need to invent.

That, of course, was where the promise really came in—and the peril. As Clarke put it, "*need* is the operative word here." Will a world with artificial ultra-intelligence have any use for humans at all? Perhaps people will be reduced to purely menial tasks, leaving all the thinking to computers. Tragic folksongs might be written about this, along the lines of John Henry versus the steam drill. But another, even more extreme possibility loomed just beyond the horizon. "The main problem of the future," Clarke asserted, "and a future which may be witnessed by many who are alive today, will be the construction of social systems based on the principle not of full employment but rather full *un*-employment." This might sound like a formula for total economic collapse. But unlike Butler, Clarke believed that the "de-invention of work," as he put it, could usher in utopia at last. If governments were to provide a thousand dollars a year to every human being, starting at birth, then people could simply let the robots see to all their needs. Concepts like labor, capital, and private enterprise would take on entirely new meanings, or simply fall into disuse. "And then," he concluded with a flourish, "our work will be done. And it will be time to play."[2]

Clarke's essay impressively anticipated debates that are still with us today—concerning artificial intelligence, human obsolescence, and the idea of a universal basic income. Yet what really surprises is how commonplace these ideas were at the time. Already in 1952 Kurt Vonnegut, in his first novel, *Player Piano*, had depicted a postapocalyptic society overseen by an all-powerful computer called EPICAC XIV. Philip K. Dick imagined something similar in his 1955 short story "Autofac." In these speculative scenarios, products were churned out by enormous factories, each overseen by just a few people. Similarly, in 1967—the year before Clarke's essay—the British sci-fi magazine *New Worlds* published a discussion about the abolition of work, including implications for gender relations: "With the advent of automation, men may find themselves in the same position as their wives within the foreseeable future."[3]

Meanwhile, in the present day, Lyndon Johnson was rolling out his ambitious Great Society legislation, and informing the public that "in the past we fought to eliminate scarcity. In the future we will also have to learn the wise use of abundance." He said this, in part, because ever since World War II, engineers had been publishing designs for "Machines without Men," as one article in *Fortune* had it—a prospect that labor leaders like the United Automobile Workers' Walter Reuther positively welcomed. They didn't see automation primarily as a threat to their jobs but rather as a method of shortening the workweek and raising overall living standards.[4] Consumer goods were more available and inexpensive than ever before, and while the industrial designers who shaped them had moved on from streamlining, they were still making self-consciously futuristic products, which bore no human trace on their surfaces. Many of these goods were made of plastic, the quintessential modern material, described by the French theorist Roland Barthes in his book *Mythologies* (1957) as suggesting a thoroughly depopulated system of production: "At one end, raw, telluric matter, at the other, the finished, human object; and between these two extremes, nothing; nothing but a transit, hardly watched over by an attendant in a cloth cap, half god, half robot."[5]

This fascination with the idea of an economy without labor, running as if by magic, was also widespread within the American counterculture. Alan Watts, an English-born writer who did as much as anyone to introduce Americans to Zen Buddhism, predicted the onset of "a huge leisure society—where they're going to reverse taxation and PAY people for the work the machines do for them."[6] Jerry Rubin of the Youth International Party (the so-called Yippies) cried, "We demand full unemployment for all. The world owes us a living!" Rubin's compatriot Abbie Hoffman, fresh from having his mind blown by Clarke and Kubrick's *2001*, wrote that "the only pure revolution in the end is technology . . . that is the same as the revolution in consciousness."[7]

Whether or not the argument for de-inventing work was framed in terms of automation—indeed, whether it was cogently framed as an argument at all—this fantasy was central to the American counterculture. "The zero-hour day and freak-outs for all," as *Time* magazine satirically put it, has been the stereotype of the 1960s ever since: long-haired types in tie-dyed shirts and sandals, swaying in an invisible breeze.[8] In fact, it was a tiny phenomenon. The sociologist Lewis Yablonsky estimated in 1968 that there were only about two hundred thousand "core visible and identifiable total hippie dropouts in the United States," and perhaps a comparable number of part-timers experimenting with the lifestyle, within a population of two hundred million.[9] Yet the countercultural philosophy captivated mainstream America. It directly challenged their values while also approximating, if in a highly exaggerated form, their own widely held ideas about what a better future might look like. To outsiders, the counterculture looked like a perpetual party. It was hard for the squares not to wonder what they were missing.

The flip side of this dynamic was the counterculture's disregard for American postwar prosperity and consensus politics, which had so recently seemed to promise a better future to so many. Yablonsky hazarded that at least 70 percent of hippies came from middle- and upper-class backgrounds: "Almost all have had access to the American Nirvana, yet they voluntarily chose to drop out into scenes that Negroes and other minority groups have been trying to escape."[10] They were trying to de-invent not just work but the "establishment" in its entirety. For example: money. Rubin and Hoffman initially achieved their notoriety via a piece of "guerrilla theater" they organized in August 1967, in which a group of protestors dumped dollars on to the heads of traders at the New York Stock Exchange. They then set five-dollar bills on fire, holding them up for the cameras. For Watts, too, money was "a thing from which, if we're going to survive at all, we must be delivered."[11]

Nor did the hippies seem to care about all the things that money could buy. In 1967 the journalist Hunter S. Thompson published a vivid account of his visit to San Francisco's Haight-Ashbury neighborhood, the epicenter of the counterculture in its early years, observing bemusedly that "there is hardly anything 'to do'—at least by conventional standards." The neighborhood only had one proper restaurant. There was no such thing, really, as a hippie bar. Other businesses were closing their doors (especially barbershops). Some bus lines had been discontinued because of so-called mill-ins, where people just congregated in the streets, preventing traffic from passing through. The neighborhood's hippies didn't even attend the Avalon Ballroom and the Fillmore Auditorium, where bands like the Grateful Dead and Jefferson Airplane played, because the "genuine, barefoot, freaked-out types" couldn't afford the door price.[12]

The most radical group in Haight-Ashbury were the Diggers, named in honor of a faction of seventeenth-century proto-socialist dissenters in England who fought for the right to farm common land. Their 1960s namesakes went further, declaring that the only valid means of exchange were acts of human generosity. They opened a "free store" called Trip Without a Ticket, where surplus army clothing, remaindered clothing, used furniture, and even home appliances were given away to anyone who needed them. A sign on the wall read IF SOMEONE ASKS TO SEE THE MANAGER, TELL HIM HE'S THE MANAGER. A health clinic, also free, was established on the premises and eventually spun out as an independent initiative. A Black activist named Roy Ballard soon set up another free store in the neighboring Haight-Fillmore district, serving the African American community there. "What I'm thinking is what would happen if Black people could disaffiliate from money altogether," he said. "They did this even in slavery time when they was sharing the juice from the greens." One of the Diggers' street actions, a "funeral for $," involved handing out silver dollars to passersby. A few months before Hoffman and Rubin's stunt over in Manhattan, a Digger told a California newspaper, "We don't just burn money. Sometimes we eat it."[13] This was life at the outermost edge of the counterculture, and it's easy to see the appeal: Why predict the demise of work, if you can actually experience it?

———

PREDICTABLY, THERE WERE plenty of skeptics who didn't buy into this experiment in "pleasurable idleness," as one Marxist theorist called it.[14] Activists on the New Left—the more politicized, antiwar wing of 1960s radicalism—were dismayed to see so many prospective young revolutionaries dropping out. What would serve the establishment better, they reasoned, than peaceable nonconfrontation? There was agreement of a sort on the other side of the political spectrum. Herman Kahn, in a debate with Alan Watts, noted acerbically that "you can't manufacture goods simply by redefining money," and rather presciently predicted that most of the hippies would soon return to middle-class life, albeit with plenty of romantic stories to tell. Altogether, Kahn concluded that in the future, "there is a real possibility for a superior type of human being. But I would be very dubious that he is going to be a hedonist."[15]

In his typically mean-spirited way, Kahn was making a good point: Countercultural elective poverty was itself the product of unprecedented economic surplus. It could only be sustained at small scale, and only by relying parasitically on the very prosperity that it aimed to critique. As the cultural historian Louis Menand has put it more recently, "young people dropped out because dropping out was economically sustainable, and because there were more of them in the pipeline than the system could absorb."[16] On a very practical level, the Diggers depended on handouts, as did many individual hippies, who—as irritated journalists who visited Haight-Ashbury rarely failed to mention—constantly hit strangers up for loose change. The justification for this was simple: Economic resources should be freely shared. But it could just as well seem hypocritical. If these kids didn't believe in money, why were they always asking for it?

If hippie economics didn't exactly add up—even Watts wondered, "Where's the bread going to come from if everybody drops out?"[17]—this itself reflected the future-oriented nature of the phenomenon. Money was "merely an interim problem," said the counterculture's leading poet, Gary Snyder. A veteran of the Beat movement, he got by on occasional odd jobs, scavenging two-day old vegetables and gathering up loose rice grains that sifted out of shipping sacks in the Bay Area docklands.[18] In Snyder's view, society needed a whole new way of organizing itself, free of capitalist exploitation once and for all. He was simply trying to anticipate it. Peter Coyote, one of the founding Diggers and the group's most effective spokesman, broke it down like this: "The idea of changing anything from within has been exploded long ago. Because what you do to maintain your legitimacy precludes

Peter Coyote in 1968.

any change." The only solution was to strike out into wholly new territory: "to live and define my freedom in my own terms, not in the country's terms."[19]

This was the animating logic of the back-to-the-land movement, a supposedly quintessential 1960s phenomenon that would not actually peak until the mid-1970s, by which time thousands of people (Snyder and Coyote among them) were living in communes, also known as "intentional communities," right across the country.[20] Seen in this context, Haight-Ashbury was just the first bright bloom in a quickly growing garden—or, in Hunter S. Thompson's still more colorful metaphor, "the orgiastic tip of a great psyche-delic iceberg that is already drifting in the sea lanes of the Great Society."[21] America had been here many times before, of course; the country's history was littered with failed utopias. But it really seemed like it might be different this time. Prosperity had created the positive conditions for change, but also new forms of alienation, a deep dissatisfaction that left people wanting more without quite knowing what that might look like. Snyder, for one, believed that society had to move "through the drama of Western culture and technology in some accelerated way, before they're ready for this."[22]

The same argument was advanced by academic analysts of the counterculture, including Theodore Roszak, who coined the term in his book *The Making of a Counter Culture* (1969). The book's thesis is neatly summed up in the subtitle, *Reflections on the Technocratic Society and Its Youthful Opposition*. Roszak helpfully defined technocracy as "the social form in which an industrial society reaches the peak of its organizational integration. It is the ideal men usually have in mind when they speak of modernizing, up-dating, rationalizing, planning." This system, he thought, had successfully put the future in its cold, unfeeling grip, thanks to a "multi-billion-dollar brainstorming industry that seeks to anticipate and integrate into the social planning quite simply everything on the scene." As specific examples, he mentioned Kahn's Hudson Institute, as well as Robert McNamara, that "paradigm of our new elitist managerialism." As for the "youthful opposition," it was something genuinely novel, engaging in a form of dialectical conflict that Marx could never have imagined. As Roszak memorably put it, "The bourgeoisie, instead of discovering the class enemy in its factories, finds it across the breakfast table in the person of its own pampered children."[23]

One further, crucial thing distinguished the counterculture from earlier utopian movements: It had virtually no definite program regarding the future. Paradoxical as it may sound, this was the essence of its radicalism. Charles Reich, in another influential study of the counterculture, *The Greening of America* (1970), explained it like this: The generation that had come of age at mid-century were shaped by schools, the military, corporations, and other institutions. They therefore put all their energy into winning recognition and clearing the "formal hurdles of life." A member of this cohort was like one of Wernher von Braun's rockets, "a projectile, ready to be set in motion by outside energies," driven by motivations "constantly directed toward the future, because it is not inner satisfaction that moves him, but something extrinsic to himself." For the younger generation, by contrast, it was "a crime to be alienated from oneself, to be a divided or schizophrenic being, to defer meaning to the future. One must live completely at each moment, not with the frenzied 'nowness' of advertising, but [with] utter wholeness."[24]

This all-consuming obsession with the present, and its corresponding heedlessness toward the future, was widely shared. The *Oracle*, San Francisco's iconic rainbow-colored counterculture newspaper, told its readership, "THERE MUST NOT BE A PLAN! It has always been the plan that did us in."[25] The term *flower child* conveyed the undefined potential of natural growth, as did slogans of the period like "Go with the flow" and "Turn on, tune in, drop out." The latter, famously, was coined by the self-appointed guru Timothy Leary, who came across like a blissed-out Billy Sunday, preaching a gospel of radical redemption. (He also tried "Let's mutate, baby," but it didn't catch on.) Leary's associate Ram Dass, formerly Richard Alpert, advised his readers to "be here now" in his bestselling mystical book of that title (1971). Folk and rock songs—the most powerful cultural form of the era—spread the same message. "Let me see you get together, love one another right now" (Jefferson Airplane, 1966). "Hang it up and see what tomorrow brings" (the Grateful Dead, 1970). "Into this world we're thrown, like a dog without a bone" (the Doors, 1971). Janis Joplin perhaps said it best of all, in a 1968 interview: "You destroy your now by worrying about tomorrow."[26]

San Francisco Oracle 7, 1967.

All this poses something of a riddle: Wasn't the counterculture supposed to be about transforming society? How could this happen, if the future was left (to use another period phrase) "out of sight"? Joan Didion, in her sharply observant 1967 essay "Slouching toward Bethlehem," provided an indelible portrait of the younger generation's self-involvement: "Adolescents drifted from city to torn city, sloughing off both the past and the future as snakes shed their skins, children who were never taught and would never now learn the games that held society together."[27] But what looked like solipsism from the outside felt from the countercultural point of view like a revelatory expansion of perspective. One example is the honored place that hippies accorded to the *I Ching,* the ancient Taoist divination manual, which employs a proto-digital system of broken and unbroken lines, assembled into hexagrams into which messages about the future are encoded. Tom Wolfe, in *The Electric Kool-Aid Acid Test* (1968), an account of the Merry Pranksters and their ringleader, Ken Kesey, knocking around the country in a bus called "Furthur" (a sign on the back said CAUTION: WEIRD LOAD), was surprised to find a copy of the *I Ching* on board: "I couldn't fit it in with the Pranksters' wired-up, American-flag-flying, Day-Glo electro-pastel surge down the great American superhighway." Then it struck him. "Of course! The *I Ching* was supremely the book *of Now,* of the moment." Its oracular metaphors were not about prediction at all, just another a way of infusing the present with as much meaning as possible.[28]

The same was true for astrology. The *Oracle*—whose very name promised profound foresight—devoted a special issue to the topic, in which it assured readers that they were in the midst of a great change, guided by the stars. The present trajectory would culminate in the Age of Aquarius, "the coming age of mankind," according to the astrologer Gavin Arthur, "where everybody will be intelligent enough to have intellectual anarchy."[29] Another contributor to the issue,

Rosalind Sharpe Wall, reckoned by the stars that this mass conversion had begun in 1959 and would culminate in 1989: "Only those able to respond to the new vibration or change in consciousness will be able to stand."[30] Concurrently, Wall produced a new Aquarian Age tarot, adapting Pixie Smith's illustrations to the aesthetics of the moment. It was sold with the promise of "a direct electric emotional charge . . . a fixed image complex surrounded by anxious feelings could by contact with one of these tarot images evolve into an enlarging affirmative enlightening vision."[31]

All this may seem pretty far-out, but it was precisely the idea of "affirmative enlightening vision" that defined the counterculture's contribution to futurology. The movement was experimental, all right, and it did orient itself to the principle of transformation. But it completely opposed the idea of the future as a laboratory, in the sense that it could, or should, be subjected to advance speculation and manipulation. The straitjacketed society administered by the technocracy, and above all the calamity in Vietnam, had proven the folly of that strategy. Instead of forecasting the future, hippies wanted to create the ideal conditions for its emergence, letting it unfold spontaneously and organically, and then welcome it with open arms. In practical terms (not that it looked all that practical from the outside), this meant decentering the individual in favor of the collective, creating the immersive conditions in which new senses of self could be born.

This is why the Party was so vital to the counterculture. The two symbolic high points of the movement, which also bracketed its years of greatest influence, were both huge celebrations: the Human Be-In, also known as the Gathering of the Tribes, held in Golden Gate Park on January 14, 1967 (a date chosen on the basis of astrological advice from Gavin Arthur), and the Woodstock festival, held in August 1969. "A new nation has grown inside the robot flesh of the old," proclaimed a press release circulated in advance of the Be-In. "Hang your fear at the door and join the future. If you do not believe, please wipe your eyes and see." More than twenty thousand people attended the event, which was free to all comers. The scene's biggest bands played. Jerry Rubin, Timothy Leary, and Richard Alpert all spoke. The Diggers gave out free turkeys. It was a festival of the present tense, devoted to the simple, amazing fact of existence itself. Tom Wolfe described it as "a freaking mind-blower, thousands of high-loving heads out there messing up the minds of the cops and everybody else in a fiesta of love and euphoria."[32] The psychiatrist Helen Swick Perry, in the midst of researching a book about Haight-Ashbury and finding herself more sympathetic with each passing day ("My middle-aged cynicism was vanishing," she noted, "a frightening event for the middle-aged"), said that at the Be-In she felt "initiated into this new society, this new religion, as surely as if I had been initiated into the Ghost-Dance Religion of the American Indians."[33]

The Be-In was also, according to the Beat poet Allen Ginsberg, "the last purely idealistic hippie event."[34] Just a few months later came the so-called Summer of Love, which, despite its reputation as a glimpse of paradise on earth, was actually when the problems started. As new arrivals came to San Francisco, many headed straight for Haight-Ashbury, overwhelming its fragile subsistence economy. The press, entranced by the outlandish spectacle, covered it all. By October the Diggers were moved to hold a new rite: a funeral for "Hippie, devoted son of Mass Media," complete with a black coffin and a ceremonial burning of newspapers. Swick Perry felt that she "had witnessed the end of a noble experiment—an attempt at a new kind of Utopia."[35] The editor of the *Oracle*, Allen Cohen, mused many years later that "there was this sense of having to go on to the next invention, the next myth."[36] Nationwide, though, the counterculture was just getting going. Many participants in the San Francisco scene, sick of the hassle, decamped for rural communes. Some of the Diggers, for example, moved up to Morningstar, a former ranch in Sonoma County that had an open-door policy. Anyone was welcome, and the "formula for living," as *Time* breathlessly reported, was "do what you want, wear or not wear what you want."[37]

A primary propellant of countercultural decentralization was Stewart Brand, a beaky military veteran who sometimes sported a golden disk on his forehead and had an uncanny talent for seeing around the next corner of history. He had been deeply involved in the San Francisco scene in its formative years; as part of a theater group called USCO, he helped stage an important precursor to the Be-In, the three-day-long Trips Festival of January 1966, with performances by the newly formed Grateful Dead and Janis Joplin's band, Big Brother and the Holding Company. Brand's best-known project, the *Whole Earth Catalog*, launched in 1968 with the slogan "Access to tools." Serially published until 1972, it remains a fascinating compendium of the moment, and a testament to Brand's own restless curiosity. Futurology was a persistent theme. The cover of the 1969 issue featured the famous "earthrise" photograph, taken by an astronaut from a spacecraft

orbiting the moon—a clear emblem of a
new day dawning, bringing with it a radically different perspective.

One of Brand's main inspirations was
Buckminster Fuller, and he modeled the
Catalog to some extent on the great futurologist's lectures, with their "raga quality of rich
nonlinear endless improvisation full of conver-
gent surprises." The first issue began with information on Fuller's books, as well as resources
about building geodesic domes. A 1970
supplement was devoted to Fuller's World
Game, bringing it to the awareness of a new
generation.

Stewart Brand in 1965.

The *Catalog* also exposed its readers to
many other discoveries, including *Modern
Utopian* magazine (which covered communes),
the sci-fi novel *Dune*, and even Kahn's book *The Year 2000*, which received a surprisingly positive review. "Is Herman Kahn the bad guy (as liberal opinion would have
it) or a good guy (as in some informed opinion)?" Brand asked. "Kahn will hang you
on that question and while you're hanging jam information and scalding notions
into your ambivalence."

The *Catalog* itself has often been described as prophetic, with countless
connections firing synapse-like—internet-like?—across its pages. At the same
time, it was quite a lo-fi operation. Brand didn't try to sell anything directly
through it, instead providing contact details for each manufacturer or publisher.
He had grander ambitions than commerce, taking very seriously the proposition
that the counterculture could change the world. Brand may have been all in for
the Party, but he also felt an unprecedented responsibility: "We *are* as Gods and
may as well get used to it." It seemed that the seeds the garden-thinking futurologists had planted in the 1930s had indeed germinated. Fuller, for his part, was
thrilled. "There is hope in sight," he wrote in 1969, when he was pushing seventy-
five. "The very young! The university students are intuitively skeptical of the
validity of any and all evolution-blocking establishment.... There is a good

Whole Earth Catalog supplement, 1969.

possibility that they may take over and successfully operate SPACESHIP EARTH."[38]

NOW, YOU MAY be wondering: What about all the drugs? I've waited to bring this up until now, not out of a sense of decorum but because psychoactive substances—marijuana, peyote, psilocybin, and especially LSD (lysergic acid diethylamide)—were simply too important to the counterculture to treat in passing. They played a decisive role in the rise and fall of the Haight-Ashbury scene, and, for better or worse, the lives of many of the movement's protagonists. Alan Watts, Ken Kesey, and Stewart Brand, for example, all participated in early trials with LSD, at a time

The Fool card of the tarot, designed by Pamela Colman "Pixie" Smith, 1909.

Kazimir Malevich, *The Knife Grinder or Principle of Glittering*, 1912–13.

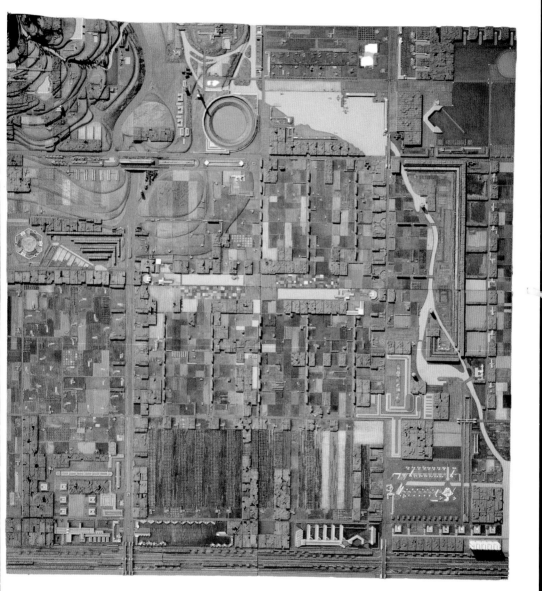

A model of Frank Lloyd Wright's Broadacre City, 1934–35.

Amazing Stories, April 1928.

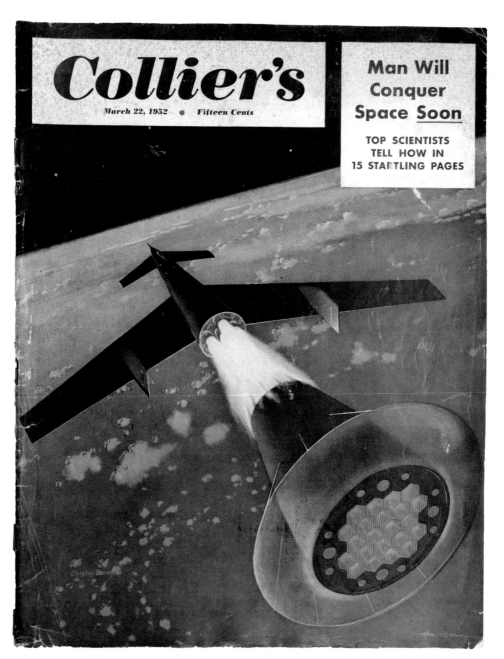

Collier's

March 22, 1952 ● Fifteen Cents

Man Will Conquer Space Soon

TOP SCIENTISTS TELL HOW IN 15 STARTLING PAGES

Collier's magazine, with illustration by Chesley Bonestell, March 1952.

Michael Bowen and Stanley Mouse, poster for the Human Be-In, 1967.

Apple I computer, 1976.

Jean-Paul Goude,
*Grace Jones Revised
and Updated*,
1978. Cut-up
transparency and
reprinted, oil-
painted photo.

when few people had even heard of it. This was a legal research program (in fact, covertly supported by the CIA, who wondered what diabolical use they might make of this powerful new chemical), and at the time the professional consensus was that access should remain tightly controlled.[39] Even Watts, in his rapturous, widely read book about the psychedelic experience, *The Joyous Cosmology* (1962), cautioned that "there should always be present some qualified supervisor to provide a point of contact with 'reality' as it is socially defined."[40] As late as 1964, even Timothy Leary—LSD's most successful, and least responsible, spokesman—said he did not support the "unrestrained civilian use of drugs."[41]

Of course, that is exactly what happened next. Over the course of the following year, Owsley "Bear" Stanley, the sound engineer for the Grateful Dead, figured out how to cheaply mass-manufacture LSD. Natural hallucinogens like psilocybin (a family of fungi), and peyote (harvested from a type of cactus) and its derivative mescaline, also entered wide circulation. In January 1966 Ron and Jay Thelin's Psychedelic Shop opened in Haight-Ashbury, followed closely by another up in Portland, Oregon. Moral panic duly ensued, then a government crackdown. Auspicious constellations may have determined the date for the Human Be-In, but the reason it was held at all was to protest the criminalization of LSD in California,

The Psychedelic Shop, Portland, Oregon, 1967.

a law that had gone into effect in October 1966. Owsley's illegal acid flowed through the Be-In anyway, like water down a mountainside.

Psychedelics were arguably the most powerful single influence on the counterculture's understanding of the future, for a simple reason: They upended the experience of time itself. Aldous Huxley had incorporated a mind-altering chemical called Soma into the satirical apparatus of his novel *Brave New World*. ("The holiday it gave was perfect and, if the morning after was disagreeable, it was so, not intrinsically, but only by comparison with the joys of the holiday.") He had the chance to try mescaline in 1953, and the book that he published about his experience the following year, *The Doors of Perception*, became a canonical description of having your mind blown. (It also inspired the name of the Doors, Jim Morrison's band.)[42] Many things impressed Huxley during his trip, including the weave of his own trousers, but what struck him most was the complete detachment that he had from the normal passage of time: " 'There seems to be plenty of it,' was all I would answer when the investigator asked me to say what I felt about time. Plenty of it, but exactly how much was entirely irrelevant. I could, of course, have looked at my watch but my watch I knew was in another universe. My actual experience had been, was still, of an indefinite duration. Or alternatively, of a perpetual present made up of one continually changing apocalypse."[43]

This arresting passage would find echoes in many later accounts. Gerald Heard, a close associate of Huxley's, noted that during a psychedelic trip, "the subject feels that time itself—time urgent, pressing, hurried, or contrariwise, time slack, lagging, heavy on his hands—is now in 'right time.'"[44] Watts, in *The Joyous Cosmology*, admitted that he was almost embarrassed when he discovered LSD. He'd spent years practicing meditation, and now he was getting enlightenment straight from a test tube. But the revelation was real, a permanent shift in perspective: "It is a dancing present," he wrote of the psychedelic trip, "the unfolding of a pattern which has no specific destination in the future but is simply its own point." Having transcended temporal flow, Watts said, one realizes "that the function of practical action is to serve the abiding present rather than the ever-receding future, and the living organism rather than the mechanical system of the state or the social order."[45] Similarly, William Braden, a journalist from the *Chicago Sun-Times*, wrote in his book *The Private Sea* (1967), based on a series of interviews with people who had taken LSD, that during a trip, "forethought is anaesthetized. Without forethought there is no anticipation. Without anticipation there is no desire. And time stops."[46]

This sounds potentially terrifying: A "bad trip"—which can result from too strong a dose, the wrong setting, or preexisting psychological conditions—can feel like a death of the ego, with the familiar moorings of time and space lost for good. For the fortunate, though, this same sense of dissolution can be euphoric. Parties like the Trips Festival and the Human Be-In were meant to make the present dance, eradicate the boundaries between the human mind and everything else. This is what Leary meant when he said, "The uncharted realm lies behind your own forehead," and why Stanley Kubrick (who didn't do drugs) used psychedelic imagery for the famous Stargate sequence toward the end of *2001: A Space Odyssey*. Filmgoers of the era—the hipper ones, anyway—would immediately have grasped what he was trying to show them, a suspension of the normal relations between time, space, and the self.

Contrary to some early claims (including by Leary, naturally), psychedelics are not technically aphrodisiacs; the sexual revolution of the 1960 owed a lot more to birth control pills than it did to LSD.[47] Nonetheless, the proverbial triad of "sex, drugs and rock and roll" did have an underlying logic to it: They were all ways of finding transcendent pleasure, living the moment to its fullest. A particularly vivid expression of this temporal release is found in the poetry of Lenore Kandel, the only woman invited to speak from the stage at the Be-In. ("There were a great number of people there I could trust with my life," she said afterward.)[48] Kandel was a well-known character in Haight-Ashbury. Peter Coyote described the bed that she shared with her lover, Bill "Sweet William" Fritsch, as an "epicurean marvel," filling the whole of a room and surrounded by candles, scented oils, dirty books, and cookies: "It was a bed you could live in for days, and they often did."[49]

Kandel gained further notoriety when a pamphlet of her erotic poetry, *The Love Book*—a paean to the "transference of ecstatic energy from one

Lenore Kandell, c. 1966.

body to another"—was confiscated by police at the Psychedelic Shop for violating obscenity laws.[50] The *Oracle* editor Allen Cohen was minding the store at the time and was arrested. Given that actual pornography was widely available in bookstores, the raid and ensuing trial were justifiably perceived as a direct attack on the community. (As is often the way with censorship, it also sent sales of *The Love Book* through the roof.) "There have been eras when the young could slip softly into their elders' lives," Kandel reflected. "This is not such a time and the choices of the young are deep and hard. At eighteen the young men must decide whether they will enter into the national pastime of death."[51] These words, more eloquent than the cliché "Make love, not war," but conveying the same idea, come from the introduction to her 1967 collection *Word Alchemy*, one of the counterculture's few major literary accomplishments. One poem, "Peyote Walk," reads, in part, like this:

> VISION: that the barriers of time are arbitrary, that nothing is still . . .
>   orgasmic infinity
>   one (!) second long . . .
> protean the form encloses space and time
>   moving
> NOW NOW NOW NOW NOW NOW NOW NOW
>   NOW NOW NOW NOW
> VISION: that yes
>   (we) is (god)

Kandel captures the drug-induced suspension of time better than any prose could. It's difficult to imagine a better evocation of presentness as grace, the vivid perception, as Kathryn Schultz has put it more recently, "that the false and true are reversed: that the unreal is, so to speak, the real real."[52]

There was a serious problem, though. When private utopias collided with other notions of the public interest, things got messy, fast. Kandel's run-in with the cops was a minor incident compared to what followed. The illegalization of LSD proved totally counterproductive, as professional dealers moved into Haight-Ashbury, bringing harder drugs like heroin with them. Crime skyrocketed. Even the Diggers' free store was burglarized, in what was, as one historian points out, "perhaps the most pointless robbery in the history of the United States."[53] There were also, inevitably, conflicts out in the rural communes. The "real real" had a way of reasserting itself; intentional communities had to contend with problems ranging from the annoying (like leaky geodesic domes) to the existential (like malnutrition and mental health problems). The division of labor, particularly between women and men, was a constant source of tension. The rejection of mainstream family values was liberating, but also raised questions that were difficult to answer in practice. Are we just talking about gender equality, or living it? Who's doing the laundry? What happens to children who aren't taken care of? (When someone asked Peter Coyote that question, he shot back, "They grow up and become presidents.")[54]

It didn't help that the communes were under constant assault from without. Morningstar, for example, prompted an angry town meeting in nearby Occidental, California, at which one concerned citizen complained, "You have not seen a truly disgusting sight until you have seen a row of naked men standing on their heads."[55] Eventually the local government bulldozed the supposedly illegal structures on the land. They were rebuilt, knocked down, rebuilt, and destroyed again before the communards finally gave up and left, in 1973. This is the difficulty with understanding the future as a party: You can try to invite everyone, but inevitably it will get too crowded. Or people will feel left out anyway. Or won't want to join you in the first place. It's telling that the key psychedelic metaphor, that of the trip, implies leaving others behind. Previous utopian travelogues—Bellamy's *Looking Backward*, Gilman's *Herland*—were devised for instructive purposes. Anyone could read those books and get the message. In the case of acid and the other psychedelics, you had to try it out for yourself. Are you, as Jimi Hendrix asked in 1967, *experienced*? The very question imposes a boundary between in-group and out-group, to use common terminology of the period—a border that was bound to be patrolled. For most Americans, in any case, the doors of perception stayed firmly closed.

In 1962 Leary and Richard Alpert set up an unregulated LSD center in Zihuatanejo, Mexico, under the auspices of what they called the International Federation for Internal Freedom (the acronym, IFIF, suggested infinite possibility). It was meant to inaugurate a new future, fulfilling Leary's lofty pronouncements of a change in consciousness, which he compared to the replacement of horse-drawn carriages by automobiles. "Our current reliance on substantive and 'closing-off' concepts," he predicted, "will be the amused wonder of coming generations."[56] Zihuatanejo was explicitly intended as a "transpersonative" environment—a term coined by Alan Watts, referring to a sense of unity brought about by the complete breakdown of social divisions. The isolated site, a resort hotel 180 miles north of

Acapulco at the end of an unsurfaced road, in "a village of fishermen and woodcut-
ters, on a large and beautiful surf-fringed bay," was chosen with this in mind, as
was the structure of the retreat.[57] Participants took turns getting high, both literally and figuratively, in "the tower," a ten-foot-tall platform on the beach. The rest
of the group—about thirty-five people at any given time, all white, mostly
professionals—were encouraged to tune into this quasi-ritual presence. They also
partook of the drug themselves at set intervals, under supervision in a special
"sessions room."

A psychiatrist named Joseph Downing who visited Zihuatanejo as an observer
concluded that LSD did indeed help the gathered strangers overcome "the conven-
tionality, mechanical adjustments, and social artificiality that insulate one human
being from close personal contact with another." (For what it's worth, he also
recorded that "sexual activity was seemingly less frequent than might be expected
from vacationers.")[58] But he also reported problems. One man tried to assert leadership over the group, was rebuffed, and stormed off to find magic mushrooms in
Oaxaca. Another, whom Downing judged to be mentally ill, was nonetheless given
LSD and eventually had to be taken off to a hospital. Meanwhile, pot-smoking
hippies who heard about the project gathered nearby on the beach, attracting
unwanted attention from local law enforcement. In the end, the colony at
Zihuatanejo lasted only six weeks before authorities shut it down. "As a Utopian
society, the Mexican center barely got started," Downing wrote. "It had only to
exist. It could not accomplish this. Nevertheless, the IFIF goals of closer empathic
relations, self-knowledge and transpersonative experience seemed to be on the way
to attainment when the group was broken up."[59] Zihuatanejo's brief run came early
in America's psychedelic adventure, but this sense of potential, oh so promising but
perpetually unfulfilled, would remain.

In many ways, the counterculture marked the high tide of a certain current in
futurology. More Americans than ever before, or since, came to believe that
anything was possible; that if the present could be made sufficiently abundant, the
future would take care of itself. One can certainly criticize those ideas as naive, but
there is no question that the counterculture put its convictions to the test with
imagination, humor, and no little commitment and courage. Peter Coyote is one of
many who gained wisdom from his youthful experiences in the movement. (He has
since gone on to a successful acting career, most prominently as the voice of several
Ken Burns documentaries, including one on the Vietnam War.) Ultimately, Coyote

came to believe that the concept of a counterculture was itself misguided, because it implies too much separation from the majority culture: "We missed the opportunity to organize those people by being so attached to our own freedom." Yet if the movement did intentionally marginalize itself, it also had tremendous impact. Its energies have migrated along myriad pathways, changing attitudes to sex and drugs and helping to inspire art, music, fashion, the slow food movement, mindfulness practices like yoga, alternative medicine, and environmental activism. "We failed in all our political agendas," Coyote says, "but on a cultural level, we won everything." Another paradox: It was in its very collapse, which scattered its energies far and wide, that the counterculture may have had its most positive effects. "It means we're all together, and you can't tell who's who," Coyote continues. "You can't tell who's a change agent. So every single place that any one of us touches the culture is a juncture point at which we can press for change."[60]

ONE NOVEMBER MORNING in 1893, the government ethnographer James Mooney—then conducting research for his comprehensive report on the Ghost Dance—took a photograph of thirteen Comanche men and women, wrapped with blankets against the cold. The group had just emerged from a tepee at the

Quanah Parker and companions, photographed by James Mooney in 1893.

conclusion of an all-night peyote ceremony. Second from left in the front row, with his eyes closed, is Quanah Parker, a man with an extraordinary past who was—no less than his contemporary, the prophet Wovoka—setting out to reshape the future of his people. His story begins back in 1836, when a nine-year-old white girl called Cynthia Ann Parker was captured in a raid on a fort in Texas, and brought back to live among the Comanche. She adopted their way of life, marrying a chief called Peta Nocona, and they had three children together, one of them Quanah. In 1860, however, when Quanah himself was about nine, a contingent of Texas Rangers located and attacked the band and recaptured Cynthia Ann. Much against her will, she was forced to go back and live with her original white family.

All this may sound familiar, because Parker's kidnapping and "rescue" helped to inspire John Ford's classic western *The Searchers* (1956), starring John Wayne. But the tale doesn't end there. Young Quanah remained with the Comanche, rising to fame as a military leader in the struggle against the U.S. Army. Finally defeated in 1875, he was brought to a reservation in what is now Oklahoma. There he took up two new vocations: first as a rancher, one of the most successful in the territory; and second as a proselytizer for peyote worship. In this latter guise, he would formalize a set of futurological customs that would enthrall the counterculture, decades later. The practice was an ancient one, though, as is attested by millennia-old archaeological finds and depictions in rock paintings. Quanah Parker's modern version of the ceremony, which is held from dusk until dawn, centers on a crescent-shaped mound facing east toward the morning sun and is conducted by a spiritual healer known as a roadman, assisted by a cedar man, fireman, and drummer.[61] A skilled political strategist who cultivated close ties to white leaders—Theodore Roosevelt among them—Quanah took a dim view of the Ghost Dance when it began attracting adherents, fearing correctly that it would bring about reprisals. (Many Native people did follow the two spiritual pathways, which were alike in that both were intertribal, and formed bridges between traditional and modern life.) One of Quanah's associates was Cavayo "Name Giver," who was entrusted with the task of assigning Comanche words to technologies like guns and cameras as they were introduced to the community.[62] One could say that Quanah did the equal and opposite thing with peyote, shaping a set of customs around it that became popular with Natives, and eventually with white America too.

At first the Bureau of Indian Affairs was determined to suppress the use of peyote, seeing it as a threat to their ongoing project of forced assimilation. On one occasion James Mooney was obliged to testify before Congress in defense of the practice, alongside a number of Native peyotists. Quanah died in 1911, and soon after, groups in Oklahoma—colloquially known as "mescal bean eaters"—began to incorporate themselves as religious organizations, establishing a secure legal basis for the sacrament. This was the origin of the Native American Church, which has remained the primary institutional infrastructure for peyote worship ever since. In its early years, the religion developed exclusively within the Indigenous community, so not many white people had the experience of taking peyote before the 1950s. One of the few who did was Mabel Dodge Luhan, who was introduced to it by her husband Tony (not in a ceremonial context). Her account of the experience reads much like Huxley's in *The Doors of Perception*, but was written almost two decades earlier: "It acted like an organizing medium coordinating one part with another, so all the elements that were combined in me shifted like the particles in a kaleidoscope and fell into an orderly pattern. Beginning with the inmost central point in my own organism, the whole universe fell into place . . . system within system interlocked in grace. I was not separate and isolated any more."[63]

Around the time that LSD began to catch on, psychoactive plants too began attracting attention. The *New Yorker* ran a story about peyote in 1954, and psilocybin was introduced to wide readership in 1957, when the normally mild-mannered *Life* magazine published a (startlingly disrespectful) photo-essay of a Mazatec ritual in Oaxaca, entitled "Seeking the Magic Mushroom." The term stuck.[64] A Canadian branch of the Native American Church welcomed its first white participants to a peyote ceremony in 1956, initiating a shift to a more open policy. (The church was also cited as a precedent by white advocates of drug legalization.) Meanwhile, natural psychedelics began circulating in the "hip" community. The Beat poets Allen Ginsberg and William Burroughs, impressively, had already managed to get hold of some peyote by 1952.[65] The actor Dennis Hopper recalled that in his apartment, in the late 1950s, "there was peyote cooking on the stove all day and night like it was a pot of coffee."[66] It was the introduction to a career of epic substance use, and abuse; in 1967 Hopper starred in a film called *The Trip*, one of several sensationalistic psychedelic films that came out in the period. After shooting the counterculture classic *Easy Rider* (1969) in Taos, he would end up buying Mabel Dodge Luhan's house, where he presided over a chaotic, drug-fueled bacchanal.

Another early adopter was Ken Kesey, who wrote his breakout novel *One Flew Over the Cuckoo's Nest* (1962) while serving as an experimental subject in a psychedelic research center in Menlo Park. He was administered with a dose of peyote, and while in mid-trip drafted the first few pages of the novel, which is narrated by a half-Native, half-white character called Chief Bromden. "I was flying on peyote, really strung out there, when this Indian came to me. I knew nothing about Indians, had no Indians on my mind, had nothing that an Indian could even grab onto, yet this Indian came to me. It was the peyote, then, couldn't be anything else. The Indian came straight out of the drug."[67] Kesey was one of the first counter-cultural leaders to explicitly acknowledge Native Americans as an influence, and he would eventually wonder if it was right to have done so, writing in 1973: "If you keep thinking the Indian was your creation, won't you eventually be forced to think of yourself as Tom Wolfe's creation?"[68]

By that time, though, the cult of indigeneity was absolutely pervasive in the counterculture. Much of this was superficial: the wearing of fringed jackets and beaded moccasins, the casual use of words like *pow-wow* and *tribal*. But many of the movement's protagonists were profoundly shaped by their encounters with Native culture. Peter Coyote adopted his *nom de paix* (his original name was Peter Cohon) after he saw a spirit animal during a peyote ceremony. He described the Diggers' activities in shamanic terms, drawing an analogy to the book *Black Elk Speaks*—mentioned in chapter 1 for its description of the massacre at Wounded Knee—which describes how "the whole village acted out the dream of the young Black Elk, assuming roles and costumes and moving according to his directions. This realization of a dream in the flesh," Coyote said, "is precisely what the Diggers were trying to accomplish."[69] While he was an undergraduate at Reed College, Gary Snyder conducted folklore research on the Warm Springs Reservation in Oregon—home to members of the Warm Springs, Wasco, and Paiute tribes—and then got a job in the tribal logging operation. Indian ancestral wisdom is a constant theme in Snyder's poetry, and he constantly encouraged other Americans to learn from Native people about ecology: "Since you've been living in a house all your life, you probably don't know what the climate is. Find out what the Indians were up to in your own area, whether it's Utah, or Kansas, or New Jersey."[70]

Stewart Brand's conversion to psychedelic activism might never have happened had he not encountered Native people. In 1963, while working as photographer, he received a commission to take pictures at the same reservation where Snyder worked, Warm Springs. There, the romantic image of Indians he'd had since child-hood fell apart. He saw something of the residents' real lives, and grasped the seriousness of ongoing threats to their cultural integrity and land rights. Then by chance, immediately after his return from Oregon, Brand was given a copy of *One Flew Over the Cuckoo's Nest*. Impressed by the novel's portrayal of Chief Bromden, he mailed some of his Warm Springs pictures to Kesey, met up with him, and soon fell in with the Merry Pranksters. He also began planning a multimedia spectacle called *America Needs Indians!*, which was originally meant to include a simulated peyote ceremony. By 1965 he was screening the program, in which images of Native cultural vibrancy were contrasted with depictions of white American soullessness; a soundtrack of drumming and the scent of burning mesquite and sage completed the experience. The following year, Brand married Lois Jennings, a mathematician who had Ottawa heritage on one side of her family. He also joined the Native American Church. Among the cornucopia of cultural resources in the *Whole Earth Catalog* were many books about Native history and religion, including *Black Elk Speaks* and Carlos Castaneda's newly published *Teachings of Don Juan: A Yaqui Way of Knowledge* (1968), represented as an account of a traditional medicine man's wisdom, including about peyote. "I don't have the words for the importance I consider these books to carry," Brand wrote.

From today's vantage point, when we are so attuned to concerns about cultural appropriation, this rush of earnest interest in Native culture obviously sets off alarm bells—beginning with the liberties taken by the white author of *Black Elk Speaks*, and the fact that *The Teachings of Don Juan* was a total fabrication. Certainly, the counterculture's representations of Native culture said a lot more about hippies than it did about Indigenous people. In May 1967, the *Oracle* published a special issue on the American Indian. The cover, by a British psychedelic artist, depicted the head of Chief Joseph of the Nez Percé floating in midair, with a trio of flying saucers soaring underneath. The contents included an unusually bitter poem by

San Francisco Oracle 8, 1967.

Snyder, in which he summoned the spirit of the Ghost Dance and declared his intention to "kill the white man, the 'American' in me." The issue also included a proposal to remake Haight-Ashbury, spiritually speaking, in the image of a Hopi kiva, described as "a broad, all-inclusive matrix for liberation." Another poem, by John Collier Jr.—son of the man who implemented the "Indian New Deal" in the 1930s—was written in the assumed voice of a Pueblo ancestor, and addressed to "you long-hair people, Beatniks, Hippies, call yourself what you will. . . . You turn your face from the future / You seek the child within you." The only Native contributor to the issue was an Ojibwe author called Vincent LaDuke—also known as Sun Bear—who was all too willing to tell the *Oracle*'s readership what they wanted to hear: "Sex is the He rains and She rains. The light and heavy rains that bring strength to the crops in the desert. Sex is the ceremony of the Return of the Sun." (LaDuke would go on to an opportunistic career as a New Age healer—in the words of one critic, a "plastic medicine man.")[71]

This cringe-making pastiche of Native Americana was obviously problematic. Yet, as the historian Sherry L. Smith has argued, the counterculture's admiration for Indigenous people was part of a genuine politics of solidarity, and it was backed up by support for their struggles for sovereignty.[72] The hippies were not politicized like the New Left was, but they were certainly opposed to imperialism, and saw clear parallels between what was happening in Vietnam and what had long been happening in the United States itself. (Some Native people saw it that way too; the Tuscarora activist Wallace "Mad Bear" Anderson went to Vietnam and said, "When I walk down the streets of Saigon these people look like my brothers and sisters.")[73] Certainly, never before had so many white Americans approached Native people as respected equals and honored elders, or attempted to form productive alliances with them. Richard Alpert fantasized about a "Hopi-Hippie Be-In" in Taos, as a successor to the San Francisco event; perhaps predictably, that came to nothing, but there were many genuine cultural exchanges in the vicinity. Some of the many communes established there, among them New Buffalo, Lama (cofounded by two of Brand's collaborators from USCO), and Morningstar East (a successor to the community in Sonoma), forged deep ties with some of the local Puebloans, learning from them about not only peyote but also adobe building and desert land management. Little Joe Gomez, a leader of the Native American Church, served as a mentor to many of the young arrivals and helped them construct their buildings;

One commune leader, Drop City's Peter Rabbit (born Peter Douthit), described Gomez as "the only fully realized human being that I've ever met in my life."[74]

As such personal connections indicate, there was a real alliance between the counterculture and Native people—some of them, anyway. Indians had themselves undergone tremendous change in the immediate postwar years, much of it resulting from the Indian Relocation Act of 1956. This was the latest tactic in the U.S. government's ongoing policy of assimilation, a reversal of John Collier's "Indian New Deal" and an explicit assault on tribal sovereignty. Natives were forced off reservation lands through a combination of vocational training in designated cities (a carrot) and decreased subsidies to tribal governments (a stick). The result was a dramatic increase in the number of "urban Indians," notably in San Francisco, where the Native population tripled within a single decade. These young men and women, along with others who were radicalized on campuses, were the main players in the so-called Red Power movement that emerged in the late 1960s.

That term, echoing Stokely Carmichael's recent popularization of the term *Black Power*, was coined by a Ponca activist called Clyde Warrior. He had been raised in a traditional manner by his maternal grandparents in Ponca City, Oklahoma. Segregation was a fact of life there: Public buildings typically had two entrances, one for whites and one marked "Negro/Ponca." Warrior responded by adopting an unusually wide spectrum of identities. A champion pow-wow fancy dancer, he also played tuba in his high school band (performing at the Rose Bowl on one occasion) and worked as a tour guide at Disneyland one summer, "playing Indian" in full Native dress. In college he became a student radical, winning presidency of the Southwest Regional Indian Youth Council with an election speech that consisted entirely of three sentences: "I am a full-blood Ponca Indian. This is all I have to offer. The sewage of Europe does not run through these veins."[75]

Clyde Warrior in 1961.

Warrior's intensity, and his biting sense of humor, are evident in his most well-known piece of writing, a short essay called "Which One Are You? Five Types of Young Indians," which anatomized his generation with deadly wit, while simultaneously mocking anthropologists who separate Native people into typologies. Warrior's own five types were the hood, or slob, who "receives his definition of self from the dominant society" and turns to criminality as a result; the joker, who "does stupid, funny things" to skirt the reality of racism; the white-noser, or sellout, who "may mingle with Indians, but only when it is to his advantage, and not a second longer than is necessary"; the ultra-pseudo Indian, who emulates traditional ways without understanding them; and finally the angry nationalist, who "resents the others for being ashamed of their own kind." Warrior himself seemingly belonged to this last category, but in fact he saw the limitations of that view—the way that the activist could "alienate himself from the general masses of Indians, for speaking what appears, to him, to be truths." What was really needed, he argued, was a new approach, "based on true Indian philosophy [and] geared to modern times."[76]

This was the animating vision behind Warrior's conception of Red Power. He first used the phrase, amid other slogans including "Custer Died for Your Sins," at a protest in Oklahoma City in 1966, which he organized together with his wife, Della, and friend Mel Thom (who was so radical that he was nicknamed Mel Zedong). Tragically, Warrior would die just two years later, at the age of twenty-eight—too soon to see the movement he had started begin to claim national attention. That transpired only when a group of "urban Indians" and students slipped across San Francisco Bay in the early morning hours and landed on Alcatraz Island—site of the notorious prison, which had closed a few years earlier. Proclaiming themselves to represent "Indians of All Tribes"—hence repossessing the tag line for the Human Be-In—they declared "the Rock" to be sovereign native territory, satirically offering to buy it for "24 dollars in glass beads and red cloth," the same amount that Dutch colonizers supposedly paid for Manhattan in 1626. Radio Free Alcatraz broadcast from the island to a nationwide, primarily Native American audience, and a plan was developed to transform the old prison grounds into Thunderbird University.[77]

The occupiers would manage to hold the island for nineteen difficult months, effectively setting up a commune there and drawing both practical and moral support from near and far. Meanwhile, other Native groups associated with the American Indian Movement (AIM), the main national organization for Native

activism, were staging "fish-ins" on lakes and rivers, asserting their traditional rights
to natural resources. Fenicia "Lou" Ordonez, wife of the Alcatraz group's lead
spokesman, John Trudell, summarized the cause of Red Power like this: "The Indian
has had a tragic past, needless to say a tragic present but we are here on Alcatraz and
on Rattlesnake Island and in Pit River to prevent a tragic future."[78] (Ordonez and
Trudell had a baby boy during the course of the occupation; they called him
Wovoka.)

These territorial claims ran in parallel to back-to-the-land communalism:
attempts to enact a futurological, perhaps utopian, social arrangement in the here
and now. Unlike the peaceable hippies, though, AIM was becoming increasingly
militant in its methods. In November 1972 they trashed the headquarters of the
Bureau of Indian Affairs in Washington, D.C. Then, in February 1973, a group two
hundred strong—mostly from the Oglala Lakota tribe—seized the town of
Wounded Knee, all but daring the U.S. government to repeat the violence that had
happened there in 1890. During this second major occupation of the Red Power era,
which ultimately lasted ten weeks, the medicine man Leonard Crow Dog, whose
great-grandfather had been a Ghost Dancer, led a ceremony paying tribute to his
ancestors' own acts of resistance. "The white man says that the 1890 massacre was
the end of the wars with the Indian, that it was the end of the Indian, the end of the
Ghost Dance," the AIM leader Russell Means said. "Yet here we are at war, we're
still Indians, and we're Ghost Dancing again."[79]

Red Power developed closely alongside the New Left and the civil rights movement, and shared some of their key tactics. But symbolic and philosophical connections to the counterculture can be glimpsed too. The historian Sherry Smith points
to a hand-painted pennant discovered at Wounded Knee, in the aftermath of the
occupation, which read AMERICA NEEDS INDIANS—Stewart Brand's old motto.
Clyde Warrior was every bit as critical of the cultural mainstream as his contemporary Peter Coyote; in his "Five Types" essay, he wrote, "I am disturbed to the point
of screaming when I see American Indian youth accepting the horror of 'American
conformity' as being the only way for Indian progress."[80] Vine Deloria Jr., in his
bestselling book *Custer Died for Your Sins: An Indian Manifesto* (enthusiastically
recommended in the *Whole Earth Catalog*), did have hard words for the counterculture: "It was by rejecting customs that the hippies failed to tribalize and became
comical shadows rather than modern incarnations of tribes."[81] Yet elsewhere he
summarized his own philosophy in the familiar terms of presentness: "Live a full

life, right now. Be really human, right now. What a man does with his life right now is what he will do in the future. That's the Indian way. So you might say the Indian is 'future-oriented' in the present. The urban man says he lives for the future. He doesn't really. He lives by the time clock and the calendar and the bank check. As a result he hardly lives at all. Now or ever."[82]

Deloria's words may sound perilously close to John Collier Jr.'s implication that Indians turn their face from the future, or indeed his father's earlier claims about natives as inhabiting another temporal universe. ("We think now that any other time than linear, chronological time is an escapist dream," Collier Sr. wrote in 1949. "The Indians tell us otherwise, and their message and demonstration addresses itself to one of our deepest distresses and most forlorn yearnings.")[83] The leading Native novelist of the era, N. Scott Momaday, rightly critiqued this presumption of ahistoricism: "The Indian has been for a long time generalized in the imagination of the white man. Denied the acknowledgment of individuality and change, he has been made to become in theory what he could not become in fact."[84] The stereotypical assumption of cultural stasis was quite different, however, from the idea that living fully in the present might be the best possible approach to shaping the future. That belief was widely shared in the 1960s, and belonged to no one group, ethnic or otherwise.

Equally, there was no shared perspective within the Native community about how best to respond to countercultural idealization or, still more crucially, navigate the complex intersection of ancestral and modern identity. It's a question that Clyde Warrior, for one, faced head-on. So it seems fitting that in 2006 a building named in his honor in White Eagle, Oklahoma, was inaugurated with the ceremonial burial of a time capsule. Constructed of stainless steel and filled with inert gas, the capsule was designed in consultation with the Smithsonian Institution; like the time capsule for the 1939 World's Fair, it was conceived as a comprehensive picture of a culture, in this case that of the Ponca tribe. Placed within were recordings of songs and stories, dried foods, photographs, tools, clothing, a large ceremonial drum, and an outfit much like the regalia Warrior himself would have worn as a competitive dancer.[85] It was determined that the capsule would remain sealed until 2136. Until then it will travel through time, poised between the past and the future.

ONE OF THE worst moments of Lyndon Johnson's presidency—and he had quite a few—occurred in Queens on April 22, 1964, seven months to the day since he was sworn into office. He was speaking at the opening of the 1964 World's Fair, which had returned to New York City. Johnson began, "I understand that at the close of this fair, a time capsule will be placed in the ground. Every possible precaution has been taken to make sure that it will be opened several thousand years from now." This led him smoothly into a speech that was all about the world to come, continuing the theme established in 1939. Johnson even indulged in a bit of futurology himself, saying, "I prophesy peace is not only possible in our generation, I predict that it is coming much earlier. If I am right, then at the next world's fair, people will see [an] America in which no man must be poor. They will see an America in which no man is handicapped by the color of his skin . . ."

The problem was, the audience could barely hear him. A group of demonstrators behind a nearby police cordon were so loud that they overwhelmed Johnson's

Congress on Racial Equality protest, New York World's Fair, 1964.

amplified Texas twang. "Jim Crow Must Go!" and "Freedom Now!" they chanted. One held up a sign reading A WORLD'S FAIR IS A LUXURY BUT A FAIR WORLD IS A NECESSITY. When Johnson got to the bit about racial equality, the protestors just laughed at him. Furious and embarrassed, the president of the United States could only struggle to his conclusion—"I am sure that speakers at the next world fair will look back with amusement at how greatly I underestimated [the] capacity and the genius of man"—and then stalk off, fuming. A police commissioner who observed the proceedings put it well: "The President came to the world of fantasy, and encountered the world of fact."[86]

The shouting-down of Johnson was the culmination of weeks of planning by the Congress on Racial Equality (CORE), which had risen to prominence in the early years of the civil rights movement. Its cofounder and director, James Farmer, played a leading role in planning the first Freedom Rides in 1961 and worked closely alongside Martin Luther King Jr. in implementing the strategy of nonviolent resistance in the South. By 1964, however, CORE was concentrating its efforts in northern cities, partly in response to pressure from Black Nationalists—including Malcolm X and the Nation of Islam—who were reviving the separatist philosophy and confrontational strategies of Marcus Garvey. "Once a middle-class cadre of idealists," as Farmer wrote in his 1965 book *Freedom—When?*, "we have become increasingly a mass movement, our attention turned inward to the ghetto—our support, our leaders, our goals, our temper, set by the people of the ghetto."[87]

This new focus, and the certainty of a media spotlight, made the World's Fair an irresistible target. Some members wanted to stage an extreme action: a so-called stall-in, during which hundreds of drivers would intentionally run out of gas on the roads leading to the fairground, their cars blocking traffic, effectively shutting down the opening day. The city prepared itself for a pitched battle, even readying a helicopter to physically lift offending automobiles from the street. In the end somewhat cooler heads prevailed, and the CORE demonstrators—a mix of about 750 Black and white activists and college students—opted for a more traditional approach of picketing and sit-ins. Ugly conflicts still ensued, however; a reporter for the *New York Times* overheard white fairgoers shouting things like "Ship 'em back to Africa" and "Get the gas ovens ready."[88]

Farmer himself was arrested when he helped to block the entrance to a pavilion that featured a newly made scale model of New York City. It was one of the few memorable displays at the 1964 World's Fair, which was less successful than its predecessor—though General Motors' Futurama II, with a people-mover taking visitors past imagined scenes from the year 2024, was once again the most popular exhibit. Billed as "a future not of dreams, but of reality," it nonetheless included some wildly speculative scenarios, realized with the support of Walt Disney's imagineers: a weather-forecasting center buried under the Antarctic ice cap; a resort hotel on the ocean floor; a road-building project in the equatorial jungle, with laser beams razing the trees to the ground.

As it turned out, the CORE protest was a much better indication of where the future would actually lead. Yet the civil rights movement was not, in itself, much concerned with speculation and prophecy. Its rhetorical high point may have been King's famous "I Have a Dream" speech, which looked ahead to an America where prejudice had finally been overcome. But the spirit of the movement was also captured in the rank-and-file chant, "What do we want? *Freedom.* When do we want it? *Now.*" For generations—indeed, since before the nation was even founded—advocates for racial justice in America had been told that they were asking for too much, too soon. The civil rights movement was virtually defined by its rejection of this perpetual waiting game. Like the counterculture, it emphasized the importance of the present moment. If hippies thought of "now" as a permissive zone of possibility, in which the future could unfold of its own accord, civil rights activists demanded immediate, concrete action.

James Farmer would soon find himself on the wrong side of this dynamic, despite having foregrounded it in the title of his own book *Freedom—When?* His answer was artful: "Freedom is not an end: it is a beginning and a process. We feel further from the end now than we did before a decade's progress was wrought. We have settled down for a long haul."[89] That was not what his own constituents wanted to hear, though; they constantly pushed him to be more oppositional with the white establishment. The breaking point came at the annual CORE convention in July 1966, held in Baltimore. Stokeley Carmichael spoke, as did the southern organizer Fannie Lou Hamer, a self-made activist well known for her hard-hitting, epigrammatic style ("I don't want equal rights with the white man, if I did I'd be a thief and a murderer").[90] Both of them openly criticized Reverend King for what they perceived as his hesitancy, and issued a call for Black Power—a term Carmichael had begun using the previous month, following the shooting of the activist James Meredith by a member of the Ku Klux Klan. In the face of this increasing urgency, the comparatively moderate Farmer stepped down from his post, making way for a more audacious leader.

This was Floyd McKissick, a lawyer and veteran activist. In 1948 he had taken it upon himself to single-handedly break the color line at the University of North Carolina, at one point jumping into a whites-only swimming pool with his clothes on and announcing, "It's integrated now!" McKissick briefly led CORE in a newly radical direction. He was among the first civil rights leaders to denounce the Vietnam War. He embraced the call for Black Power and controversially argued that nonviolent strategies had "outlived their usefulness," thus aligning CORE with the newly formed Black Panthers, who were just beginning their armed patrols to guard against police brutality. Here was a "party" in the sense of a full-fledged political entity, not a social gathering. McKissick also believed strongly in Black capitalism, that is, the development of business opportunity and ownership within the African American community. He saw this as the crucial next step in the onward march of the civil rights movement. "If Black Power is to be more than illusion," he wrote, "it must include, if not begin with, economic power."[91]

Many other activists shared this orientation toward future-building, finding in their cause an affinity to the economic self-determination of Ghana and other post-colonial African states. Fannie Lou Hamer set up her Freedom Farm Cooperative in rural Mississippi, which included a self-replenishing "pig bank," begun with fifty donated animals. In Detroit, an organization calling itself the Republic of New Afrika advocated a separatist strategy in which Blacks would do business only among themselves, based on the concept of *ujamaa*—a Swahili word literally meaning "cooperation" or "fraternity," here used to signify cooperative economics. Its members attired themselves in outfits similar to those of the Black Panthers, with the addition of leopardskin epaulettes. The group's leading voice, Robert S. Browne, revived an idea that had circulated during the Depression era, under the banner of the 49th State movement: to allocate part of the country exclusively to African Americans. The Republic of New Afrika could, Browne proposed, occupy all of South Carolina, Georgia, Alabama, Mississippi, and Louisiana.[92]

McKissick aimed at an all-but-unexplored middle ground between Hamer's small-scale enterprise and Browne's grand but improbable scheme. Having left CORE in 1968, he began several business ventures, of which the largest was a new town of about fifty-two residents. He called it Soul City. Like Ebenezer Howard and the garden city planners of the 1930s, he hoped to attract investment through thoughtful design. The difference was that this would be a hub for Black business and innovation. An unusual opportunity was in the offing, too, because the federal government was just about to earmark funding for civic projects through the Urban Growth and New Community Development Act of 1970. Seeing his opening, McKissick did something even more unexpected than setting out to build a Black city from scratch: He forged an alliance with Richard Nixon. This was obviously a marriage of political convenience. Nixon was a sworn enemy of the Black Power movement, and a more-or-less open racist.[93] But he was also a champion of free enterprise, and McKissick was able to find agreement with him on this narrow ground. As the design journalist Katie Mingle has put it, "Nixon believed in Black capitalism because Nixon believed in capitalism."[94]

The gambit earned McKissick considerable distrust in the Black community, but it did work—for a time. Soul City was indeed awarded development funds administered through the Department of Housing and Urban Development (HUD). Construction duly began in 1972, on the site of a former slave plantation in Warren County, about an hour north of Raleigh, North Carolina. McKissick was from North Carolina originally, and the state had a long tradition of Black-owned companies, going back to the North Carolina Mutual and Provident Association, so it must have seemed a propitious place to build his dream. Unfortunately, just as construction crews were breaking ground, something terrible happened: Jesse

Floyd McKissick in 1966.

Helms was elected U.S. senator for the state. The reactionary politician made it his business to ensure that Soul City would fail, arranging for legal challenges and onerous audits and spreading baseless claims of corruption. Other white interests also lined up against the project, including the major regional paper, the *Raleigh News and Observer*. At one point the *Wall Street Journal* cited, as proof of McKissick's personal greed and vanity, the fact that he owned a microwave oven (he had lived on-site in a mobile home for five years). The real fear, of course—despite promotional materials that showed racially integrated residents in peaceable coexistence—was that Soul City was a manifestation of Black separatism.

Meanwhile, McKissick was desperately trying to attract companies to create jobs for the new community, with a business incubator called Soultech serving as a base of operations. His economic development efforts proved unsuccessful, though; General Motors, for one, seems to have declined his invitation to build a factory in Soul City largely because they were put off by the name of the place. Eventually, in the midst of a national downturn, the project's reserves began running low. The government finally withdrew funding in 1979, effectively ending the experiment. "Hard-pressed American taxpayers are sick and tired of paying for foolish dreams," gloated Helms, obviously making no mention of how he had prevented said dreams from being realized. The official HUD report stated, "The average prospective white buyer sees Soul City as having a negative connotation. He conceives of it as a community built by Blacks for Blacks and is concerned that he would be living in an alien atmosphere." It seems not to have occurred to the report's authors that the reverse had been true of white neighborhoods across America, for three hundred and fifty years and counting.[95]

McKISSICK WAS A utopian of sorts, but one who tried to play by America's rules. Given the challenges he faced, it is unsurprising that so many others in the Black community embraced outright separatism, as emblematized by the charismatic, confrontational Black Panthers. There were other ways to be radical, though. Some of the most significant statements of Black futurology in the 1960s and '70s came in musical form—after all, what is music but the art of shaping time? Jazz players often speak of "stretching out," referring to the way that linear and sequential experience can be transformed into something else, in the full flow of improvisation, something complex, layered, and malleable: a space of possibility that is more than just sonic. The aims of the civil rights movement might have remained frustratingly unfulfilled, but some measure of liberation could be had readily, onstage or in the studio, in the realm of story and sound. Sun Ra, a progenitor of this approach, put it like this: "Politics, religion, philosophy have all been tried, but music has not been given a chance."[96]

To be sure, similar ideas circulated in the psychedelic counterculture. The sprawling jam sessions of the Grateful Dead, to take the most obvious example, were explicitly intended to create a capacious mental space; as the band's drummer Mickey Hart put it, "We're in the transportation business. We move minds."[97] But it was Ra who was music history's most committed futurologist, a sort of Buckminster Fuller of jazz, intensely idiosyncratic, wildly imaginative, and hyper-generative. If Fuller proposed that we all live on Spaceship Earth, Ra was farther out. "Space is the place," he said, and more provocatively and mysteriously, "It's after the end of the world, don't you know that yet?"[98] He was born Herman "Sonny" Blount in Birmingham, Alabama, to a family with Garveyite sympathies. A musical prodigy and autodidact, he read his first science fiction in the public library in Birmingham—actually, not *in* the library, because it was whites-only, but he was able to have books slipped out the back door by sympathetic Black staffers. He read plenty of other things, too: books on history and philosophy, science and technology, and mysticism and the occult, and the Bible, constantly.

Who knows what part these varied sources might have played in the big event of his life: an extraterrestrial visitation, which occurred around 1936, when he was twenty-two years old. "It looked like a giant spotlight shining down on me," he later said. "I call it trans-molecularization, my whole body was changed into something else. I could see through myself. And I went up." Up to the planet Saturn, that is, where he beheld a railroad track leading to a vacant lot, then a stadium. He found himself on the stage, face-to-face with a group of alien beings. They told him that he must discontinue his other worldly activities and commit to being a messenger. After teleporting him back to Planet Earth, they placed one of their own robes on him, and told him to set forth: "Go out there and speak to them."[99] This youthful revelation set Sun Ra's career on its improbable orbit. For him, the aliens were not metaphorical, or make-believe. They had truly spoken to him, and this gave him a sense of mission, as well as a deep conviction that he forever inhabited a place apart. "Those of the reality have lost their way," he rhymed. "Now they must listen to what myth has to say."[100] He was the man to tell them.

It took him a while. During World War II, still Herman Blount, he claimed conscientious objector status, and when he failed to report for alternate service he was briefly imprisoned—a traumatic experience that left him permanently distrustful of the government, and of authority generally. At the close of the war he moved to Chicago and took up the life of a gigging musician, playing lounges like the beautifully named Wander Inn. At the time, the country's most avant-garde jazz musicians were creating "the harsh, anti-assimilationist sound of bebop," as LeRoi Jones (later Amiri Baraka) put it in 1963.[101] The new idiom was challenging, even for some Black insiders, and definitely for the white mainstream that had embraced swing and big band before the war. Ra briefly adopted the style, then pushed into new, even more experimental territory. He seems to have been the first jazz musician to use an electronic synthesizer, playing a Hammond Solovox on his 1953 track "Deep Purple." In 1952 he legally adopted the name Le Sony'r Ra—Sun Ra was a kind of shorthand—and in 1957 he released his first full-length albums. One of these, the bebop classic *Jazz by Sun Ra, Vol. 1* (there was no volume two), featured track names like "Transition," "New Horizons," and simply "Future." Advertised as "A Fantastic New Jazz Conception by SUN RA, SUN God of Jazz," the record was, unusually, distributed with a manifesto, which read in part, "The real aim of this music is to co-ordinate the minds of peoples into an intelligent reach for a better world, and an intelligent approach to the living future."[102]

The 1950s were a time of intellectual as well as musical ferment for Ra, thanks largely to his friendship with Alton Abraham, a full-time hospital radiology technician and part-time bibliophile, mystic, and polymath. The two men readily became soul mates, and for a time they ran a small secret society they called Thmei Research—named for an ancient Egyptian goddess—and circulated typescript flyers in Washington Park in Chicago. These documents, which have been published in facsimile, give a detailed insight into the formative period of Ra's thought. They are densely typed, often in all caps, with an ample provision of exclamation marks ("WAKE UP!! FOR PETE'S SAKE . . . WAKE UP!!!"), and packed with Bible references, elaborate wordplay, and portentous declarations: "The Creator can take just so much of arrogance and vicious prejudice against innocent people and after that he begins to do unto others as the others have done unto others. America has only three more months to make up her mind."[103]

This sense of urgency can be recaptured today by watching Edward O. Bland's short film *The Cry of Jazz*, made in Chicago in 1959. Using a debate between white and Black listeners as a narrative framework, Bland advances a theory of jazz as in perpetual conflict with itself, with restraint, embodied by repetitive chord changes, in structural opposition to freedom, expressed in improvisation. This dual structure symbolizes the condition of Black America, which is trapped in "a futureless future," from which it yearns to break free. The music, in this analysis, is a "joyous celebration of the present, the Negro's answer to America's ceaseless attempts to obliterate him." Ra's band is featured in the film's soundtrack, and he is presented as the most visionary of all contemporary musicians, providing a "portrayal of everything the Negro really was, is, and is going to be, with emphasis focused on the Negro's triumph over the demonic currents of his experience."

On a more practical front, Ra was also setting up (with Abraham's help) an independent record label, El Saturn Research, to distribute his increasingly experimental music. And what music! Working with an ever-revolving constellation of players called the Arkestra, a name that suggests a vessel bearing survivors away from a traumatic past, Ra defined the new idiom of free jazz, then transcended it. Listen, for example, to the A side of his 1965 album *Magic City* (the nickname of Birmingham, where he grew up), which is given over entirely to the twenty-seven-minute-long title track. Ra's electronic keyboard meanders as if on a spiritual quest through a landscape of thrumming basslines, birdlike flutes, and rattling percussion. At the fifteen-minute mark there is a sudden assault: Every member of the band plays at full volume, the reeds and horns screeching in ecstasy, or pain, or both. The cacophony lasts an almost unbearable two minutes before the music shifts abruptly again, now wending its way downward past craggy outcroppings of saxophone into a rollicking multi-instrumental conversation centered on frantic piano lines (also played by Ra, who was double-tracked). This yields, in turn, to another shattering crescendo of noise, then a final, quiet passage of profound irresolution. Through it all, there is no consistent time signature or chord progression, nothing at all to anchor you. Listen to it in the right mood, though, and you may find it gripping beyond belief.

"Sometimes I hook up with the cosmos," Ra once said, "and out of the cosmos comes this sound."[104] Far more than Kubrick's exactingly executed special effects in *2001*—simultaneously being produced in London, a cultural world away—*Magic City* conjures the wonder and terror of what it might actually feel like to drift in the domain of infinite blackness. That points to the political subtext of Sun Ra's "space jazz," which was separatism by other means. Stewart Brand was certain that the first photos of Earth taken from orbit, floating fragile in the void, helped to inspire the environmental movement.[105] Sun Ra's belief in his own extraplanetary origin had a similar distancing effect, positioning him at a point far outside America's racial politics. It was for the same reason that, beginning in the late 1950s, Ra began attiring himself and his bandmates in elaborate Egyptian-style robes and head-pieces. This symbolized one of his key ideas: that the most powerful way to escape the tragic dimension of Black America was to step into another dimension entirely, to refuse sequential time itself, fuse deep history and the far future together into one undifferentiated frame of reference.

Sun Ra would eventually come to be seen as an originator of Afrofuturism, a term coined by the critic Mark Dery in 1994 in the context of a trio of interviews—with Samuel Delany, the cultural analyst Greg Tate, and the music scholar Tricia Rose. Afrofuturism has since become an extremely influential idea, finding expression in everything from pop music and contemporary art to the Marvel film *Black Panther* (2018).[106] One way to understand it is as an extension of an intellectual tradition that began with the nineteenth-century African colonization movement, continued in Marcus Garvey's Black Nationalism and pan-Africanism, and ultimately led to the Black separatist movement of the 1960s. In all these contexts, despair over the prospects for racial equality inspired African Americans to establish a place apart, beyond the sphere of white power and influence. With the serial failure of these movements, however, and the foreclosure of the spaces of freedom that they imagined, the Black imagination turned instead to tomorrow. Seen in this light, Afrofuturism can be defined as—in Tate's words—"simply put, how human truths crushed to Earth rose to engage in symbolic warfare."[107] It is a utopian impulse that reflects, as if in a mirror darkly, what has been called "Black pessimism."[108]

If this is Afrofuturism, then Ra may indeed have been its first exponent, even though—as his biblical interests and Egyptian iconography suggest—he was just as much into the Afropast. As Tricia Rose noted in her interview with Dery, "Sun Ra's flying saucer imagery is about accepting the mystical powers that one knows. . . . If you're going to imagine yourself in the future, you have to imagine where you come from; ancestor worship in black culture is a way of countering a historical erasure."[109] The theorist Kodwo Eshun argues that by summoning the legacy of ancient Egypt, a glorious African civilization that dated to long before the Atlantic trade in human beings, Afrofuturists like Ra have provided an alternative to "the collective trauma of slavery as the founding moment of modernity."[110] Yet, if Ra did manage to achieve escape velocity on these terms, it's difficult to see quite how one could follow him. Even the first step—believing that he had been to Saturn and back—is probably beyond the reach of most people. Much less is it possible to live outside racism, a fact that Ra himself acknowledged, as on the occasion when he stood in front of the White House and remarked, "I'm looking across the street and don't see the Black House."[111] Ultimately, Ra is most inspiring not as a symbolic figurehead for escapism but precisely because his work is a sublime, searing response to the world we actually live in. As the curator John Corbett puts it, Sun Ra and his Arkestra "may force us not just to question *their* sanity, but to question our own."[112]

Also preeminent in the Afrofuturist pantheon is George Clinton, the mastermind of 1970s funk and leader of Parliament-Funkadelic, two separate bands with overlapping sensibilities and personnel. While the direct influence from Sun Ra seems to have been limited—Clinton has said that he didn't know much about the older musician until the 1980s—the parallels between the two men are striking.[113] Clinton, too, created his own utopian version of America, reimagining it as "One Nation under a Groove." Clinton never claimed to have been instructed by aliens, but he did play one onstage: At the height of his popularity, the Mothership Connection tour of 1975, he started each concert by descending in a model spaceship, announcing himself as the Starchild (possibly an allusion to *2001: A Space Odyssey*), come to address the citizens of the universe. "Ain't nothing but a party," he'd jive, as a chorus chanted a version of the gospel standard "Swing Low, Sweet Chariot." "Time to move on, light years in time ahead of our time. Free your mind and come fly with me."

Parliament-Funkadelic's "Dr. Seussian astrofunk" (to quote Dery) was more fun than anything happening in jazz, Sun Ra included, but it was also sophisticated in its own way.[114] Clinton was omnivorous, synthesizing ideas from both Black and white music, "fusing the hippie counterculture with parodies of black pop, pimp, and prayer culture," as Tate put it.[115] Psychedelia was a particularly important ingredient in this hot, sometimes messy stew. Clinton routinely invoked the Beatles' trippy *Sgt. Pepper's Lonely Hearts Club Band* (1967), and for a time—unlike Ra, who avoided alcohol and drugs—he was a devoted acidhead, producing the entirety of his Funkadelic album *Free Your Mind and Your Ass Will Follow* (1970) in a single day while on LSD. (Sample lyric: "The kingdom of heaven is within. Freedom is free of the need to be free.") In his later career as a performer and producer, Clinton would continue to bridge musical cultures, immediately embracing German electronic music by bands like Kraftwerk when it emerged, and mixing it with hip-hop, the new breaking genre of Black music.

One kind of music Clinton definitely didn't dig was disco, which he mocked as "the Placebo Syndrome," and regarded, with considerable justification, as a dilution of his music for white audiences. Tate once went so far as to describe disco as "a form of record industry sabotage," because it displaced independent Black musical acts.[116] Parliament-Funkadelic got hardly any airplay on white radio during their most creative years, even as the disco craze was sweeping the nation in the wake of *Saturday Night Fever* (1977), starring John Travolta. Many then and since have found the music itself to be thin and bloodless, "clean, a product of the deodorant movement, reveling in crystal clear white polyester, cocaine, and mirrored balls, in perfumes that mask and repress the funk in its carnal primality," as the music critic Scot Hacker writes.[117]

But there's another way of telling this tale, in which disco figures not as a sellout genre but rather a culmination of postwar musical futurology. That version begins at the Stonewall Inn in New York City, the site of the uprising against Vice Squad cops in June 1969 that began the gay liberation movement. The Stonewall was itself a proto-disco, a party every night with a racially mixed crowd. One Latino regular says, "There were other bars in which you sometimes squeezed in a little dancing, assuming that the circumstances were OK, but dancing was the central activity at the Stonewall. The Stonewall was the biggest and the most fun."[118] It was also, therefore, dangerous. Police harassment and gay bashing by members of the public were commonplace. For this reason, the queer community just as often celebrated behind closed doors, in privately owned spaces.

This is where a gay kid from Utica, New York, came in: David Mancuso, a hippie and a high school dropout who moved to New York City in 1964. He got by on odd jobs, but lived for the nighttime, when he would go to the Manhattan equivalents of San Francisco's psychedelic scene. He was deeply impressed when he saw Timothy Leary speak at a venue called Fillmore East, backed by a light show. Mancuso began hosting small LSD gatherings—five people or fewer—at a time when the drug was still legal. Deeply interested in music, he invested what little money he had in vinyl records and a terrific sound system. All these factors came into beautiful alignment on Valentine's Day, 1970. Low on funds, Mancuso decided to throw a rent party, like those of the Harlem Renaissance. Everyone would be welcome—and that meant everyone. The majority who showed up were queer, but unlike at a typical gay or lesbian bar of the era, quite a few straight people came too. The crowd was also strikingly interracial, a reflection of Mancuso's own diverse circle of acquaintance. He called the event Love Saves the Day—notice the initials—and based the pacing of the night-long set on one of Leary's guides to the psychedelic experience.[119] The party was such a success that he made it a regular thing, calling it simply the Loft.

The historian Tim Lawrence, author of a groundbreaking study of early disco culture, notes that the invitation for Love Saves the Day had an image of Salvador Dalí's painting *The Persistence of Memory* (1931), the one with the melting pocket watches; and that there were no clocks at the Loft, which "contributed to the dance dynamic. In the everyday world the clock signifies the unstoppable forward movement of teleological time, but party time unfolds in a different dimension."[120] It was an effect borrowed directly from the psychedelic scene, here amplified by the music, the mix of people, and—not to be forgotten—the mirror ball hanging from the ceiling like a miniature geodesic dome. It was a winning formula, and was rapidly replicated within the gay community, both in the city, at venues like the Paradise Garage and the Flamingo, and also out on Fire Island, then in its heyday as a gay pilgrimage destination. Up in Harlem, drag queens—mostly Black and Latino/Latina—organized themselves into "houses" and competed against one another for official trophies and the acclaim of the crowd.[121] As Andrew Holleran put it in his pioneering novel of queer New York life, *Dancer from the Dance* (1978), the scene was "a strange democracy where the only ticket of admission was physical beauty—and not even that sometimes. All else was strictly classless."[122]

Disco and drag manifested yet another conception of the future-as-party. As another early participant told Lawrence, "[After] the repression of the Black Panthers, the next youth wave realized that they couldn't change the world," and in any case, most of the disco crowd "couldn't tune in and drop out because they had nothing to drop out from."[123] These were not people who lived communally, or off donations from home, but had grinding nine-to-five jobs (which, to be fair to *Saturday Night Fever*, was a major plot point in the film). In one sense, the scene was escapist; but from another perspective, it *was* the "real real," the only place where people could feel truly themselves. Tina Turner spoke for many when she sang, in 1978, "night time is the right time."[124] By then, admittedly, disco had lost much of its inclusive, racially integrated character. The celebrated epicenter of the scene, Studio 54 (which opened in 1977), was just as famous for its restrictive door policy as its sexy, cocaine-snorting, science-fiction-styled glitterati.

As disco jumped the rails from subculture to the mainstream, losing its avant-garde character, the genre began to attract widespread backlash.[125] That reaction was exemplified by the ugly, indeed neofascist spectacle of Disco Demolition Night on July 12, 1979, when thousands of white baseball fans at Comiskey Park in Chicago shouted antigay slurs while a great heap of vinyl albums was blown up on the field. (Only some of the records were in fact disco; many recordings by Black musicians in other genres were mixed in too.) The crowd then had a small riot to celebrate.

Ultimately, though, it wasn't homophobia and racism that ended the utopian promise of the disco era; it was the AIDS epidemic, first reported in 1981. This tragedy robbed America of many of its most optimistic and imaginative souls. Queer life, of necessity, became increasingly politicized, with groups like ACT UP formed to urge government action against the disease. Given what happened right after, the unbridled hedonism of the disco era takes on a terrible poignancy. Yet for all the mockery and the subsequent heartbreak, it is worth reconnecting with disco's original, futurological character. In musical terms, its clinical, beats-driven aesthetic laid down the tracks for subsequent house music and techno. More importantly, it allowed for a thrilling exploration not just of the present moment but also of fluid identity—a spectrum that would not be explored in public with equal boldness until very recently.

The potency of disco culture in its glory days is perhaps best embodied in an extraordinary 1978 portrait of the performer Grace Jones, made by her style guru at the time, Jean-Paul Goude. Born in Jamaica, Jones had established herself as a fashion model in Paris before launching herself as a disco diva in New York City, initially playing to gay clubs, then becoming one of Studio 54's most recognizable habitués. Goude's image depicts her in a taut arabesque, clothed only in sweatbands.[126] A power cord snakes from the wall to her upheld microphone, as if she herself were plugged in. It takes a moment to realize that, even for someone of Jones's athleticism, the pose is physically impossible. In fact, we are looking at "*Grace Jones Revised and Updated*," as Goude put it, assembled from numerous photographs and then retouched by hand. In its seamless perfection, the clever collage eerily anticipates later manipulations, including the synthetic avatars that have more recently come to populate our film and computer screens. Equally, Jones's perpetually changing public image during these years presaged the serial restylings of current celebrities like Janelle Monáe (a latter-day avatar of Afrofuturism).[127]

Such maneuvers bear the traces of a still-provocative idea: that what counts as "real" is something one decides for oneself, in the moment. If that precept still feels futuristic today, one can nonetheless trace its origin story back several decades, taking in the sights and sounds on the way: David Mancuso's loft, George Clinton's mothership, Sun Ra's Arkestra, the dance circle at Wounded Knee, the Human Be-In, and countless other gatherings, convened across time and space. All those people, in their different ways and for their own reasons, having the time of their lives.

6

FLOOD

CARE ABOUT THE NOW, SURE. If I had a good day of work in, I wouldn't mind going for a walk. But it's not enough for me to just live in the now. I hate every day that goes by when I haven't made some kind of landmark. Because it goes so fast, and it just drifts on, and I hate the shapelessness of it." The year is 1967, and a young woman called Shulie is completing her degree at the School of the Art Institute of Chicago, while working part-time at the post office. She is just twenty-two years old, but already she feels unmoored by the flood of time. She wants desperately to escape from the present moment—the immediacy worshipped by so many in her own generation. That, she says, is why she is studying painting. Art survives its creator, transcending the organic cycle of life and death. It is an act dedicated to the future.

Shulie is explaining all this to a team of four film students (all male) from Northwestern University, who have decided to make a documentary about her life. They've been following her around Chicago: on the train, taking photographs, and enduring a critique of her work, during which she is subjected to the opinions of the faculty (also all male). Toward the end of the half-hour film, which is simply called *Shulie*, one of its directors asks her about personal matters—about her relationships with men, for example. It's difficult, she replies, because most of them do not respect women as intellectuals or artists. They "want you to be interested in them, before anything else," and also expect you to have children, a prospect that holds little appeal for her. "I'm not trying to say it's meaningless to be a mother, but you're just concerned with one baby and taking care of its needs," Shulie explains. Her own friendships with women were compromised when they had children: "It can be very limiting, because if you're not interested in that particular baby, you have nothing to talk to them about." And what she wants to avoid, at all costs, is limitation. "In some way, I want to be a master of time, because it's not enough for me to just live and die," she declares. "I'm twenty-two, and what have I done? I want to do something. Instead of beauty and power occasionally, I want it all the time. In every word, in every painting, in every brushstroke. Not just now and then."[1]

In 1998 the director Elisabeth Subrin made a shot-by-shot re-creation of *Shulie*, filmed in exactly the same Chicago locations, with a lookalike actress in the lead role. She undertook this forensic replica partly in homage. Subrin was deeply impressed by Shulie's forthright questioning of the gender norms of her day: the way she called out sexism; her honesty in suggesting that motherhood could be more a burden than a joy. In remaking the film, and thus collapsing the past into the present, Subrin also implicitly posed a larger question about what had changed for women in the intervening three decades, and what hadn't. "Why, if we had reaped the benefits of second-wave feminism," she asked, "should Shulie's life seem so contemporary?"[2] This question was especially provocative because, in fact, Shulie was not just any art student. She had indeed gone on to "do something." Her full name was Shulamith Bath Shmuel Ben Ari Firestone, and shortly after the documentary about her student life was completed, she emerged as the most brilliant and controversial theoretician of the women's liberation movement.

Right at the start of *Shulie*, Firestone speaks of her plan to move to New York City, "the place to go when you don't belong anywhere." By that time she had already started a feminist group in Chicago. Now, out east, she sought new allies, cofounding the New York Radical Women (NYRW). Though relatively short-lived—it lasted only two years before splintering into other groups—it was the most influential of the pioneering women's liberation organizations. In fact, the NYRW brought the feminist movement to national attention for the first time, in 1968, when, following the suggestion of their member Carol Hanisch, they staged a protest at the Miss America Pageant in Atlantic City, symbolically throwing corsets, bras, makeup, magazines,

Shulamith Firestone, c. 1970.

and other accoutrements of mainstream femininity into a "Freedom Trash Can." The protestors also organized a boycott against companies advertising at the pageant, and—in a nice touch—declared that they would only give interviews to women journalists, and only submit to arrest by female police officers. Those stipulations were made in a press release written by another leader of the NYRW, Robin Morgan, in which she vociferously critiqued the pageant as a cult of objectification and obsolescence, the principles of consumerism applied to human beings. "What is so ignored," Morgan asked, "as last year's Miss America?"

As fearless on the front lines as Elizabeth Gurley Flynn had been in the days of the Wobblies, Firestone also proved to be an effective organizer behind the scenes and a gifted writer. She helped found a successor to the NYRW called the Redstockings, which staged abortion "speak-outs," at which women shared their own experiences and demanded legal autonomy over their bodies. For a 1968 publication that she coedited, *Notes from the First Year*—the very title suggested futurity, the inauguration of a new epoch—Firestone edited a conversation among a group of her movement sisters in which they discussed their sexual relationships with men.[3] As an early account of "consciousness-raising" (a term that originated within

New York Radical Women protest, Atlantic City, 1968.

the NYRW), it is a historically important document.[4] Thanks to the women's perceptive examination of their pleasures and frustrations, it is also deeply affecting to read—and occasionally hilarious, as at the end, when one participant says with a sigh, "Sometimes, you know, you'd almost rather play ping-pong."[5] In the same vein, Firestone also wrote her own essay on love, which begins, "Wait! I'm not ready for this one yet, give me at least a few more years," but then does proceed to a trenchant exploration of romantic relationships. Love, Firestone argued, was "the pivot of women's oppression today." While partnership could provide freedom from isolation, it too often subjected women to an unequal balance of power, making it an obstacle to half the world's happiness.[6]

In short, Firestone was exploring the idea that "the personal is political"—another saying she helped to popularize.[7] In 1970 she developed that premise into a full-length treatise, *The Dialectic of Sex: The Case for Feminist Revolution*, in which she aimed to do for gender relations what Karl Marx had done for economics and Sigmund Freud for psychology. It made her famous—and infamous. Amazingly erudite, given that Firestone was still only twenty-five when it was published, *The Dialectic of Sex* frames women's liberation as the "ultimate revolution," a transformation in power relations that run deeper than class or even race. She asserted that achieving true gender parity meant confronting not just culture but nature itself: "changing a fundamental biological condition." To the extent that women remain the primary childbearers and carers in society, Firestone argued, they will never be truly free. They must be relieved of this burden, or at the very least, share it equally with men.

This was a vision right out of Charlotte Perkins Gilman's *Herland* or Ursula K. Le Guin's *Left Hand of Darkness*. But Firestone was writing a political manifesto, not a piece of speculative fiction, and she squarely faced the consequences of what she was proposing. As she put it in the book's introduction, "Many women give up in despair: If that's how deep it goes, they don't want to know. Others continue strengthening and enlarging the movement, their painful sensitivity to female oppression existing for a purpose: eventually to eliminate it."[8] After two hundred ensuing pages of closely argued critical theory—integrating Marxist and Freudian analysis into the feminist project, and vice versa—she finally turned her attention to that possible future. "I am aware," she commented drily, "of the political dangers in the peculiar failure of imagination concerning alternatives to the family." It was easy enough to condemn the patriarchy; feminists had been doing that for well over a century. But she would do more, outlining a whole new social order devoid of gender discrimination.

This final section of *The Dialectic of Sex* is what made it notorious. In one passage, which recalls her discussion of motherhood in *Shulie*, she dismissed pregnancy as "barbaric," something that nobody should have to endure. ("Like shitting a pumpkin, a friend of mine told me when I inquired about the Great-Experience-You're-Missing.") But the ordeal of childbirth might soon be a thing of the past. Citing the recent development of birth control pills, Firestone predicted that technology would continue to reshape human reproduction. There would be oral contraceptives for men, artificial insemination and inovulation, and even artificial placentas, which would enable parthenogenesis—the "virgin birth" that Gilman had imagined. Then Firestone took an even greater leap, making "some 'dangerously utopian' concrete proposals." (The scare quotes are hers.) Once sex was decoupled from conception, and gestation from the female body, she hypothesized, the family structure itself would become obsolete. So would social prohibitions against homosexuality and incest(!). Children, no longer under parental control, would acquire a totally different legal status. The physical fabric of society would also be thoroughly reshaped, as it would no longer require residences for nuclear families.

Firestone didn't stop there. Having thoroughly neutralized gender as a social force, her argument turned to a well-established futurological theme: artificial intelligence, "cybernetics, machines that may soon equal or surpass man in original thinking and problem-solving." She recognized that this prospect was "a double-edged sword." In the short term, it might well be a means of further oppression: "To envision it in the hands of the present powers is to envision a nightmare. We need not elaborate. Everyone is familiar with Technocracy, 1984." But Firestone saw artificial intelligence as potentially emancipatory, too—and not only in that it would free people from work, as Arthur C. Clarke and others had imagined. It might open up whole new patterns of mental life—"Why store facts in one's head, when computer banks could supply more comprehensive information instantaneously?"—and would almost certainly produce dramatic social upheaval. Clerical and domestic jobs, the forms of employment most open to women in 1970, would be swiftly automated; that process was, in fact, already underway. Eventually this would result in a dramatic shift in the female consciousness: "Cybernation may aggravate the frustration that women already feel in their roles, pushing them into revolution."

Men, too, would gradually see their jobs taken over by machines, first low-skilled manual laborers, then middle management, and finally the technocratic elite itself.

As we've seen, many futurologists foresaw this same process, but Firestone was the first to see that it could also radically alter gender relations: "We will be beyond arguments about who is 'bringing home the bacon'—no one will be bringing it home, because no one will be 'working.'" Firestone was thus predicting a three-part revolution—sexual, economic, and cultural—that would bring about unprecedented freedom. Crucially, she saw all these changes playing out against a crisis incurred by rapid population growth. At the very moment that people were being displaced by machines, leaving them with less and less to do, there were going to be more and more of them. This too was a widespread concern among futurologists in the 1970s, as we'll see; but Firestone had a unique perspective on it. "The two issues, population control and cybernetics, produce the same nervous superficial response," she said, "because in both cases the underlying problem is one for which there is no precedent: qualitative change in humanity's basic relationships to both its production and its reproduction."

With this insight, Firestone brought *The Dialectic of Sex* to its logical conclusion: The politics of gender could only be resolved by making them *impersonal*. Only by abandoning the traditional family structure, and women's subjugated place within it, could the existential double threat posed by demographic and technological change be met. In this future scenario, human reproduction would no longer be an exclusively private matter, driven by individual desire and obligation. It would instead be a question for society as a whole to determine: The guiding principles of Gilman's *Herland* had to be applied to the impending flood of people, before it was too late. In this sense, women's liberation was the necessary step toward a viable future for all. Firestone did not understate her case: "The feminist movement has the essential mission of creating cultural acceptance of the new ecological balance necessary for the survival of the human race."

Whatever one might think of this argument, it was certainly ambitious, and in some ways genuinely prophetic. Today, while the family remains the basic unit of social organization, its shape and character have clearly been reconfigured. In the immediate aftermath of its publication, others echoed and extended *The Dialectic of Sex*. The activist Ti-Grace Atkinson, who had similarly speculated about technological alternatives to natural birth, asked "how 'love,' as a psychological phenomenon, operates as a response and support to power, and thus to oppression."[9] The radical lesbian feminist Jill Johnston declared a "new approach: all women are lesbians except those who don't know it, naturally; they are but don't know it yet."[10] Johnston dedicated her book *Lesbian Nation* (1973) to her mother, "who should have been a lesbian," and her daughter, "in the hopes that she will be one," and advanced the notion of "*psychic* parthenogenesis," a rebirth of the same-sex-desiring self into a political revolutionary.[11] In the longer term, Firestone's optimism about the radical potential of technology made her the foremother of cyberfeminist theorists like Donna Haraway, author of "A Cyborg Manifesto" (1985).[12] Her refusal to see sexual difference as an irrevocable social distinction anticipated ideas of gender as fluid. And the connections she illuminated between capitalism, patriarchy, and environmental degradation still form the matrix of ecofeminist critique today.[13]

By the time *The Dialectic of Sex* was published, though, Firestone was already stepping back from activism. She had been disheartened by internecine struggles within the early feminist groups, and the anger directed toward her personally. Many of her compatriots found her all too similar to men who had tried to boss them around; philosophically speaking, they believed that her style of charismatic leadership was incompatible with the movement's egalitarian principles. Jo Freeman, an ally of Firestone's from Chicago days, took her side on this question, describing a "tyranny of structurelessness," while another feminist historian has commented that "sisterly communalism made consensus a matter of endurance."[14] It was not a style of politics that Firestone could accept; she was no more temperamentally inclined to living in the indeterminate "now" than she had been in art school. And so she left.

Firestone had a hard life thereafter. After the suicide of her brother Daniel, in 1974, she began suffering from mental illness. Her only subsequent book was *Airless Spaces* (1998), in which she addressed her own experiences of psychiatric treatment through a series of short stories, applying her old excoriating honesty to herself: "She was lucid, yes, at what price. She sometimes recognized on the faces of others joy and ambition and other emotions she could recall having had once, long ago. But her life was ruined, and she had no salvage plan."[15] When Firestone died, in 2012, Freeman said at her memorial: "When I think back on Shulie's contribution to the movement, I think of her as a shooting star. She flashed brightly across the midnight sky, and then she disappeared."[16]

A certain way of thinking about women's liberation faded from view as well. The movement's center of gravity shifted toward "cultural feminism," often anchored in a positive conception of essential womanhood—one of the ideals that Firestone had worked hard to dismantle.[17] This second wave of second-wave feminism directly paralleled the eclipse of the New Left by the rising counterculture. Feminist communes became commonplace. A separatist movement gained ground across the United States, especially among lesbians, who attempted a real-life realization of Gilman's *Herland*. One of the pioneers of lesbian separatism, Betsy Warrior, went so far as to proclaim man "an obsolete life form." As far as she was concerned, "sperm banks and test-tube babies can take over his last function, his only function that has positive effects for the human race." ("If females feel some compunction about eliminating him entirely," she added, "man preserves and zoos might prove a rational alternative."[18]) Other women worked to create "counterinstitutions," as Robin Morgan called them—"concrete moves toward self-determination and power," such as health clinics, rape crisis centers, underground abortion clinics, and feminist bookstores.[19]

These efforts, comparable to those of the Diggers and Black Panthers, were pragmatic steps toward an alternative infrastructure. But this was not at all what Firestone had imagined. She saw communal childcare centers, for example, as "timid if not entirely worthless as a transition" because they would "buy off women," serving only to diminish the pressure that was necessary to bring about true social change.[20] Firestone was ready for a new world, and she was ready for it now. On the last page of *The Dialectic of Sex*, she rewrote a mythic origin story. When Adam and Eve ate the apple of knowledge, they were banished from the Garden of Eden, and inflicted with a double curse: "Man would toil by the sweat of his brow in order to live, and woman would bear children in pain and travail." But it was possible to win freedom from this ancient state of affairs. "We now have the knowledge to create a paradise on earth anew. The alternative is our own suicide through that knowledge, the creation of a hell on earth, followed by oblivion."[21]

FOR ALL OF Firestone's forward-thinking radicalism, her advocacy of "ultimate revolution," *The Dialectic of Sex* was a book absolutely of its moment. In at least one respect, its concern about rampant population growth, it was in the futurological mainstream. "Books come out all the time on the subject," Firestone noted, and she was right. She mentioned just three examples—*Too Many Americans* (1964), *Famine 1975!: America's Decision: Who Will Survive?* (1967), and *The Population Bomb* (1968)—but she could easily have cited many others, beginning with William Vogt's *The Road to Survival* and Fairfield Osborn's *Our Plundered Planet*, both published in 1948. Firestone used a simple analogy to explain the disturbing logic of all these books, which was that of exponential growth: If you put a certain number of rats in a room, they will breed at an ever-escalating rate, as each generation reproduces itself in larger numbers along a steeply rising mathematical curve. Inevitably, they will start competing for what food is available. Then starving. Then killing one another.

The Population Bomb, by far the most widely read book of this "demographic panic" genre, was published under Paul Ehrlich's name alone, even though it was jointly written with his wife, Anne; as Firestone would have been unsurprised to learn, the publisher thought it would sell better as the work of a sole male author. The book was a runaway success, and brought the concept of exponential population growth to popular attention. To grasp its core argument, though, you didn't need to read any further than the cover of the 1978 paperback edition: "While you are reading these words, three children are dying of starvation—and twenty-four more babies are being born." Within, you would find one Cassandran scenario after another, some of them in the form of didactic short stories, describing terrible things to come: a crashing halt to postwar affluence; mass famines, probably within the next decade; a "super-flu" killing one of every three people on the planet. To their credit, like Firestone, the Ehrlichs emphasized the impact of population growth not just on people but also on ecosystems (the book was prominently endorsed by the Sierra Club).[22] How could they not, when they had such a totalizing view of the disaster that lay ahead? "The battle to feed humanity is already lost," they wrote, adding, "*No growth rate can be sustained in the long run.*"[23] The only solution was to bring the birth rate and death rate into alignment, so that the world population would remain stable at a manageable number—ideally, 1.5 to 2 billion. (The world population in 1968 was already 3 billion, but the authors thought this was far too high.) This brought them to a set of recommendations for population control, some of which were quite similar to Firestone's utopian schemes: widening access to abortion, IUDs, and vasectomies, and ultimately overcoming the familial ideal as the unquestioned basis of social organization. Some of their other proposals were more disturbing. The Ehrlichs advocated social engineering, so that more babies would be born male—the total number of women in the population being the more important constraint on the birth rate. They also, notoriously, espoused the use of coercive population control, particularly in "underdeveloped" countries, including the linking of food aid programs to preset population targets and "sterilizing all Indian males with three or more children."[24]

While arrestingly bleak, the Ehrlichs' thinking was not particularly original. One of their most striking scenarios imagined "a continuous 2,000-story building covering our entire planet," with people allotted just three or four square yards of floor space each. They credited that thought experiment to a recent physicist, but Constantinos Doxiadis (the founder of the Ekistics movement and Delos Symposium, encountered in chapter 3) and other garden thinkers had already speculated about the possibility of such a globe-spanning "Ecumenopolis," and J. G. Ballard had written stories based on the same idea. One of them, "Billiennium," published in *New Worlds* in 1961, features a protagonist living in the bend of a stairway, in a city where it's not possible to walk across the street due to the oncoming rush of pedestrians. Buckminster Fuller ran numbers similar to the Ehrlichs' back in 1927, when he calculated how much elbow room humanity would have if we were all packed on to the landmass of the British Isles. Indeed, as critics of *The Population Bomb* were quick to point out, the book's central premise was identical to that put forward by the British political economist Thomas Malthus, all the way back in 1798. "Population, when unchecked, increases in a geometrical ratio," he had written. "Subsistence increases only in an arithmetical ratio."[25] From this simple, unproven (in fact, false) premise, Malthus predicted mass calamity. The ensuing 170 years did little to confirm his predictions. Worldwide food production actually outpaced population growth over that time, and while famines occurred, they were generally the result, not the cause, of political disruption. These facts did not give the Ehrlichs or their like-minded peers much pause. Logically, they figured, there must come a point when a finite planet is overwhelmed by its inhabitants, and Spaceship Earth founders under the weight of its own crew. They were sure this flood was coming, and that they were the last generation with a chance to stem the tide.

In 1972 another book arrived that bolstered the claims of *The Population Bomb*, making its arguments look flimsy (which was not too difficult) and its projections of the future insufficiently alarmist (which is really saying something). This was *The Limits to Growth*—for better or worse, the single most influential futurological work of the late twentieth century. It was written primarily by a biophysicist at MIT, Donella Meadows, based on a two-year research project she undertook with her husband, the social scientist Dennis Meadows, and a starchy, self-convinced systems analyst called Jay Wright Forrester. Though Forrester's name did not ultimately appear on *The Limits to Growth*, he was the senior figure on the team: a quintessential lab-style futurologist who had spent his early career in computing, then transitioned to MIT's Sloan School of Management. There, he developed computer simulations that could be applied to supply chains, business cycles, and city planning—the usual apparatus of futurological consulting.

In his 1969 book *Urban Dynamics*, Forrester had used his computer models to show that low-income Blacks would be better served by "diffusion into existing economic activity" than by "coalescing into a self-respecting, self-disciplining, and self-leading group." Why? Because, as he showed by running the numbers, an economically integrated city is far more efficient than one that is divided. Lacking such internal coordination, he concluded that "outside money can produce only fleeting benefit, if any"— that is, that direct federal aid to struggling cities was a waste of taxpayer money.[26] (As he later put it, "Most policies in a system are very low leverage. They don't really matter and most of them are what people debate. They debate things that don't matter.")[27] This was an extremely provocative argument—managing to contradict racist zoning codes, Black separatism, and Great Society policy all at once—but in *Urban Dynamics*, it was presented as objective fact. Numbers don't lie, right?

Forrester would now be just another forgotten futurologist had *Urban Dynamics* not come to the attention of a private think tank called the Club of Rome. This was an initiative led by the corporate executive Aurelio Peccei, whose long and successful career had included stints at the Italian industrial giants Fiat and Olivetti. In 1968, under the influence of Bertrand de Jouvenel's Futuribles group in Paris, he invited prominent European politicians, economists, and businessmen to join him in an "invisible college" that would deliberate the destiny of humankind. The group's first meeting was hosted by Peccei in Rome, hence its name. Two years on, it published a report entitled "The Predicament of Mankind," which recapitulated the currently fashionable themes of futurological speculation: Society did indeed have the chance to enter a post-scarcity age, but that could only be achieved if global imbalances of wealth, politics, and technology were drastically reduced. The Club of Rome dubbed this array of threats, rather stylishly, "the *problematique*," and declared its intention to solve them. This grand objective, the group said, would initially require "an initial, coarse-grain, 'model' or models of this dynamic situation," which they hoped would "reveal those systemic components that are most critical and those interactions that are most generally dangerous for the future."[28]

This is where Forrester came in. In June 1970 he met with members of the Club of Rome in Bern, Switzerland, and persuaded them that his computer-based techniques were just what they needed to rigorously study the *problematique*. Funding was secured from the Volkswagen Foundation (its president, Eduard Pestel, was a club member), and Donella and Dennis Meadows were soon at work under Forrester's direction. Working with a team of researchers, they set up a computer model with five quantifiable trajectories—world population, industrial capitalization, natural resources, agricultural investment, and environmental pollution—and then began testing various scenarios, seeing how each of these sectors would mutually interact. They did their calculations on IBM machines, using a bespoke computer language called DYNAMO (a portmanteau of "DYNAmic MOdels"). It was an experiment right out of the RAND playbook, but with an important difference: The study had an extremely high level of generality and a very long timescale, claiming to assess the fate of the entire planet all the way out to the year 2100—a full century beyond Herman Kahn's concurrent speculations.

The Limits to Growth research team, ca. 1972.

The MIT group's first output was Forrester's *World Dynamics* (1971), a follow-up to his earlier study of urban planning. Based on the MIT team's computer modeling work, the book was packed with technical commentary, charts, and equations, even extracts from the DYNAMO code used in the lab. Hardly easy reading, it sank without trace.[29] So it wasn't until the following year, with the publication of the more accessible *Limits to Growth*, that the world learned of the astonishing conclusion the team had reached: In Donella Meadows's concise, dismaying formulation, "The basic behavior mode of the world system is exponential growth of population and capital, followed by collapse."[30] The models adopted different underlying assumptions, yet even when ameliorating factors—curbed pollution, increased crop yields—were fed into the computers, the results were the same, give or take a few years. The population curve rises steadily until, at some point in the twenty-first century, it swoons and then plummets, reflecting a mass die-off. After that, the authors wrote, their models no longer had predictive value: "We find it difficult to imagine what new forms of human societal behavior might emerge and how quickly they would emerge under collapse conditions."[31] But they insisted on the validity of their analysis, right up to the point of apocalypse.

The Limits to Growth was launched in March 1972 at a symposium in Washington, D.C., jointly sponsored by the Club of Rome and the Xerox Corporation. The event was held in the Smithsonian Castle's Great Hall, under the watchful gaze of a bust of the Smithsonian secretary Joseph Henry; he had orchestrated his weather forecasting network from the same building in the 1850s. Dennis Meadows, standing in front of large-scale reproductions of the study's charts, spoke to a large and presumably horrified audience of politicians, journalists, and academics. It was a McNamara-esque performance with precisely the opposite message: Business as usual was a recipe for disaster. It would only lead to ever-increasing economic inequality, depletion of natural resources, and, ultimately, ruin at an epochal scale. Technological solutions alone, he emphasized, "can serve only to postpone the collapse." The only hope was that humanity would somehow find its way to a zero-growth plateau, but that would require nothing less than a revolution in human nature itself. As Donella Meadows put it, in her characteristically restrained yet terrifying prose, "Is the future of the world system bound to be growth and then collapse into a dismal, depleted existence? Only if we make the initial assumption that our present way of doing things will not change."[32]

Swiftly following the presentation in Washington, D.C., the Club of Rome orchestrated a press campaign, pushing *The Limits to Growth* as a "rediscovery of the laws of nature." Response was immediate, dramatic, and mostly appalled. Here and there, the report did find allies. A few professional economists were sympathetic, agreeing that humanity had somehow to embrace equilibrium, rather than expansion, as a core principle. The long-term goal should be "a steady-state economy."[33] In Britain, a team of environmental scientists produced their own study, incorporating some of the MIT group's findings, and similarly arguing against the principle of boundless growth. They released the text first in installments in the *Ecologist* magazine, and subsequently as a book titled *A Blueprint for Survival*. Humanity, they asserted, was worse than a bull in a china shop: At least the bull doesn't think the china shop will adapt itself to him.[34] As for Paul Ehrlich, he thought the MIT researchers were entirely too optimistic: He reckoned it would be twenty years, tops, before "utter catastrophe overtakes the western world."[35]

The more common initial reaction to *The Limits to Growth*, however, was that it was nonsense. Many people found the idea of simulating all of reality in a computer to be inherently absurd—an understandable view, given that even top-of-the-line IBM machines of the day had only eight megabytes of core memory. The *Village Voice*, broadsheet of hip New York City, dismissed the book as "a clever computer exercise in futurology and fear mongering."[36] Even one of the Meadows's own colleagues at MIT told a journalist, "What they're doing is providing simple-minded answers for simple-minded people who are scared to death."[37] One of the most damning reviews came from John Maddox, editor of the venerable science journal *Nature*. His book *The Doomsday Syndrome: An Attack on Pessimism* (1972), published just a few months after *Limits to Growth*, was principally devoted to exposing the junk science in demographic panic literature like *The Population Bomb*. As far as Maddox was concerned, there was still plenty of planet to go around. "Tiny though the earth may appear from the moon, it is in fact an enormous object," he wrote, then ran some of his own calculations. He figured that every person alive had, all to themselves, a million tons of air and half a cubic mile of water. Buckminster Fuller's much-traveled analogy of Spaceship Earth was, Maddox wrote, "probably not yet applicable to the real world. Human activity, vast though it may be, is still dwarfed by the human environment." It was not inconceivable that civilization could eventually affect such a vast, powerful system, but that was not about to happen anytime soon. Limits to growth might exist in theory. In reality, they were nowhere in sight.[38]

Other, more attentive critics of *The Limits to Growth* zeroed in on its methodology. Just a month after the book's launch, the *New York Times* published a devastating assessment by three leading social scientists. They summarized the argument even more concisely than Donella Meadows had—"Either civilization or growth must end, and soon"—then comprehensively demolished it. The main problem, they wrote, was oversimplification. For example, the book did not adequately consider the potential efficiency gains of new technologies, or account for price rises, which tend naturally to protect resources (as they get scarcer, they also become more expensive, incentivizing alternative means of production). Had someone in the year 1900 written a book like *The Limits to Growth*, they would have predicted that future society would require twenty million telephone switchboard operators, and that every city on earth would be completely buried in horse manure. In sum, the MIT group had rediscovered not a fundamental law of nature but rather one of computer science: "Garbage In, Garbage Out."[39] (The British innovation expert Christopher Freeman basically agreed, though he thought it was more a case of "Malthus in, Malthus out.")[40] The *Times* reviewers also took issue with economists who defended *The Limits to Growth*, simply because it alerted the general public to the dangers of economic expansion. Actually, they wrote, this sort of pessimism was completely counterproductive. It is ongoing capitalization that provides the conditions for innovation; investment is what allows society to keep pace with itself. Whatever problems might lie ahead for society, preaching against growth, as such, could only make matters much, much worse.

This acrimonious debate over *The Limits to Growth* was itself a premonition of sorts, in that it anticipated arguments about the future right down to the present day. To a degree that is most unusual in the annals of social science, the book's findings have been continually, bitterly contested over the years. Detractors contend that the subsequent development of technology, including into virtual space, has shown the economy can indeed keep expanding, perhaps indefinitely, and certainly along routes unthinkable back in 1972. They also argue that a steady-state economy is nothing to be desired: As a zero-sum scenario, it all but assures an age of global warfare. It's not growth but the collapse of virtuous cycles of capitalist exchange that will plunge society into that chaos. "It's hard to see how a global plateau could last indefinitely," writes the Silicon Valley mogul Peter Thiel, an outspoken libertarian and one of the most prominent recent critics of the Club of Rome.[41] For Thiel, attempts to constrain growth through regulation are invariably wrongheaded, pushing us all toward "a world of technological stagnation and demographic collapse . . . sclerosis in government and banal repetition in culture."[42]

The champions of *The Limits to Growth* and its legacy, conversely, argue that it got at least one huge thing right—climate change is a real and existential threat—and that its projections about resource depletion look increasingly prescient as the twenty-first century wears on. Fossil fuels turn out to be harder to replace than horses. The Club of Rome, still in action, has restated the central arguments of the book with ever-increasing urgency, including in volumes published on its thirtieth and fiftieth anniversaries.[43] As for Donella Meadows, she died in 2001, convinced that she and her colleagues had gotten the future basically right. Their main mistake had been in expecting people to believe them. "The way we thought about the future was utterly logical," she wrote in 1999. "If you tell people there's a disaster ahead, they will change course. If you give them a choice between a good future and a bad one, they will pick the good. They might even be grateful. Naïve, weren't we?"[44]

THE LIMITS TO GROWTH sold at least eight million copies in its first decade, and was translated into thirty languages. (Its British sibling, *A Blueprint for Survival*, sold about five hundred thousand copies.) It has been credited with influencing government at the highest level, from Jimmy Carter's inaugural address in 1977— "We have learned that more is not necessarily better, that even our great nation has its recognized limits"—to China's One-Child Policy, implemented in 1980 in an attempt to curb its own population.[45] *The Limits to Growth* also found echoes and dissent in the work of other futurologists. In 1972, Barbara Ward—still making her annual trips to Greece for the Delos Symposium, and now advising Robert McNamara in his role as the president of the World Bank—published *Only One Earth*, coauthored with René Dubos, the environmental scientist who popularized the slogan "Think globally, act locally." In the book's conclusion, titled "Strategies for Survival," they argued that while the future might be fundamentally unknowable, it was definitely subject to constraint: "Above all, we know that there are limits to the burdens that the natural system and its components can bear, limits to the levels of toxic substances the human body can tolerate, limits to the amount of manipulation that man can exert upon natural balances without causing a breakdown in the system, limits to the psychic shock that men and societies can absorb from relentlessly accelerating social change."[46]

Robert Jungk was more suspicious of the MIT group, and of Forrester in particular, whom he described as "a Stalinist type . . . very cold, very inhuman, who actually tries to impose his pattern on reality." Jungk worried that the Club of Rome presaged an "expertocracy" which would be given unprecedented powers in order to stave off the disasters it was predicting.[47] Yet he did share many of the concerns expressed in *The Limits to Growth*, and accepted the idea that computer simulations—what he called "serious games"—could play an important part in understanding the threats ahead. All the more reason, he thought, to democratize these tools, and give everyone the opportunity to use them.

We can well imagine how intensely annoyed the futurist Daniel Bell felt, seeing the debate over *The Limits to Growth* eclipse his own, much more nuanced work. The author of "Twelve Modes of Prediction" summarily dismissed *The Limits to Growth*, again on the grounds of its oversimplification: "It assumes that no qualitative change in the behavior of the system takes place, or is even possible. But this is not so." Anyway, it was ridiculous to think that futurological techniques could be applied to such an expanse of time and space. "It is easy—and particularly so today, to set forth an extravagant theory which, in its historical sweep, makes a striking claim to originality," he wrote. "But when tested eventually by reality, it turns into a caricature." He made this argument in his book *The Coming of Post-Industrial Society: A Venture in Social Forecasting* (1973), which accurately predicted the shift away from manufacturing and toward an economy based on services and information. This shift from physical to intellectual property would place "technical decision-making" at the heart of the political process, he thought, resulting in exactly what Jungk feared: "the pre-eminence of the professional and technical class." This was a further reason that Bell was not worried about the predictions in *The Limits to Growth*. However the math worked out, there would be experts in charge of the postindustrial society, people like Bell himself. Surely they would be able to manage the process of continual expansion.[48]

Lewis Mumford had long been delivering warnings of the kind issued in *The Limits to Growth*, though without arousing such dramatic response. In the mid-1960s he started musing about the "mega-machine," a hypertrophied version of industrialism in which people, rather than mechanical components, were the moving parts, controlled by forces they could not fathom. He agreed that the "removal of limits," in modern industrial society, was perilous in the extreme. But like Jungk, he viewed the prospect of rule by "expertocracy" as a nightmare. In his last major published work, *The Pentagon of Power* (1970)—a Vietnam-era title if ever there was one—Mumford took as a cautionary tale the "crazy, cruel and murderous" computer in *2001: A Space Odyssey*, then summoned a much older fable: Goethe's 1797 poem "Der Zauberlehrling" ("The Sorcerer's Apprentice"), which Americans would have known from Disney's 1940 film *Fantasia*. In this poem, a trainee wizard enchants a broom and instructs it to clean his master's workshop, but he cannot control the spell. The broom takes on a life of its own, fetching bucket after bucket of water, and nearly destroys the place. "The moral should be plain," Mumford wrote. "Unless one has the power to stop an automatic process—and if necessary reverse it—one had better not start it." Humanity had not observed this basic principle. "As a result, we are already, like the apprentice, beginning to drown in the flood."[49]

The Flood: a central metaphor of late twentieth-century futurology. It is, of course, an image rich in religious association, and its currency marked a return to the prophetic mode that had prevailed decades earlier. Once again, across a wide spectrum of opinion, there was consensus that society was in a race against time. Shulamith Firestone wasn't the only one talking about heaven and hell; the Ehrlichs and the Meadows weren't the only ones worried about the very survival of the human race. The impending torrent would be global in its reach, and would over-whelm us all. There was just going to be *too much*. Too much population. Too much pollution. Too much information. Too much complexity. Above all, "too much change in too short a time," which is how Alvin Toffler defined the concept of "future shock." His 1970 bestseller of that title was the only book of the era to rival *The Population Bomb* and *The Limits of Growth* in shaping the general public's understanding of the future.[50] And like those books, Toffler's premise was a simple one: Just as you can experience "culture shock" by traveling to a foreign country, you can also experience "future shock" by encountering an unfamiliar timeframe—which, according to Toffler, is what was happening to everyone, all the time, at least in the industrialized West.

Future Shock sold five million copies. It was also the basis of a short documentary, released in 1972, that makes for strange viewing half a century later. Technologies, fashions, and social changes that now seem quaintly nostalgic are presented in a tone of insistent paranoia. The presence of Orson Welles as narrator enhances the ominous atmosphere. Portly, bearded, draped in a long black coat, and puffing on a cigar, he presides with his trademark air of bemusement over a portrait of society in flux. (A few years later he would repeat the performance as host of a documentary about the sixteenth-century French astrologer Nostradamus, who supposedly foresaw the calamitous events of the future, including the French Revolution and World War II.) In the film, as in Toffler's original book, a huge number of topics are circumscribed within a single phenomenon. Future shock is seen as writ large in the globalized economy—Turkish workers in Germany, flamenco concerts in Sweden—and at smaller scale in ephemeral commodities like paper dresses, disposable diapers, and rental cars. "We're in an endless combat with our own environment," Welles intones in the film, "with all its pace and variety, its choice and over-choice."

If rampant consumerism was an index of future shock, though, so was the anti-consumerist counterculture. The younger generation, Toffler thought, was addicted to new experiences, like LSD, and to transient relationships. Intimacy was an instant thing among the hippies, literally here today and gone tomorrow. The home was just "a place to leave." The women's liberation movement, with its rejection of traditional gender roles, was another "symptom of a society that is cracking under the pressures for change," the book argued, as was the breakdown of the traditional family in favor of experimental alternatives like "homosexual family units" and "wife-swap clubs." And all of this was only the beginning. There was more change coming, and fast. Shifts in sexual mores augured the rise of "psych-corps," which would "vie with one another to create the most outlandish, most gratifying experiences," including "brain-stimulating pleasure probes." (Tuned in or not, Toffler's descriptions of dystopia often seem strangely turned on.) There might soon be "babytoriums," where parents could purchase an embryo to their liking. Based on his conversations at RAND, Toffler also predicted massive networks for combined human and machine decision-making—a development that he expected to arrive by about 2020. All these innovations, he wrote, "will fire off like a series of rockets carrying us out of the past, plunging us deeper into the new society."

Alvin Toffler had a lot in common with Paul Ehrlich, and not only because he too coauthored his book with his wife and failed to credit her. (Heidi Toffler was a former union shop steward and civil rights activist; she went on to write several more books with Alvin, receiving credit only beginning in 1993, with their book *War and Anti-War: Survival at the Dawn of the 21st Century*.) Like *The Population*

Bomb, the title *Future Shock* was a catchphrase that felt novel, even though the idea had been kicking around for more than a century—hadn't Marx and Engels said, in the *Communist Manifesto* (1848), "All that is solid melts into air"? (Less famously, they remarked that the bourgeoisie of their own time had "created more massive and more colossal productive forces than have all preceding generations together. . . . There is too much civilization, too much means of subsistence, too much industry, too much commerce.") Also like the Ehrlichs, the Tofflers made breathtakingly bold predictions on the basis of selective anecdotes and wholly imaginary scenarios. When Alvin Toffler capitalized on his newfound success with an edited anthology called *The Futurists* (1972), including texts by Margaret Mead, Robert Jungk, John McHale, Daniel Bell, Ossip Flechtheim, and Buckminster Fuller, he gave the first spot to Paul Ehrlich's story "Eco-Disaster!" It forecast the extinction of ocean life, "smog disasters," the accidental destruction of grain worldwide by a newly intro-duced pesticide, and other climate catastrophes, all before the decade was out.[51] Ehrlich was right to be worried, as we now know, but his wild guesswork, swiftly proved incorrect, was just the sort of thing that threatened to discredit the environ-mental movement in its early years. At least Toffler was right about one thing; the

Alvin and Heidi Toffler in 1974.

writers he had gathered "share a wish to shape the future. And each, in his or her own way, already has!"

THERE WAS ONE area where Toffler's concept of "future shock" really did make sense. This was in the rapidly developing field of computers, which "combine facts to make new knowledge at such high speed that we cannot absorb it." The logic of exponential growth—all those rats, breeding themselves to oblivion—was omnipresent in late twentieth-century futurology, the futurology of the Flood. In most cases, it proved completely misplaced. In the case of world population, for example, the overall rate of increase has steadily declined; there are still more people on earth with each passing year, but the uncontrolled demographic rise foreseen by the Ehrlichs has simply not materialized. Where exponential growth has occurred, and completely reshaped society, however, is in computer power.

This phenomenon is indelibly associated, both in the industry and in the popular imagination, with Moore's law. Actually it's not a law, just a prediction, but a strikingly prescient one. It was originally put forward in 1965 by Gordon Moore, an engineer at Fairchild Semiconductor, in the pages of *Electronics Magazine* (later, Moore would cofound the chip-manufacturing giant Intel). He had noticed that in the few years integrated circuits had been manufactured so far, their capacity—that is, the number of transistors and other components they could hold, and therefore the number of operations they could perform—had approximately doubled on an annual basis. He boldly speculated that this compound rate of increase would continue for at least a decade. In one way, that proved a little overconfident; when the decade was up, it looked like capacity was actually doubling every two years or so, rather than annually. But in another sense, Moore was not optimistic enough. Exponential growth of computing power would continue far longer, right into the twenty-first century, making possible the digital revolution we all know today. Fueled by this ever-increasing capacity, the computer industry has embraced future shock as its modus operandi. Every product is launched as a transformative game changer. Consumers are habituated to the idea that their devices will have short lifespans. There had long been a conscious strategy to "instill in the buyer the desire to own something a little newer, a little better, a little sooner than is necessary," as industrial designer Brooks Stevens put it. But for a product to stop working because it can no longer keep up with technology, after just a few years? This is truly planned obsolescence.

The industry has yet to honestly debate that issue, but they have been arguing among themselves about another question ever since Moore promulgated his prediction: Should we be putting all this power into automation, or augmentation? This distinction, often framed with pleasing symmetry as an opposition between AI and IA (short for artificial intelligence and intelligence augmentation), has to do with the amount of human involvement in a digital system. In the case of total automation, there isn't any. This is the world of the "lights out" factory, with machines working away hyperefficiently in complete darkness, apart from occasional maintenance checks by human supervisors. The final destiny of this sort of automation, theoretically, would be "strong" or "general" artificial intelligence, in which machines transcend the level of human understanding, and thus the need for our guidance or control. I'll get back to that thrilling, terrifying prospect in this book's conclusion. Here, though, I want to consider the contrasting idea of intelligence augmentation, which is much less widely discussed, despite the fact that it defines the digital world we inhabit. It's worth noting, at the outset, that this is not how most of the pioneers of computer science thought things would go. Robots like the ones in Karel Čapek's *R.U.R.* provided the conceptual template for researchers in the 1960s. As the historian of technology John Markoff explains, "the era was dominated by a belief that Artificial Intelligence was at hand and would soon create a world populated by thinking machines."[52] But some saw the augmentation of the human mind as holding much more promise.

One of those was a farm boy from Portland, Oregon, named Doug Engelbart. He joined the U.S. Navy as a radar technician near the end of World War II, and was actually shipping out on VJ Day when news came in of the Japanese surrender. The sailors on board started shouting, "Turn around!" but off they went anyway, to the Philippines.[53] An introvert by nature, Engelbart spent a lonely and tedious year on the base there, but it was punctuated by a momentous discovery. Flipping through a copy of *Life*, he encountered an article by Vannevar Bush, who was at the time the head of the U.S. Office of Scientific Research and Development—the bureau charged with developing experimental technology for the military, including the atom bomb. Entitled "As We May Think," the essay is deservedly famous today for its forecast of a future device called a "Memex"—a remembering machine—"in which an individual stores all his books, records, and communications, and which is mechanized so that it may be consulted with exceeding speed and flexibility." Such a device, Bush thought, would look something like a traditional desk, but it would probably have a slanting translucent screen, buttons, and a keyboard. It would be able to store many thousands of pages' worth of information, all of which could be linked via trails through the maze of content. "Such machines will have enormous appetites," Bush wrote, and "some of them will be sufficiently bizarre to suit the most fastidious connoisseur of the present artifacts of civilization."[54]

Engelbart was transfixed. At that time, as he later put it, a computer "was an underpaid woman sitting with a hand calculator," but he had the strong intuition that Bush's vision would be realized, sooner or later. It was a premonition of the Flood. The idea stayed with him as he first got a PhD in the emergent field of computer science and then, having turned down a job offer from RAND, founded a short-lived company called Digital Techniques. After this proved unsuccessful, in 1957 he joined the Stanford Research Institute, another think tank founded immediately after the war. An unpublished manuscript of Engelbart's from this time suggests the direction that his thoughts were taking: "It may well be that the true picture of what computer technology is going to do to our social structure represents too drastic a change to expect our inelastic little minds to face up to. On the other hand, it is clear that almost everything in our society is experiencing an accelerated evolution."[55] He anticipated Gordon Moore's thinking about miniaturization, giving a lecture on "microelectronics" in 1960, in which he suggested computers would become ever smaller and more powerful. Such machines would, he thought, "baffle the intuition and the understanding which has been developed in working with normal-sized devices."[56] A decade before Alvin Toffler began promoting the idea of future shock, Engelbart was already thinking about the speed of change, and considering how it might best be channeled.

What really made Engelbart an outlier, though, was his commitment to augmenting the human intellect.[57] While his colleagues at Stanford were determinedly pursuing robotics and other applications of artificial intelligence, he instead focused on the "man-machine interface," which he saw as nothing less than the next step in human evolution. By way of explanation, he liked to ask people to write with a pencil that was tied to a brick, an experience he described as "de-augmentation." Imagine freeing yourself from such a burden: How much faster could you think and work? This, he said, would be a way of "bootstrapping" the intellect (as in, pulling yourself up by your own bootstraps). Aided by computers, people would not only learn more quickly but learn *how* to learn more quickly, in an ever-faster rush of new knowledge—another vision of compound or exponential growth, which computer interaction specialists since have nicknamed "Engelbart's law."

In 1963, Engelbart managed to secure funding for his Augmented Human Intellect Research Center—later shortened to Augmentation Research Center, or ARC. The acronym prompted Engelbart's workplace nickname, Noah, appropriate for someone at the crest of the Flood.[58] Around this time, he also tried LSD. This was, after all, the Bay Area; he and his fellow computer programmers were surrounded by the burgeoning counterculture, and their tastes tended to lean hippie. (Engelbart was a folk-dancing enthusiast, and some of the ARC researchers sat at "yoga workstations," on floor cushions in front of five-inch monitors.) Despite his unit's extensive connections to the military-industrial complex—it received its core funding from the Advanced Research Projects Agency, descendant of Vannevar Bush's wartime bureau, later renamed DARPA, the *D* standing for *Defense*— Engelbart also subscribed to a philosophy of individual transformation, decentralized community building, and mind-expanding tools, the countercultural formula for social transformation as presented in the *Whole Earth Catalog*.[59]

In fact, the *Catalog*'s founder, Stewart Brand, would play a minor role in the signal event of Engelbart's career, which has gone down in history as the "mother of all demos." For two years, ARC had been developing something they called the On-Line System, an array of interactive technologies that allowed multiple users to collaborate in a single network. It incorporated several innovative elements, including the first computer mouse, a contraption of wheels and sensors contained in a lacquered pine box.[60] The mouse had been developed by a talented engineer named Bill English, who also had enough expertise to orchestrate a complex multimedia event, which would communicate all the discoveries ARC had been making. This demo occurred on December 9, 1968, with Engelbart as the presenter. It was witnessed by a live audience of perhaps a thousand people, assembled for a computer conference in San Francisco.

Doug Engelbart in the "Mother of all Demos," 1968.

Separate cameras were trained on Engelbart's face and on his controls, a mouse and keyboard. These were electronically linked to the system on the Stanford campus, thirty miles away. There, another crew—including Brand, whose experience with the Trips Festival and other events qualified him as a cameraman—captured the computers' screens, as well their sounds, a futuristic patter of clicks and beeps. English directed the broadcast from afar, communicating with Engelbart via headset and superimposing the various video streams on top of one another.

What the live audience actually saw, on a twenty-two-foot projection—you can too, in online archival footage—was an astonishing demonstration of all the main elements of personal computing, a full decade before they became available to the general public. Engelbart began with a rhetorical question, complete with Freudian slip: "What if you in your office, you as an intellectual worker, were supplied by a computer display backed up by a computer that was alive for you all day, and was instantly responsible . . . responsive, heh heh, to every action you had, how much value could you derive from that?" He then proceeded to demonstrate a dizzying array of operations: word processing, including cut-and-paste functions; saving a file to storage; the hyperlinking of content; collaboration across multiple workstations; even, astonishingly, a precursor to teleconferencing, with an inset video of one of his colleagues at Stanford. The transmission was, admittedly, only one way; at one point he joked to Bill English, "Don't worry, there's nobody here but a large audience." Engelbart closed by suggesting that within a year, he might be able to give a similar presentation remotely, viewable anywhere in the country. But already he had seemed to transcend the normal boundaries of space and time. The unspoken analogy for the presentation was that of another kind of trip, through the previously uncharted territory of cyberspace.[61]

Rarely has the future seemed to arrive quite so suddenly. But if Engelbart came across, on that day, as a prophet of the electronic age, he was also about to be blindsided by unforeseen events. As his mention of the "intellectual worker" as the intended user of the On-Line System suggests, he saw its potential in elitist terms. Releasing it to the general public was of little interest for him, because he saw augmentation as a method of advanced training for the human mind. But it turned out that it was no easier to contain in a lab than LSD had been. Over the course of the early 1970s, Bill English and several other ARC engineers were lured to a competing think tank, Xerox's Palo Alto Research Center (PARC), where they set about making a more user-friendly version of the On-Line System. One of PARC's founders was an engineer called Alan Kay, the first to envision the laptop computer, in 1972, and also the man who coined the well-known aphorism "The best way to predict the future is to invent it." Ultimately, however, their efforts would also be superseded. Engelbart's biographer has remarked that "Xerox is famous for not being famous for the invention of the computer." Photocopying was the company's core business, and PARC was too isolated from corporate leadership to assume a central role in their strategy.[62]

Instead we got Apple, incorporated in 1977 by Steve Jobs and Steve Wozniak. They'd worked together at the Homebrew Computer Center, a regular gathering of hobbyists partly inspired by the *Whole Earth Catalog*.[63] Unlike Engelbart, Jobs and Wozniak were populists, positively obsessed with making their devices appealing to the general public. That meant affordable, and it meant easy to use. When developing their first computer, ultimately released as the Apple II, they set a target of just thirty minutes for a user to gain operative fluency.[64] Did this mean that they didn't care about augmentation? Far from it. "The computer is a bicycle for the mind," Jobs said, and he often spoke of how the "man-machine interface" would empower a new generation of entrepreneurs. He, too, had taken LSD, and considered it one of the transformative events of his life: "It reinforced my sense of what was important—creating great things instead of making money, putting things back into the stream of history and of human consciousness as much as I could."[65] (Wozniak, for the record, wasn't interested in psychedelics: "I felt I had a great mind and wanted to be judged as myself, not myself plus an aid.")[66]

Whatever it was that Jobs ultimately put into the stream of history, he certainly did make a lot of money—especially after the release of the Macintosh desktop computer. (He briefly considered calling it the Bicycle.)[67] It was launched in 1984 with an extraordinary advertisement directed by Ridley Scott, inspired by the idea that humanity actually had arrived at the future, the year so ominously depicted in George Orwell's dystopian novel.[68] In the commercial, which ran during the Super Bowl and thus reached nearly half of American households, we see a rank-and-file of miserable-looking workers, all clad in dingy gray. They are harangued by a gigantic, bespectacled talking head on a giant screen, surrounded by superimposed text. (The striking resemblance to Engelbart's famous demo was presumably coincidental.) "We have created for the first time in all history a garden of pure ideology," this Big Brother figure snarls, "where each worker may bloom, secure from the pests of any contradictory true thoughts." At the same time we see, pursued by a squad of policemen, an incongruously contemporary figure: a blonde woman in a tank top and red shorts. She is carrying a long-handled throwing hammer, as if she has just jogged over from an ad for that year's Olympic Games. (The actress, Anya Major, was in fact a former track-and-field athlete.) With a dramatic pirouette, she hurls the hammer into Big Brother's face. The screen explodes in a flash of light, which washes over the slack-jawed crowd. And then text fills our own TV screen: "On January twenty-fourth, Apple Computer will introduce Macintosh. And you'll see why 1984 won't be like *1984*."

The meaning of this allegory was left unstated. An expression of antiauthoritarianism, akin to Pink Floyd's *The Wall* (1982)? A victory of energized capitalism over sclerotic communism? Of upstart Apple over its enormous competitor IBM, nicknamed Big Blue? These were all possible subtexts (especially the last one), but the ad also had a deeper significance. Burrell Smith, who designed the motherboard for the new Mac, had said, "I want to build the computer of the 90's. Only I want to do it tomorrow."[69] And this is essentially what had happened. The first Macintosh augured a new era in the history of computers, in which they would become a nearly universal consumer product. This would take a little while; after a strong start, Mac sales temporarily tailed off, as its functional limitations became evident. (The main problem was the total lack of internal storage capacity. This meant that users had to rely entirely on floppy disks inserted into the front of the machine, leading to the nickname "the beige toaster.") It would take a series of further launches and new product categories to install Apple into the hard drive of consumer culture. Nonetheless, it was with the first Mac that the general public began to accept the idea that computers were no longer specialist equipment but rather something that every home would have. My own first computer was a Mac II. When my father brought it home, in 1988, I remember wondering what on earth it was for. I ended up playing Tetris on it, writing essays, and doing the layout for the school newspaper. It was both toy and tool. Had I been augmented? Maybe so; all these years later, I'm a published author, typing on a battered MacBook Air. But at sixteen, staring into the cold glow of a twelve-inch black-and-white screen, I looked a lot more like the gray-garbed drones of the *1984* ad than the heroine with the hammer.

THE PLOT THICKENS now, into a fog. Just prior to directing Apple's Super Bowl commercial, Ridley Scott made *Blade Runner* (1982), his most highly regarded film, much debated by audiences at the time and by academics ever since.[70] Based on Philip K. Dick's science fiction novel *Do Androids Dream of Electric Sheep?* (1968), the movie is set in 2019, in an inky, rain-soaked Los Angeles. The sinister Tyrell Corporation is headquartered in a glowering mammoth pyramid that recalls ancient Egypt, or the cover of a Sun Ra album. The city below is saturated with neon, in the style of Times Square, Hong Kong, or Tokyo's Shinjuku district. Other references glide through the movie, too: Constructivist graphics of the 1920s, fashions from 1930s Shanghai, 1950s automobiles (some of which fly), a general ambience of postwar film noir. As the movie's visual futurist, Syd Mead, put it, "One of the principles behind designing this film is that it should be both forty years in the future and forty years in the past."[71] This mise-en-scène—a high tide of "floating signifiers," as the theorists put it—is one reason *Blade Runner* is considered a classic of postmodern cinema. The other is the storyline, which revolves around characters called "replicants," artificial intelligences who look, talk, and apparently think exactly how human beings do, and may not realize that they are, in fact, artificial. The film tacitly asks whether the main character, a replicant-hunting detective played by Harrison Ford, is himself a replicant. That mystery is never quite solved. Beguiling as it is, the film is purposefully inconclusive, refusing to cohere from its parts.

This too is typically postmodern—at least, it might be? The definition of *postmodern* is famously elusive. It originated in architectural criticism, referring primarily to the return of historic styles suppressed by modernism, in a spirit of ironic quotation. Postmodern buildings are like billboards on all sides, decorative motifs hung on them like trophies. But the concept soon migrated into other cultural forms, acquiring diverse connotations on the way. In literature, postmodernism meant arch authorial self-reference. In fine art: the appropriation of found objects and imagery. In design: the playful manipulation of kitsch pattern and color. In hip hop music: the techniques of sampling and cross-fading on turntables, transforming the track into a stuttering, malleable thing.[72] Yet there was one impulse that activated all these disparate phenomena. Postmodernism was, above all, an expression of indeterminacy. It reflected a relativist point of view (or perhaps better to say, many simultaneous points of view), in which nothing is fixed. Even the most strongly held convictions and identities are seen as contingent, provisional, not to be trusted. Like the all-too-perceptive children of accomplished parents, the postmodernists were obsessed with what came before them, but could not follow suit. *Blade Runner*, meanwhile, suggests that in the future, we will no longer even know whether our own memories and desires are authentic. They might instead be programmed into us, like code into a computer. We will no longer be living in reality, but—as the French theorist Jean Baudrillard argued was already the case—in a simulation.

This was a term borrowed straight from futurology. At think tanks like RAND, in MIT and Stanford computer labs, in corporate planning offices, and in government departments, simulations were understood as diagnostic tools. Never intended to be 100 percent predictive, they were instead meant to give insight into possible futures, and thus provide strategic guidance. Baudrillard turned this idea against itself in his brilliant, hyperbolic 1981 treatise *Simulacra and Simulation*, arguing that such techniques had become so widespread that they were now self-defeating. They had generated an endless flood of models, unmoored from reality. The attempt to achieve total control had resulted in a vast projection, impossible to escape: "The territory no longer precedes the map, nor survives it. It is the map that engenders the territory."[73]

Baudrillard particularly demonized advertising, which he saw as exemplifying the hollowness of simulation and playing the leading role in its dissemination. Decades earlier, the emergent advertising industry had helped to redefine society's relationship to the future, orienting the public toward the values of novelty and improvement. It had been propaganda for the doctrine of progress. Baudrillard believed this manipulation machine had become so effective, so pervasive, that authentic human desires had been entirely displaced by imaginary ones, implanted in service of profit. Advertising was meaningful only in the fleeting moment when it claims attention, an "instantaneous form, without a past, without a future, without the possibility of metamorphosis."[74] Apart from that transaction, it had no meaning at all.

Look again at Ridley Scott's Apple advertisement, this time through Baudrillard's skeptical eyes. Orwell's novel *1984* had been a dead-serious political allegory, a frightening vision of freedom foreclosed. In the ad, by contrast, freedom is easily won—it only takes sixty seconds—but it is emptied of content, functioning purely for promotional purposes. It has become, in Baudillard's terminology, a "lost referent." He saw this effect multiplied all across contemporary culture. Postmodern society was a Disneyland version of reality, with the actual Disneyland, by the way, "presented as imaginary in order to make us believe that the rest is real, whereas all of Los Angeles and the America that surrounds it are no longer real, but belong to the hyperreal order and to the order of simulation."[75]

Blade Runner could almost have been designed to visualize this condition: The only bright light in the film comes from illuminated billboards. But these ideas were pervasive in postmodern art and culture. It was a global phenomenon, but we can get the flavor by looking at what was happening just in New York City. The metropolis had bottomed out into near-ungovernable chaos in the 1970s, then roared back as the nexus of late capitalism in the 1980s, exemplifying the transition from manufacturing to financial and information services that Daniel Bell predicted.[76] The representative sculpture of this sudden inflation, Jeff Koons's *Rabbit* (1986), is quite literally a simulation—a more-than-perfect copy of a blow-up toy, in stainless steel—that reflects everything around it in funhouse curvature. Koons himself has spoken of the work as an image of immortality, holding its breath forever. But if *Rabbit* is a quasi-religious icon, expressive of infinite faith in its own improbable existence, it is also (again, both literally and metaphorically) hollow, and supremely blank. To behold it in person is to confront the chilling logic of simulation in the nonflesh; you're just standing there, looking at yourself.

At the same time, the postmodern torrent of symbols could also be channeled into works of arresting emotional depth. The avant-garde performance artist Laurie Anderson, for example, shot to unlikely fame when her track *O Superman* climbed the pop charts in 1981. It is a poem about love, longing, and the military-industrial complex, set to synthesizer accompaniment. The lyrics could have been plucked from stray TV broadcasts—"Hold me, Mom, in your long arms, your petrochemical arms, your military arms, in your electronic arms"—and Anderson delivers them mesmerically, her voice transmuted to merge seamlessly into the soundscape, using a Vocoder. (This electronic device, invented in 1938, was mentioned by Vannevar Bush in "As We May Think" as one way his imagined Memex machine might communicate.) The following year, Anderson released her first album, *Big Science*, appearing on the cover all in white, wearing opaque eyeglasses. She is the postmodern incarnation of an ancient archetype: the blind seer.

In the album's title track, an unnamed narrator who seems to be wandering around in search of utopia ("golden cities, golden towns") stops to ask for directions. "Well," she's told, "just take a right where they're going to build that new shopping mall, go straight past where they're going to put in the freeway, take a left

Laurie Anderson performing in Amsterdam, 1982.

at what's going to be the new sports center, and keep going until you hit the place where they're thinking of building that drive-in bank. You can't miss it." Anderson's vision of America as a nation entranced by its own myriad possibilities, and therefore utterly lost, found its most capacious outing in her eight-hour concert piece *United States* (1983), in which she gave her audience a whirlwind tour of hyperreality. At one point she seemed to describe her own modus operandi: "a language of sounds, of noise, of switching, of signals... the language of the future." In Baudrillard's theory, simulation is impenetrable, a domain of appearances without meaningful substance. Anderson, though, showed that you could get inside it.

Another emissary of the future in Manhattan's art world was Keith Haring, once described by Timothy Leary as "a Greek god Pan in track shoes."[77] He'd arrived in 1978, a queer, nerdy teenager from Kutztown, Pennsylvania, who had briefly been an LSD-tripping deadhead. In New York he had one of those instant self-reinventions that the city seems to specialize in. While still an art student, he plunged into the queer nightlife and hip-hop scenes and began a guerrilla art project, making rapid-fire drawings all over the subway system. This wasn't exactly graffiti; he drew in chalk on the black paper that was used as a placeholder when advertisement space was left unoccupied (a frequent occurrence at that recessionary moment). The subway drawings were the laboratory for his quickly developing graphic style, which he soon applied in myriad other contexts. Constantly guzzling Coca-Cola, music blasting on his boom box, he'd populate any surface that came to his attention, covering it with intriguing, hieroglyphic motifs: breakdancing figures, barking dogs, crawling babies, televisions, computers. Whatever he was working on, he'd occupy every available bit of space. As Haring explained: "I absorb information at an increasingly rapid rate. We all do. Information is coming from all kinds of sources, new sources every day. Technology is moving faster, perhaps, than we can keep up with. I digest information from these sources, channel it through my own imagination, and put it back out into the world."[78] It was the iconography of the Flood.

Haring was constantly looking for new channels to broadcast his work. "It has become increasingly clear to me that art is not an elitist activity reserved for the few, but for everyone," he said in 1984.[79] Acting on this instinct, he made numerous public murals, theater sets, and music videos—including one for Grace Jones's song "I'm Not Perfect (But I'm Perfect for You)"—even a full-scale zeppelin. In 1986 he opened his Pop Shop to sell merchandise based on his own work, as if he were a living museum, and this was the gift shop. The move was widely criticized at the time, but has since come to seem a bold predictor of art world populism. He also put his boundless energy into raising awareness about political issues such as South African apartheid, domestic racism, and especially the AIDS crisis, which was devastating the queer community, including his immediate circle of friends. In symbolic defiance of the disease, he organized a massive celebration called the Party of Life. First held at the Paradise Garage, the celebrated gay disco, in 1984, it was such a success that he did it again the following year, even bigger and better. This time the venue was the Palladium, newly opened by the Studio 54 founders Steve Rubell and Ian Schrager (it was their comeback after imprisonment on tax evasion charges). Designed by the Japanese postmodernist architect Arata Isozaki, the club had as its spectacular centerpiece one of Haring's huge polychrome murals, an image of ecstatically entwined bodies towering over the dance floor, flanked by twin phalanxes of video monitors. Unlike the hippies at Golden Gate Park, who were in some respects their predecessors, the attendees at the Party of Life actually were experiencing an apocalypse. Haring himself would perish from AIDS-related symptoms in 1990, only thirty-one years old. Until then, though, he and his friends danced like there was no tomorrow.

The Palladium with a mural by Keith Haring, 1985.

Among Haring's many interests was science fiction, signified by his frequent use of flying saucers right out of *The Day the Earth Stood Still*; sometimes his UFOs "zap" other motifs, like pyramids (in his work, too, ancient Egypt and the future seemed to cohabit). Baudrillard, with his customary brutality, had consigned the whole genre of sci-fi to obsolescence: It "will never again be a mirror held toward the future, but a desperate hallucination of the past."[80] He was soon proved wrong, though, as writers absorbed his ideas and those of other postmodern theorists and used them to reinvent the genre yet again. The break-through came with William Gibson's *Neuromancer* (1984), subtitled, as if in direct response to Baudrillard, *Remembering Tomorrow*. The novel's terrific opening line—"The sky above the port was the color of a television, tuned to a dead channel"—plunges the reader into a richly described world, in which technologically augmented humans contend with artificial intelligences for supremacy: the central opposition of computer science, reprised as epic dystopian struggle.

Neuromancer inaugurated an aesthetic that came to be called cyberpunk, which assumed the mantle of 1960s New Wave sci-fi, demonstrating the genre's continuing avant-garde potential. Fittingly for a postmodern literary phenomenon, cyberpunk's influence came mainly through stylistic tropes. Particularly enduring were the neologisms scattered through Gibson's novels, predictions of a digital age yet to come: *cyberspace, wetware, the matrix.* The last of these described a virtual reality that hackers could jack into and surf, "bright lattices of logic unfolding across [a] colorless void," a "consensual hallucination." When Hollywood finally caught up to *Neuromancer*, this was the metaphor it claimed. *The Matrix* (1999) stars Keanu Reeves as Neo, a perpetually stunned-looking messiah figure who discovers that he lives in a simulated reality and leads a revolt against his AI overlords. At least the debt was acknowledged: *Simulacra and Simulation* features as a prop in an early scene (the book is hollowed out, and Neo stores his cash and computer files inside). Baudrillard, unamused, executed a final lap around the circular track of self-reference: "*The Matrix* is surely the kind of film about the matrix that the matrix would have been able to produce."

Speaking as a child of postmodernism myself—I was born in 1972—I'll say that my own favorite trips into hyperreality came courtesy of the Talking Heads, the postmodern pop act par excellence, once described by *Spin Magazine* as "the first American band to go to art school."[81] Their frontman, David Byrne, defined a new archetype, beguiling and intellectual, making an elaborate game of his own celebrity. At the outset of the Talking Heads song "Road to Nowhere" (1985), his stentorian baritone is joined by a full chorus singing a series of outright contradictions—"We know where we're going, but we don't know where we've been . . . the future is certain, give us time to work it out"—before launching into a lurching anti-travelogue in march tempo. Accompanied by rattling snare drum, jaunty accordion, and a crescendo of backing vocals, Byrne alternates between stirring affirmation and exquisite ambiguity. Never did inconclusiveness sound so good.

David Byrne in 1983.

For those who somehow missed the deadpan irony in the song's lyrics, there was an accompanying music video in which Byrne jogs perpetually in place against a blank background; like the Red Queen in *Through the Looking-Glass*, he can only stay where he is by running as fast as he can. Meanwhile, a bewildering cascade of superimposed images courses past him, as if he's fallen into a live-action Keith Haring painting: We see Byrne with his head in a spinning cube, Byrne enthroned as the king of a cut-paper puppet show, an old man crawling into a cardboard box from which a baby later emerges. Such is the overflow that the screen must fragment in order to hold it all, at one point running five scenes concurrently. Again and again, the video returns to the "road to nowhere" of the title, a highway through the featureless American West, lined with hitchhikers who never get picked up. We seem to be stuck *somewhen*, outside of linear time. The critic Dick Hebdige, in a masterly piece of scholarly analysis—one of the first ever written about a music video—described the effect like this: "We get bound into a writhing chain of signifiers, and dragged backwards into the here and now."[82] Byrne put it even better, in the earlier Talking Heads song "Once in a Lifetime": "Same as it ever was. Same as it ever was. Same as it ever was. Same as it ever was."

———

THE POSTMODERNISTS MADE the best of their historical situation, dancing on the grave of an earlier, heroic age. But a road to nowhere is also a dead end. As one of Baudrillard's peers, the theorist Jean-François Lyotard, influentially argued, progress was a "grand narrative" that could no longer be sustained: "Anytime we go searching for causes in this way we are bound to be disappointed."[83] If the machine-age modernists had charged confidently ahead, media-saturated post-modernists were transfixed by an awareness of the complexity all around them, frozen in the glare. This paradoxical mindset, a stasis borne of too much speed, found its ultimate visual expression in the enigmatic film *Koyaanisqatsi* (1982), directed by Godfrey Reggio. Scored by the minimalist composer Philip Glass, but free of dialogue, the movie follows an implied historical arc beginning with sublime scenes of unspoiled nature, which give way to scenes of resource extraction—mines and oil fields—and finally the city, which is portrayed as an endless rush hour, a frenzy of purposeless motion. As the music historian Alex Ross has pointed out, the structure essentially reprises that of *The City*, Lewis Mumford's didactic film from the 1939 World's Fair, with Aaron Copland's open-hearted prairie rhythms replaced by Glass's churning, relentless soundtrack.[84] At the conclusion, a rocket blasts off and then explodes in midair, its detritus falling back to Spaceship Earth in a hail of smoke and fire. A caption informs us of the title's meaning: appropriated from the Hopi language, it can be translated "crazy life, life out of balance . . . a state of life that calls for another way of living." Finally, three Hopi prophecies flash on-screen: "If we dig precious things from the land, we will invite disaster. Near the day of Purification, there will be cobwebs spun back and forth in the sky. A container of ashes might one day be thrown from the sky, which could burn the land and boil the oceans."

What could professional futurologists possibly say to this? Plenty. This era of anxiety witnessed tremendous growth in the prediction business, eager to offer guidance for the future-shocked. The new forecasting companies recycled long-established techniques, distributing subscription newsletters with titles like *Changes* and *Future Abstracts*—the descendants of Roger Babson's stock market reports—and trend analyses comparable to those of Margaret Hayden Rorke's TCCA.[85] Given the far greater size and complexity of the consumer marketplace, however, they lacked the critical advantage of centralization that these predecessors had exploited. There was no way they could move markets with a single prediction, as had happened with the "Babson break" of September 1929; nor could they coordinate fashions, colors, or product lines through back-channel management, which had been Rorke's stock-in-trade. Futurologists of the postmodern era could never mount that kind of self-fulfilling prophecy. They compensated with a new technique that, in the brand-happy spirit of the 1980s, I'll call the Big Idea. By this I mean a general prediction about culture at large that initially feels like an important insight, but is actually either so general as to be beyond dispute, or so vague as to be immune to disproof. The Big Idea, in Baudrillard's terms, is a simulation of futurology itself: a baseless projection, a "sign without a referent," whose primary purpose is to gain market traction.

Big Ideas weren't worth the voluminous amounts of paper they were printed on, but at a time of rising uncertainty, they kept the business of futurology riding high. In the 1980s and '90s, two of their most successful purveyors were the trend forecaster Faith Popcorn (not her real name, obviously; she was born Faith Plotkin, and rebranded herself), and the corporate consultant John Naisbitt. Popcorn was much the more colorful of the two. A fast-talking New Yorker with a distinctive cropped haircut, she had parlayed a background in advertising into a forecasting company called BrainReserve. The firm was typical for its time until she took over sole leadership in 1984, and began pitching herself as a singularly oracular figure: "I guarantee you everything I'm going to tell you today is going to happen, but you won't believe it," she likes to say, claiming that she has a 95 percent prediction success rate.

Given the nature of her forecasts, it's hard to see how such a calculation could possibly be made, much less verified. Popcorn specializes in catchy slogans about emergent cultural dynamics: "down-aging" (older people emulating the buying habits of the young), "ego-nomics" (the desire to assert individuality), "99 Lives" (juggling various professional and personal roles), and, most famously, "cocooning" (hiding out in the comfort of one's home). Her method is to briefly explain each of these ideas, offering a few reasons why the trend might be happening, then smoothly pivot to how it can be monetized by her savvy clients and readers. Generally, Popcorn's underlying observations are trite, impossible to validate statistically, and certainly open to challenge. But that's just fine, because "the clichés of a culture sometimes tell the deepest truths," and "consumers are people— full of contradictions."

In 1991, having successfully dispensed her trend forecasts through her consultancy, Popcorn capitalized further with a book called *The Popcorn Report*.[86] Here she cleverly framed her various trend ideas as aspects of a single, ongoing "socioquake!" Her argument was, intriguingly, the exact reverse of Baudrillard's: the public had gotten so wise to advertising gimmicks that they were now practically immune to them. The more manipulated they felt, the more turned off they became. Also, they were increasingly suspicious of corporate types, panicked about climate change, and disaffected with capitalism itself. All of this meant that in the future, they were going to be harder and harder to sell to. This diagnosis sounds more like a description of what consumers say about themselves than an analysis of how they actually spend their money. But it was an ingenious rhetorical maneuver on Popcorn's part. Her clients, and the book's nominal readership, actually *were* corporate types—so it initially seemed like she was giving them bad news. But of course she had a solution, which she sloganized as "Decency Positioning" (today we might call it virtue signaling). The idea was that the company should present the most ethical version of itself, persuading consumers that it had a "Corporate Soul."

If Laurie Anderson was the bard of postmodern inauthenticity, then Popcorn was its head cheerleader. Even she, however, didn't think of writing *Megatrends*, a book that, even in its title, perfectly epitomizes the Big Idea. Authored by John Naisbitt—with, lo and behold, uncredited support from his then wife and collaborator Patricia Aburdene—it was published in 1982 and was immediately, staggeringly popular, sitting on the *New York Times* bestseller list for two years and reportedly selling more than fourteen million copies, about as many as *The Population Bomb*, *The Limits to Growth*, and *Future Shock* combined.[87] And yet, not to put too fine a point on it, *Megatrends* is a truly bad book. Its central argument is harmless enough: "The most reliable way of anticipating the future is by understanding the present." (The inverse of computer scientist Alan Kay's more provocative line, "The best way to predict the future is to invent it.") Naisbitt's way of substantiating this truism, however, is laughably reductive. He identifies ten "megatrends" transforming society, each encapsulated in a neat formula:

Industrial Society ⟹ Information Society
Centralization ⟹ Decentralization
National Economy ⟹ World Economy
Hierarchies ⟹ Networking

And so on. Naisbitt pounds each of his dichotomies flat, draining them of nuance and explicating them with suspiciously tidy aphorisms like "Farmer, laborer, clerk: That's a brief history of the United States," or "Money is information in motion." It doesn't help that his reliance on dichotomies to explain historical change is directly contradicted by one of his own megatrends:

Either/Or ➠ Multiple Option

Naisbitt's ten megatrends are all either derivative—like "Information Society," which Daniel Bell had discussed with far greater subtlety a decade earlier—or just plain wrong. Naisbitt thought new tools for participation in decision-making were leading to the "death of representative democracy and the two-party system," and that the country was becoming "a nation of independents." The exact opposite has happened, of course, as American politics has become increasingly polarized, while (just about) holding on to its long-established democratic procedures. Naisbitt also made oppositions out of things that were entirely compatible. Communication networks do not necessarily weaken hierarchies—quite the contrary, as should already have been obvious in 1982. Similarly, a society can experience centralization in some respects and decentralization in others; the two processes may even amplify one another.

For all its glaring faults, *Megatrends* still needs to be taken seriously. It marks an important moment in the history of futurology (which I promise not to explain using two words and an arrow). It was the harbinger of many other equally dumbed-down books about the future, usually aimed at the self-help or business markets—a publishing phenomenon that continues to this day, as a visit to any airport bookstore will confirm. This superficiality is nothing new; most of the responses to Bellamy's *Looking Backward*, nearly a century earlier, had been equally reductive. But books only become sensations for a reason. The appetite for Naisbitt's simplistic pseudoscience was driven by the same conditions that postmodern artists, writers, and musicians were responding to: the much-too-muchness that I've been calling the Flood. Naisbitt's insistence on making the future legible was perfectly attuned to its particular moment.

It wasn't long before the charlatanism of postmodern futurology was called out, by the business consultant William Sherden in his book *The Fortune Sellers* (1997). Sherden had been a professional predictor himself, having worked in the field of inflation forecasting in the 1980s. Over time, he became more and more struck by the difficulty of his task. He and his colleagues were aggregating and analyzing ever more data, supported by ever more computing power. But statistically speaking, they could do no better than they would have simply by assuming that present trend lines would continue. Once he realized this, Sherden began noticing how unreliable other forecasters were. Hundreds of thousands of analysts, he observed, completely failed to predict the 1987 stock market crash. No one foresaw the fall of the Berlin Wall, or the Gulf War, or the floods that struck the Mississippi Valley in 1993 and California in 1995.

Sherden came to the conclusion that futurology was a sham, and that, as a "poacher turned gamekeeper" (as a reviewer in the *New York Times* put it), he was in the position to write a devastating exposé of his own profession.[88] He lampooned *Megatrends* and the *Popcorn Report* for their myriad inaccuracies, noting that Naisbitt's prediction of economic decentralization could not have been more wrong—the late 1980s were a boom time for corporate mergers—and that far from "cocooning," Americans of the early 1990s were eating at restaurants, visiting museums and amusement parks, joining clubs, and generally getting out of the house more than ever before. But Sherden was not just looking for isolated errors, as satisfying as that must have been. He saw two systemic problems that, in combination, were making prediction futile. The first was complexity. As Sherden put it, "If society is a complex system that is affected by almost everything, including popular attitudes and beliefs, economic conditions, technological advances, population trends, political events, wars, the weather, and all of these forces are unpredictable, then society itself must be unpredictable."[89] This was partly a matter of perspective: Access to the internet proliferated right around the time *The Fortune Sellers* was published, and information was not just more plentiful but more available, more psychologically present. What had seemed like a flood in the 1970s and '80s began to look, in retrospect, like a mere trickle. In this unprecedented deluge, forecasters were apt to drown.

A second, related dilemma for futurology was that it had become a flood in its own right. Sherden reckoned that the forecasting industry annually furnished two hundred billion dollars in services. If he was correct that most of this advice was false or misleading, then this was a massive distortion field which compromised economic and policy planning—as he nicely put it, a "reign of error." The situation called to mind an old witticism of Arthur C. Clarke's: "For every expert there is an equal and opposite expert." Theodore Roszak, the sociologist who had coined the term *counterculture*, now observed that government strategy was "to counter fact with fact, number with number, research with research. It even becomes advantageous to have lots of contention about facts and figures, a statistical blizzard that numbs the attention."[90]

Meanwhile, even as the "dataglut" (a term of Roszak's) was clogging the arteries of public discourse, it created anxiety in people's heads. When Sherden's book came out, *The Population Bomb* was twenty-five years old and looking more foolish all the time. But there had been new scare stories—among them, Ravi Batra's bestselling *The Great Depression of 1990* and its sequel, *Surviving the Great Depression of 1990*, published in 1985 and 1988, respectively.[91] (There was no depression in 1990.) It seemed that the more uncertain the future became, the more demand there was for futurology. And the more futurologists there were, the more bewilderment they caused. This is why Sherden called his book *The Fortune Sellers*. He thought the professional predictors of the late twentieth century were no better than soothsayers of days gone by, with their crystal balls and their decks of cards. "The world's second-oldest profession," as he liked to call forecasters, were leaving the world no better than they found it—probably worse. Certainly, they had no idea what might happen next.

AMERICA, IT SEEMED, was suffering from a strange new malady: a complexity complex. Sherden concluded that futurology was a symptom rather than a remedy. In the brief conclusion to his book, he offered some advice. It was important to be skeptical, he said, as well as humble, about what forecasting could achieve. Above all, one had to be adaptable, ready for just about anything: "The only certainty is that we are destined to live in an unpredictable world filled with endless uncertainty."[92] As insights go, this sounds about on a par with *The Popcorn Report*. But at a higher level of analysis, these apparently banal principles of flexibility and readiness were indeed reshaping the future, and how it was approached. This is the final twist in the tale of twentieth-century tomorrows.

Back in 1973, Daniel Bell had predicted a general rise in the influence of experts. He thought this would be a characteristic feature of what he called postindustrial society. His reasoning was simple: Increasingly complex systems would require more analysis to navigate; this meant that the intersecting fields of futurology and technology would come at a higher premium; and this, in turn, would translate into greater political and economic leverage for the technocracy. For Sherden, this elitist vision of "herds of intellectuals" in charge of everything was anathema, a fulfillment of the prophecies of *1984* (and he meant the novel, not the Apple commercial).[93] But Bell had also made another, subtler point. In an ideal technocracy, he noted, people would respect the authority of experts, "just as one obeys the instructions of a doctor or an orchestra conductor or a ship's captain." But no society has ever been ideal. In practice, he thought that as power converged on experts, controversy about their predictive mechanisms would immediately follow: "The post-industrial society will involve more politics than ever before, for the very reason that choice becomes conscious and the decision-centers more visible."[94]

Bell did not place much emphasis on this observation, but it would prove to be among his most prescient. Not only was information becoming more and more visible; so too were the processes by which that information was gathered, analyzed, and deployed. It had long been possible for professional futurologists to act as if they were disinterested observers of tomorrow. Edward Bellamy, Christine Frederick, Norman Bel Geddes, Catherine Bauer, Lewis Mumford, Buckminster Fuller, Barbara Ward, Robert Jungk, Herman Kahn, Bell himself: While far from apolitical, they all presented themselves as providing a useful public service, untainted by self-interest. After the 1960s, that was just no longer an option. Vietnam, the New Left, the counterculture, the civil rights movement, women's liberation, and environmentalism all, in their different ways, challenged the authority of established expertise. Postmodernism cast doubt on the possibility of objectivity itself. In the process, the technocracy—the supposedly disinterested professional management class overseeing government policy and corporate strategy—was unveiled as an ideological force, and perhaps a highly dangerous one.

The sociologist Ulrich Beck had a fascinating take on this shift, which he summarized as follows: "The gain in power from techno-economic 'progress' is being increasingly overshadowed by the production of risks. In an early stage, these can be legitimated as 'latent side effects.' As they become globalized, and subject to public criticism and scientific investigation, they come, so to speak, 'out of the closet,' and achieve a central importance in social and political debates."[95] This is from his book *Risk Society* (1986; translated into English in 1992), in which he incisively analyzed a new dynamic in futurology. Like so many postmodern phenomena, it was becoming "meta"—which in this case meant an increasing focus on the management of uncertainty itself. The job was no longer to predict the future accurately, but instead to work out the most advantageous position possible within an environment of pervasive risk. This was technocracy raised to the second power:

Each company, each nation-state, sought to shield itself as much as possible from exposure to hazards like economic instability, environmental pollution, military conflict, and political unrest by shifting those risks on to others, whenever possible. As a result, futurology was being reinvented once more, this time as a domain of outright political conflict. This, Beck thought, was what it really meant for a society to be "postindustrial." In a process that he called "reflexive modernization," the techniques of classical industry—its methods of efficiency and rationalization—were being applied to the oversight of change as such. The economy was thus becoming "self-referential, independent of its context of satisfying human needs," no longer organized around the production and distribution of commodities, but instead the manufacture and allocation of risk.[96] Uncertainty was no longer just an unavoidable fact of life, but an instrument wielded by powerful interests.

A good way to understand this argument is to see how it applies to the insurance industry. As noted in chapter 2, the French theorist François Ewald (who was writing in dialogue with Beck) thought that insurance was basically a wonderful thing, virtuous and egalitarian. It spreads economic risk across a large population, helping to shelter individuals from harm. Confidence in this safety net, furthermore, encourages innovation, entrepreneurialism, and other positive forms of investment. However, the onset of what Ewald called a "precautionary mindset"—a similar formulation to Beck's—was a malicious demon eating away at the system and the solidarity it fostered. At the time when he and Beck were both writing, insurance companies' relationships with policyholders were becoming less actuarial and more adversarial. A similar mistrust was becoming endemic in many other areas, from politics to medicine to patent law, resulting in a general atmosphere of wary suspicion (and in the United States, out-of-control litigation).[97] In such a circumstance, all the incentives are on the side of avoiding responsibility, shifting it onto someone else. As Ewald put it, "Morality becomes a sort of negative morality: it is not so much turned toward the positive quest for the best as toward the avoidance of the worst." And all this was only the symptom of an even larger crisis in faith. Ever since *The Limits to Growth*, Ewald wrote, society had contended with the possibility that progress is the greatest threat of all: "It is necessary to 'kiss the utopian ideal goodbye' and to denounce the psychological danger of the promises of prosperity." With a flourish that perhaps only a French theorist could muster, he proclaimed that "with risk of development we rediscover the face of destiny, but with a difference: In the Old World, destiny wore the face of the gods, while for us it now has always and necessarily a human face."[98]

Beck (who was German) was saying the same thing, if less poetically. Far from being invalidated by the postmodern condition, futurology was more intensely contested than ever. Massive scale and interconnectedness, the very factors that persuaded Sherden that futurology was a lost cause, were crucial to this analysis. Up to the late twentieth century, Beck explained, risk had been understood as a relatively local phenomenon. Life insurance was purchased by a person or a family. Business decisions, for the most part, dictated just one company's success or failure. With the advent of globalism, however, risk assessment increasingly had to take place within a vast framework of reference. Take the example of climate change: It is a planet-wide phenomenon, but its effects are felt more swiftly and dramatically in some places than others. A company that "manufactures" risk by polluting the atmosphere may not be exposed to that risk at all. The people who suffer will be downwind, hundreds of miles away, and eventually even farther, as ice caps melt, coastal waters rise, forests burn, and hurricanes rage. The dangers involved are all too real, but they operate on a very long timeline that is itself unpredictable, sometimes unfolding in slow motion, sometimes in sudden crises. All this makes accountability very hard to establish. A scientist can try to estimate the damage caused by a given actor in the tragedy, but it will likely be very difficult to do so without controversy, and even harder to decide what should be done about it. Beck went so far as to say that "there is no expert on risk," meaning that it had become a matter of ethics and politics, not calculation and prediction.[99] Futurology had indeed arrived at a point of crisis, but this was not because it was fraudulent; rather, it bore a new and terrible responsibility, as it was conscripted into the tasks of risk assessment and administration. To live in risk society, Beck wrote, is "to live on the volcano of civilization."

THIS IS ALL rather abstract, though; what is it like to actually experience risk society? For an answer to that question we can turn, in conclusion, to the writer Octavia E. Butler. She has been celebrated in recent years as a leading exponent of Afrofuturism and an extraordinarily perceptive commentator on where America was going—the place where we now seem to have arrived. In fact, one of Butler's best-known novels, *Parable of the Sower* (1993), begins in the year 2024. It is set in a California transformed by climate change, an apocalypse ("Pox" for short) that has brought alternating floods and droughts. Fresh water is in short supply, as is any permanent safety. Roving bands of "pyros," driven insane by psychedelic drugs, light settlements on fire just for the pleasure of watching them burn. The novel's main character, Lauren Olamina, loses her home and most of her family in such an attack, and is forced out on to the road, becoming a refugee in her own country. In the sequel, *Parable of the Talents* (1998), she suffers further travails, while in the background a demagogue called Andrew Steele Jarret runs for president. He comes across as both an echo of Billy Sunday and a premonition of Donald Trump: "Leave your sinful past behind and become one of us. Help us make America great again!"

Octavia E. Butler in 1986.

Butler once said, "I began writing about power because I had so little."[100] She was born in Pasadena in 1947 and raised mainly by her mother, a domestic cleaner. A devotee of science fiction from a young age—she especially loved the work of Robert Heinlein and Theodore Sturgeon—she started writing at the age of ten and persisted, despite receiving no positive response for a long, long time. As Gerry Canavan writes in his book-length study of Butler, "She wrote through a lonely childhood, through discouragement from family and teachers, through a decade and a half of mounting rejection slips, through bankruptcy, through too many years after that of being underpaid and disrespected in the midlist. She wrote."[101] Indeed, she did so prolifically—she was among the most widely published Black women of the twentieth century—and brilliantly, transcending the genre divide between sci-fi, fantasy, and straight fiction.

In *The Parable of the Sower* and *The Parable of the Talents* (and a planned sequel, left incomplete when Butler died in 2006), Olamina is the inspired prophet of a religion called Earthseed. She preaches a doctrine of transformation—her mantra is "All that you touch you Change, all that you Change Changes you, the only lasting truth is Change, God is Change"—and gathers followers as she travels through the blasted landscape of Los Angeles. Along the way, we discover that she is afflicted with the psychological condition of "hyper-empathy": She shares in any intense emotion (pain, especially) that she witnesses. This is the inverse of how leaders often regard those around them—a point Butler makes unsparingly, for Olamina's identification with others' suffering is for the most part a crippling handicap. Nonetheless, she and her community survive, and even intermittently thrive. The first novel ends with Olamina setting up a counterculture-style commune called Acorn. Ultimately she intends to lead them to outer space—an outlandish idea that might be understood as an allusion to the African colonization project championed by Marcus Garvey, or the Black separatist movement.

Despite their fantastical elements, Butler's Parable novels are a believable continuation of the present day—much more so, certainly, than *Blade Runner*, which is also set in a dystopian future California. As she explained, "All I did was look around at the problems we're neglecting now, and give them about thirty years to grow into full-fledged disasters."[102] Yet it would be a mistake to view these stories simply as cautionary projections, fictional descendants of *The Limits to Growth*. Butler did intend to warn her readers of potential trouble ahead, but she also realized that crises like the ones she described were nothing new: "Things have always been sorry."[103] The literary scholar Stefanie Dunning, in her discussion of Butler's work, expands on this point, observing that "apocalypse is neither new nor unexpected if one closely reviews the history of civilization. Arguably, many worlds 'ended' with the inauguration of the transatlantic slave trade, and those worlds have been ending in degrees ever since."[104] The collapse of a social order may seem like a disaster, especially for those on top and those standing directly in harm's way. At the same time, disruption might be necessary to redress historical inequities. From this perspective, understanding change as the most absolute of values, as Olamina does, makes a great deal of sense; it is the essence of her religion, but also a kind of pragmatism. Her belief that "God is Change" helps her face the future squarely, for it encompasses all the possibilities of historical transformation, benevolent, vengeful, and sublime. As Butler once said of religion, "I'm not saying it's a force for good, just a force."[105]

Butler seems to have had her own power of hyper-empathy, or at least a genuine understanding of hope and fear. She conveyed what it is like to be exposed to uncertainty, and it is this emotional maturity, rather than her admittedly uncanny anticipation of our present predicaments, that makes her so worth reading today. In one of her most meaningful passages, she wrote, "Our tomorrow is the child of our today. Through thought and deed, we exert a great deal of influence over this child, even though we can't control it absolutely. Best to think about it, though. Best to try to shape it into something good. Best to do that for any child."[106]

Like parenting, the future is not something we can simply get right, or solve like an equation. As the postmodernists discovered, tomorrow can only be approached with a range of complex and contradictory instincts: curiosity and caution, planning and open-mindedness, decisiveness and experimentalism. At any rate, as long as we have the future in front of us, we will have futurology. It is part of what it is to be human. Its limitations and absurdities reflect us, but its imaginativeness and insights bring out our best too. Again, a lot like raising a child. The future is a profound responsibility, and while it may feel heavy, we can't drop it in hopes that someone else, another generation perhaps, will come along and pick it up. Nor can we yield it up to heaven. "Screw inspiration," Butler said, when asked about her life writing speculative fiction. "It's certainly not a matter of sitting there and having things fall from the sky."[107] They're words to live by, today, tomorrow, and tomorrow.

CONCLUSION

N 2019 *TIME* MADE THE SWEDISH climate activist Greta Thunberg, then sixteen years old, its Person of the Year. She was photographed for the magazine's cover standing at the land's edge, looking rather like the Fool in the Rider-Waite-Smith deck. It was an appropriate—if presumably unintentional—analogy. For Thunberg is indeed something like a fool, not in the tarot but in a Shakespeare play, a clever commoner speaking truth to power; or the child in the parable of the emperor's new clothes, who sees clearly the naked vanity of those in charge. "We must change almost everything in our current societies," Thunberg said that January, in an instantly famous speech at the World Economic Forum in Davos. "I don't want your hope. I don't want you to be hopeful. I want you to panic. I want you to feel the fear I feel every day. And then I want you to act. I want you to act as you would in a crisis. I want you to act as if our house is on fire. Because it is."

In 2017 the artist Alisha B. Wormsley put up a billboard in East Liberty, a historically Black, working-class neighborhood in Pittsburgh that was undergoing rapid gentrification. It read, simply, THERE ARE BLACK PEOPLE IN THE FUTURE. Wormsley's sign was soon removed by the city, but the community's positive response motivated her to repeat the action across the nation, in Detroit, Charlotte, New York City, Kansas City, and Houston, as well as abroad (including in Accra, the Ghanaian capital, where Buckminster Fuller had built Kwame Nkrumah a geodesic dome half a century earlier). The billboard was both a simple statement of fact and an intentional provocation, rather like the slogan "Black Lives Matter," which had been launched on social media four years earlier. The simple act of asserting the ongoing presence of Black people, in a nation that has often sought their erasure, was tantamount to a manifesto—a promise, as Wormsley subsequently put it, that

Alisha B. Wormsley, *There Are Black People in the Future*, Detroit, 2019.

"not only will black people exist in the future, but . . . we will be makers and shapers of it, too."[1]

Also in 2017, the writer and activist Wendell Berry published a book with the down-home title *The Art of Loading Brush.* Raised on a tobacco farm in Kentucky, he has spent his career making the case for a conservative agrarian worldview: "an informed and conscientious submission to nature," guided by "a preference for enough over too much" and "a lively suspicion of anything new." Presumably Berry would not want to do without electricity, but he does wonder whether it is really for the best, as it makes people forever dependent on corporations whose decision-making they can neither comprehend nor control. By the same logic, he regards the rise of factory farming with sorrow, as it has also effaced the well-worn pathways of rural life. As to the future, Berry writes, "it looks to me like an unhappy place filled with a lot of disappointed people: optimists who thought it would be better and pessimists who thought it would be worse."[2]

In 2020 the company OpenAI launched a chatbot called GPT-3 (the initials are short for Generative Pre-trained Transformer), to considerable public astonishment. Pop in a prompt, and it provides prose that is fluent, grammatical, and often persuasive—though also, sometimes, untrue. The world soon learned how the thing worked. It was a prediction machine, which calculated the most likely first word in a sentence, then the word after that, and the word after that. Through this deceptively simple procedure, it could convincingly mimic a human being. Arguments flew back and forth about the ethics of releasing such a technology into the wild. Would it be used in massive disinformation campaigns? Encourage kids to cheat on their homework? Put writers out of work? (Eek.) In the years since, as ever more powerful artificial intelligence platforms have proliferated, technologists have competed with one another not only to develop and commercialize these systems but also to describe them in hyperbolic terms. OpenAI's CEO, Sam Altman, has made comparisons to nuclear fission, another technology of extreme promise and danger, while Sundar Pichai, the CEO of Google, has offhandedly remarked that AI might be "more profound than, I dunno, electricity or fire."

These few examples indicate some of the contours of contemporary futurology. Taken together, they raise an interesting possibility: Even in our postdiluvian times, maybe the future hasn't changed that much after all? We can see numerous echoes between today's most pressing issues and those that preoccupied twentieth-century American futurologists. Thunberg's dire warnings of climate apocalypse, though based on an additional half century's science, would certainly not have surprised the authors of *Limits to Growth*. Wormsley's idea for her billboard initially came to her as "a Black nerd sci-fi joke," an insider allusion to Afrofuturist music, film, and literature. Had Berry been born a few decades earlier (which might have suited him better), he would have a found ready ally in Lewis Mumford, who, as a critic of progress for its own sake, would likely have endorsed this bit of Berry's homespun wisdom about the future: "If you see a squirrel in the middle of the road, you can't predict whether it will run to the right or the left (therefore you should slow down)."[3]

As for contemporary debates about artificial intelligence, as we've seen, they have precedents all the way back to Samuel Butler's 1863 essay "Darwin among the Machines," via twentieth-century speculations about the prospect of a fully automated economy and consequent "full unemployment." In 1993 the inchoate fear that humans will eventually, inadvertently, render themselves obsolescent was given sharp definition by the science fiction writer Vernor Vinge. He postulated a "coming technological Singularity," an inflection point when computers would "awake" and depose their previous masters—that is, us. Vinge wrote, "This change will be a throwing-away of all the human rules, perhaps in the blink of an eye—an exponential runaway beyond any hope of control."[4] This was something new in the annals of futurology: a potential time horizon beyond which mere mortals simply cannot make predictions. The machines will be in charge, and smarter than we are. Who knows *what* they might do? The Singularity is like an astronomical black hole, swallowing all possibility of future speculation into its gravitational field. When we are surpassed by AIs, the veil will descend. Lewis Mumford's worst fears will have come true, and the machines will sit in judgment over us, new Gods that we ourselves have enthroned.[5] What will they want from us? Perhaps not much, for as Arthur C. Clarke mused a long time ago, "the intelligent machines of the future will have better things to do with their time. . . . I often talk with my dog, but I don't keep it up for long."[6]

Strangely, however, the AI that we have so far is more like a rearview mirror than a crystal ball. Earlier generations of artificial intelligence attempted to mimic humans, duplicating our methods of reasoning and approximating our bodily actions. OpenAI had been active in this field before developing GPT, but they concluded that large language models—trained on massive quantities of information, all available on the internet—had much more potential. These machines don't need to be programmed. They teach themselves, relying on the statistical analysis of enormous preexisting data sets, turning the Flood into a power source. This is ingenious, but it does mean that these AIs can only repeat what is already "out there," though in novel configurations. Only once human beings have had their say can the tech have anything to tell us in return. I asked ChatGPT to make a long-term forecast, and it responded. "As an AI language model, I don't have the ability to predict the future. My knowledge is based on information available up until September 2021, and I cannot browse the internet or access current events beyond that point." It's the one behind the veil.

Will AIs remain subservient to humans, or will the relationship be reversed, as Vernor Vinge prophesized? It's a fiercely debated topic. In a widely cited 2022 poll, professionals working in the artificial intelligence industry assigned a median likelihood of 5 percent to the probability of something "extremely bad (e.g., human extinction)" happening as a result of their own work. It seemed pretty weird that anyone would contribute to a project with a one-in-twenty chance of eradicating life as we know it. To the extent that such a perplexing finding could be explained, it was because of the huge countervailing potential that many of these same people see in AI. They believe it could help to resolve some of our most intractable challenges, with climate change heading the list. Forecasting the weather is one thing; remediating the effects of a rise in planetary temperature is another. The great promise of artificial intelligence, in this context, is that it can assimilate far higher levels of complexity than the human mind can—and our rapidly changing environment is the very definition of a complex system.

For example, AI might help to overcome the problem of accountability that Ulrich Beck identified in his book *Risk Society*. In theory, a computer model could track and assess the real impact of pollution, so that fair and appropriate penalties could be administered. Intelligent machines can also contribute to more efficient energy production, manufacturing, and transport (for instance, self-driving cars that are never stuck in traffic). They might be able to improve the analysis of satellite data, predicting the floods, fires, and hurricanes that are becoming increasingly common, so we can better prepare for them. Then there is the more futuristic possibility that we could enter a new phase of "post-industrial society." The transition from physical to intellectual property that has already occurred might become universal, with virtual experiences generated using AI (often described as the "metaverse") gradually superseding real-world ones, a prospect akin to the simulation depicted in the *Matrix*. This might sound awful—OK, it *does* sound awful. But in theory, it could be a tremendous advance in sustainability, just as video conferencing has an infinitesimal carbon footprint compared to airplane travel. An immaterial economy could approach Buckminster Fuller's long-ago dream of "doing everything with nothing at all."

As with any technology, those speculating on the future of machine intelligence must factor in a conspicuous weak point: the continuing involvement of people. The old adage that we are our own worst enemies definitely applies here, for it seems likely that the greatest dangers posed by artificial intelligence, at least in the near term, involve its malevolent use by human beings. One can imagine AI-equipped hackers attacking information networks of all kinds, from banks to critical infrastructure. Dario Amodei, who left OpenAI to found a more safety-oriented firm called Anthropic, is deeply worried that artificial intelligence could be used by terrorists (or nation-states) to create deadly bioweapons. Even barring such a mass destruction scenario, there is the pressing question of the public interest: Are profit-seeking companies really the right decision-makers and stewards of these technologies? "Rather than AI developing towards the level of human intelligence, we are in danger of human intelligence descending to the level of AI," writes the statistician Erica Thompson, "by concreting inflexible decision criteria into institutional structures, leaving no room for the human strength of empathy [and] compassion."[7] It's a concern shared by the futurologist Jaron Lanier, a virtual reality pioneer and leading critic of AI boosterism. He believes that describing machines as "intelligent" is already a serious category error—we too easily forget that, as he puts it, "big-model AI is made of people"—and worries that our instinct to defer to such systems will make us dumber and dumber as the years go by, as the "smart" devices in our lives arguably already have, in some ways.

Lanier recommends that we "treat computers as nothing more than fancy conduits to bring people together."[8] Many twentieth-century futurologists would doubtless have concurred. Unfortunately, the twenty-first century we've got has proved to be so fractious that a unified response to AI, climate change, or just about any other risk seems a remote prospect. We find ourselves in a bitter cultural conflict that seems likely to continue, for another generation or two at least. This clash of worldviews doesn't fall neatly along familiar lines of left versus right, or progressive versus conservative (at least, not in Wendell Berry's sense of conservative). Rather, it is a symptom of the complexity complex. Is the increasingly diverse and globalized future to be embraced, or feared?

On one side of this question, we find post-postmodern futurologists like Adrienne Marie Brown, who writes in her book *Emergent Strategies* that "at this point, we have all the information we need to create a change; it isn't a matter of facts. It's a matter of longing, having the will to imagine and implement something else."[9] Like Anna Julia Cooper, Robert Jungk, and Octavia Butler's protagonist Lauren Olamina, Brown believes that change will be for the better, so long as it is generated by—she would say "emerges from"—a truly diverse range of perspectives. On the other side, of course, we have Donald Trump, with his nostalgic slogan Make America Great Again and his fantasy of building "a big, beautiful wall," a metaphor for blocking out anyone or anything unwelcome. Among his ideological allies are the racist theorists of a "great replacement," who believe that white people are being purposefully outnumbered by other ethnicities—a paranoid reprise of the demographic panic of fifty years ago, the inverse of Wormsley's declaration that "There Are Black People in the Future," and just as strongly felt.

For much of the twentieth century, futurology was structured around dichotomies: the mechanistic and organic ideals of the 1920s and '30s; the technocratic and
countercultural impulses that prevailed from 1945 to 1970. What made futurology
in these eras so intellectually dynamic, however, was a certain compatibility between
its contrary tendencies. The interwar generation, which adopted the Machine and
the Garden as master metaphors, operated according to the shared premise that
futurology should be professionalized, and that positive change could be enacted
through prediction and planning. After 1945, futurologists adopted a more explor-
atory, open-ended approach; whether they were impelled to the rigors of the Lab or
the euphoria of the Party, they embraced experimentalism. Such a common framework of reference is precisely what is missing, today—a condition that has its source
in the late twentieth-century Flood, when such dialectical operations were dislodged
from their moorings, carrying us all out to the open sea.

At one level this is a crisis specific to futurology, whose claims about tomorrow,
always tenuous, have become increasingly distrusted. But an overabundance of information also undermines expertise in a more general sense. My twin brother, Peter, a
historian of philosophy, recently published a good book about this called *Don't Think
for Yourself.* "How many of us understand enough about the atmosphere to have a
reasonably informed opinion on climate change, never mind being in a position to
critically evaluate what climatologists might say?" he asks. "On this and many other
issues, we are apparently in the politically and epistemologically uncomfortable position of choosing whose opinions we should blindly accept."[10] This is a real dilemma,
and it can't be solved simply by believing whatever experts say, or conversely, disre-
garding the value of expertise entirely. I wrote *A Century of Tomorrows* partly during
the Covid-19 lockdown, when Americans tended to instinctively adopt one or the
other of these two positions—it was either "trust the science" or "reject Big Pharma"—
resulting in a body politic more divided against itself than ever. Peter's argument is that
we somehow have to get better at making such "second-order" judgments. That is, we
need to be more effective in evaluating experts themselves. Are they self-interested?
Inconsistent? Are their arguments based on empty rhetoric, instead of evidence? If so,
best not trust them. But if they pass such tests of scrutiny—as climate scientists, in the
aggregate, obviously do—it is worth listening to what they have to say.

The same should go for futurologists, in theory, but what counts as "evidence," in
their case, remains a tough problem. In 2009, for a book called *This Will Change*

Everything, 125 experts in various fields were asked a simple but difficult question: "What will change everything? What game-changing scientific ideas and developments do you expect to live to see?" Of the respondents who hazarded a response—many were evasive—very few came up with predictions that have come true in the years since. The critic of technology Sherry Turkle probably came closest, forecasting a rise of social robots who are "preferable to an available human being." Many other contributors expressed concern about climate change—but that hardly constituted a prediction by that late date. Not one so much as mentioned a global pandemic, or a profound reckoning with racism, or a land war in Europe. Instead, as is so often the case with futurology, their forecasts were much more outlandish: quantum computing, cold fusion, the discovery of extraterrestrial life, mass technological failure, immortality, telepathy, molecular manufacturing, 100 percent reliable lie detection, economic policies based on happiness metrics, and yes, the Singularity.

It's easy to scorn a book like this—nothing dates faster than the future, as they say—though who knows, maybe all of these predictions will come to pass someday. In the meantime, what is the alternative to futurology? The musician and producer Brian Eno, in his contribution to *This Will Change Everything*, put it like this: "What if we come to feel as though there is no 'long term'—or not one to look forward to? What if, instead of feeling that we are standing at the edge of a wild new continent full of promise and hazard, we start to feel that we're on an overcrowded lifeboat in hostile waters, fighting to stay on board, prepared to kill for the last scraps of food and water?"[11] Unfortunately, that passage now seems the most prescient in the whole book. Back in the 1950s, the typical science fiction film featured aliens of some kind, perhaps dangerous, perhaps benevolent, nearly always mysterious. The future was figured as an exciting encounter with another world, intersecting our own. If there's a genre that defines our own moment, it's the zombie apocalypse, TV shows and films in which ex-humans lurch about inexorably, stupidly, and lethally. In these grim tales, the government has invariably collapsed, and people are thrown back on their own aptitude for survival—an allegory of the future as a ruined version of the present, Octavia Butler's *Parable of the Sower* without the seeds of change.

It's not surprising that the entertainment industry should serve up such nihilistic fare at a time when humanity is confronting an unprecedented collective threat, and our politics seem singularly ill suited to meet the challenge. It does feel like an endgame. It is worth remembering, though, that we have been here before. For many millions, America's very origins were apocalyptic. Black America began in unimaginable loss and trauma, a fact that has animated the work of Octavia Butler and other Afrofuturists. And for Indigenous leaders, too—Wovoka, Clyde Warrior, and so many others—there has been no choice but to see the relationship between past and future in existential terms. For that matter, anyone who was born in 1900 and lived through two world wars and the Great Depression might well wonder at the tendency to regard our own moment as uniquely star-crossed. One of the genuinely inspiring aspects of twentieth-century futurology is how it constantly reimagined itself in response to catastrophe. Can we do the same today?

This is what Brian Eno was asking. To believe that the future is a lost cause, or that all the answers to our problems are to be found in the past, can only lead us to very dark places. Futurology, too, must look forward: Its presiding twentieth-century metaphors are certainly inadequate to the present day. The Machine and the Garden have both been transformed out of all recognition, in the age of artificial intelligence and the Anthropocene. Neither the Lab nor the Party are what they used to be, either, given the epic failures of the technocracy and the ease with which countercultural energies were co-opted. We do still need compelling stories about tomorrow, though, and lots of them. For if the postmodernists were right, and reality is at least partly a matter of perspective, there are as many different futures as there are different people. They can't be constructed so as to cancel one another out, but must be mutually legible and compatible. This, it seems to me, is the work that futurology still has before it.

In this book, I have tried to set out the stories of futurologists fairly. Along the way, goodness knows, I've highlighted their many blind spots—the tragic flaws of the supposedly foresighted. But I find that here, at the end, I do look at them with a certain admiration. The anthropologist Arjun Appadurai once wrote that "the future is not just a technical or neutral space, but is shot through with affect and with sensation. Thus, we need to examine not just the emotions that accompany the future as a cultural form but the sensations that it produces: awe, vertigo, excitement, disorientation."[12] Futurologists know this better than anyone. Whatever we might make of their predictive strategies, they help us *feel* the future, the thrilling, frightening, awesome responsibility that it is. What would we want the people of tomorrow to say about our own era in futurology, our doubtless inadequate attempts

Aram Han Sifuentes, *OTRO MUNDO ES POSIBLE*, 2017.

to predict their world? We can't possibly know for sure, but perhaps we can say this: We owe the future all the enthusiasm and imagination we can summon in ourselves. The wheel of fortune will keep turning, under the sign of the riddling sphinx; no matter what happens, we're along for the ride. We may as well try and look forward, as far as we can.

ACKNOWLEDGMENTS

Like the future itself, this book has been a long time coming. It began, for me, back in 2012, when I was in the research department at the V&A. Having recently completed an exhibition about postmodernism, which I curated with Jane Pavitt, I proposed a headline exhibition that was to be called *The Future: A History*. The idea was to trace the arts of prediction over time and space. The show was to begin with a set of oracle bones, used to tell the future in ancient China; these artifacts also happen to be among the very oldest examples of extant writing (human beings were future-obsessed before there was such a thing as history). It was to continue with medieval altarpieces showing the Last Judgment, Renaissance depictions of ideal cities, objects from nineteenth-century utopian communities, and streamlined designs that strained at the leash of their own present day.

That exhibition never happened—instead, I left for New York City to direct a museum—but my discussions with curatorial colleagues at the V&A, including Cher Potter, Karen Verschooren, and Ilaria Puri Purini, left an imprint. I kept thinking about the topic, and in 2021 an opportunity to return to it came along. The Smithsonian was developing a major project that would reopen its Arts + Industries Building, the first purpose-built museum on the National Mall. Simply entitled *Futures*, it focused on the period from 1900 to the present day. When my friend and former V&A colleague Abraham Thomas left the project team, taking up a position at the Metropolitan Museum of Art, I took his place and found myself the lead script-writer for an undertaking that made the V&A's headline exhibitions look modest in scale. The show had it all—future foods, robotics, vehicles, art, and more—and despite being delivered at the tail end of the pandemic, it was ultimately seen by 650,000 people. It was while I was working on *Futures*, which was led by Rachel Goslins and curated by Ashley Molese, Brad MacDonald, and Monica O. Montgomery, that *A Century of Tomorrows* began to take shape.

This book, then, has its origins in museums—a fact that perhaps accounts for its unusual thematic structure, which more closely resembles an exhibition than a standard work of history. Even so, when I began writing, it was with the ongoing support of the team at Bloomsbury that had helped bring into being my last book, *Craft: An American History*. I especially thank my editor, Ben Hyman, who has become a crucial thought partner for me over the past few years, and also would like to express my gratitude to Morgan Jones, Barbara Darko, Ragav Maripudi, Katya Mezhibovskaya, Miranda Ottewell, Helen Mules, and Krister Swartz. Likewise, the team at the Wylie Agency—Sarah Chalfant, Rebecca Nagel, Luke Ingram, George Morgan, and Bonnie McKiernan—provided crucial feedback on an early proposal and subsequent drafts, and organizational help with concurrent writing projects. Cindy Hernandez provided early research support, charting a whole constellation of research materials for me to navigate.

The history of the future is hardly a new topic. As the endnotes for this book attest, I have drawn on many scholars' work in constructing my own account, among them Jenny Andersson, Alice Echols, Nicolas Maffei, John Markoff, Greg Tate, and Louis Warren. Mark Dery generously shared his time (and a cascade of great ideas) with me, as did the Buckminster Fuller biographer Alec Nevala-Lee, who in turn also connected me to Thomas L. Turman, who traveled to Ghana with Fuller to construct a geodesic dome. The book is also inflected in ways great and small from conversations with Sarah Archer, Spencer Bailey, Marc Benda, Tim Britton, Scott Bodenner and Fabio Toblini, Stephen Burks, Ned Cooke, Adam Edelsberg, Tanya Harrod, Wendy Kaplan, Julia Kunin, Joris Laarman, Ethan Lasser, Chris Petrie and Ben Platts-Mills, Jon Prown, Jennifer Roberts, Seph Rodney, Sarah Thornton, and Christopher Wilk.

This book is much concerned with life as a game of chance. My own has been marked by incredible good fortune, first in having been born to wonderfully supportive parents, with a twin brother who I like to call "the smart one in the family." Peter was the first person to read the manuscript for *A Century of Tomorrows* and, unsurprisingly, made many excellent suggestions.

Then there is the greatest stroke of luck of all: that I have been able to share my life with my partner, Nicola, facing whatever tomorrow may bring, together.

IMAGE CREDITS

INTERIOR IMAGES

Introduction

3   Wikimedia Commons

6   Courtesy of Princeton University Library

8   Steven R. Shook/Flickr

Chapter 1: HEAVEN AND HELL

13   ETH-00174, Nevada Historical Society

19   Library of Congress Prints and Photographs Division, LC-USZ62-42652

23   Used with permission of the Rev. Clarence Larkin Estate, P.O. Box 334, Glenside, PA 19038, USA, 215-576-5590 • www.larkinestate.com

25   National Portrait Gallery, Smithsonian Institution

30   From the collection of Stanford University (tobacco.stanford.edu)

33   George Rinhart/Corbis via Getty Images

43   Library of Congress Prints and Photographs Division, LC-USZ62-48852

45   © James Van Der Zee Archive, The Metropolitan Museum of Art

49   Pictures From History/Universal Images Group via Getty Images

Chapter 2: MACHINE

62   Hulton Archive via Getty Images

64   Gamma-Keystone via Getty Images

68   Schlesinger Library, Harvard Radcliffe Institute

71   The Edith Lutyens and Norman Bel Geddes Foundation, Inc., Harry Ransom Center, The University of Texas at Austin

72   Milwaukee Art Museum

FACSIMILE EDITION The Psychedelic Newspaper of the Haight Ashbury (Digital Version) available: www.regentpress.net. Reproduced with kind permission of Letterform Archive.

179 Ted Streshinsky via Getty Images

180 RBC TS199 .W5 March 1970. Courtesy of the Department of Special Collections, Stanford University Libraries.

181 © The Oregonian. All rights reserved. Used with permission. Oregon Historical Society Research Library, 0358P197.

183 Frontispiece photograph from *Collected Poems of Lenore Kandel*, copyright © 2012 by the Estate of Lenore Kandel, photograph courtesy of the Estate of Lenore Kandel. All efforts to determine the name of the photographer were unsuccessful. If you have any information about the photographers, please contact North Atlantic Books. Reprinted by permission of North Atlantic Books.

187 National Anthropological Archives, Smithsonian Institution, gelatin glass negative BAE GN 01778a 06305400

191 Images from the *San Francisco Oracle* provided courtesy of the estate of Allen Cohen and Regent Press, publishers of the SAN FRANCISCO ORACLE FACSIMILE EDITION The Psychedelic Newspaper of the Haight Ashbury (Digital Version) available: www.regentpress.net. Reproduced with kind permission of Letterform Archive.

193 Oklahoma Publishing Company (OPUBCO) Collection. Courtesy of the Oklahoma Historical Society, #2012.201.B1396.0200.

197 Bettmann via Getty Images

201 © CORBIS/Corbis via Getty Images

Chapter 6: FLOOD

213 Courtesy of Laya Firestone Seghi

214 Alix Kates Shulman Papers, David M. Rubenstein Rare Book & Manuscript Library, Duke University. Photograph copyright Alix Kates Shulman; used with permission.

223 Courtesy of the Donella Meadows Project at the Academy for Systems Change

231 Susan Wood via Getty Images

235 SRI International/Courtesy of the Computer History Museum

242 Rob Verhorst via Getty Images

244   © Tim Hursley
246   Luciano Viti via Getty Images
256   The Estate of Octavia Butler

Conclusion

260   Alisha B. Wormsley, *There Are Black People in the Future.* Part of *Manifest
      Destiny*, curated by Ingrid LaFleur. Image by Alessandra Ferrara, courtesy of
      Library Street Collective, Detroit.
268   Courtesy of the artist

PLATE SECTION

Page One
—Fool card: The Fool card from the Rider-Waite Tarot decks used with permission of
U.S. Games Systems, Inc., Stamford, CT, c. 1971 by U.S. Games Systems, Inc. Rider-
Waite is a registered trademark of U.S. Games Systems, Inc. All rights reserved.

Page Two
—*The Knife Grinder*: Image from Yale University, Gift of Collection Société
Anonyme

Page Three
—Model: © 2024 Frank Lloyd Wright Foundation. All Rights Reserved. Licensed by
Artists Rights Society.

Page Four
—*Amazing Stories*: Internet Archive

Page Five
—*Collier's*: *Collier's* magazine

Page Six
—Poster: Blank Archives/Archive Photos via Getty Images

Page Seven
—Apple I: Division of Medicine and Science, National Museum of American History, Smithsonian Institution

Page Eight
— Grace Jones: Jean-Paul Goude, *Grace Jones Revised and Updated*, 1978. Cut-up transparency and reprinted, oil-painted photo. Courtesy of the artist.

NOTES

Epigraph

Ursula K. Le Guin, "It Was a Dark and Stormy Night; or, Why Are We Huddling about the Campfire?" *Critical Inquiry* 7, no. 1 (Autumn 1980): 199.

Introduction

1. Helen Farley, *A Cultural History of Tarot: From Entertainment to Esotericism* (London: I. B. Tauris, 2009), 107.
2. Arthur Edward Waite, *The Key to the Tarot: Being Fragments of a Secret Tradition under a Veil of Divination* (London: Rider, 1910), 1.
3. The first popular guide was Eden Gray, *The Tarot Revealed* (Gravesend, UK: Bell, 1960).
4. Will Dowd, "The Nearly Forgotten Mystical Artist Who Still Foretells Fates," *Boston Globe*, October 14, 2021.
5. Stuart R. Kaplan, et al., *Pamela Colman Smith: The Untold Story* (Stamford, CT: U.S. Games Systems, 2018). Smith also published her Jamaican folktales in an illustrated volume called *Annancy Stories* (New York: R. H. Russell, 1899).
6. M. Irwin McDonald, "The Fairy Faith and Pictured Music of Pamela Colman Smith," *Craftsman* 23, no. 1 (October 1912): 34.
7. Arthur Waite, *The Occult Sciences: A Compendium of Transcendental Doctrine and Experiment* (London: Kegan Paul, 1891), 3.
8. James Gleick, *The Information: A History, a Theory, a Flood* (New York: Pantheon, 2011), 147.
9. John Elfreth Watkins Jr., "What May Happen in the Next Hundred Years," *Ladies' Home Journal*, December 1900, 8.
10. H. G. Wells, *The Discovery of the Future: A Discourse Delivered to the Royal Institution* (London: T. Fisher Unwin, 1902), 33, 22.
11. E. P. Thompson, *The Making of the English Working Class* (London: Victor Gollancz, 1963), 12.
12. Henry Luce, "The American Century," *Life*, February 17, 1941, 61–65.

13. Campbell was paraphrasing the psychoanalyst Carl Jung. Joseph Campbell, "The Vitality of Myth," lecture 1.1.5, recorded 1974, transcribed by Harrison Patrick Stewart, Medium, June 29, 2016, online source.

14. Spencer Bailey and Andrew Zuckerman, *At a Distance: 100 Visionaries at Home in a Pandemic* (New York: Slowdown/Apartamento), 209.

Chapter 1: HEAVEN AND HELL

1. L. A. Dorrington, report, May 12–13, 1917, 5–9, Bureau of Indian Affairs, RG 75, National Archives, reprinted in Omer C. Stewart, "Contemporary Document on Wovoka (Jack Wilson), Prophet of the Ghost Dance in 1890," *Ethnohistory* 24, no. 3 (Summer 1977): 222.

2. James Mooney, *The Ghost Dance Religion and Sioux Outbreak of 1890* (Washington, D.C.: Government Printing Office, 1896), 771; and Michael Hittman, *Wovoka and the Ghost Dance* (Lincoln: University of Nebraska Press, 1990), 8.

3. A. I. Chapman to John Gibbon, December 6, 1890, in Hittman, *Wovoka*, 8; and Mooney, *Ghost Dance Religion*, 772.

4. Mooney, *Ghost Dance Religion*, 777.

5. *Black Elk Speaks, as Told through John G. Neihardt* (1932; repr., Albany: State University of New York Press, 2008), 270.

6. See Hélène Valance, "Vanishing Indians: Nostalgic Reminiscence and Haunting Presence," in *Nocturne: Night in American Art, 1890–1917* (New Haven, CT: Yale University Press, 2018).

7. Louis S. Warren, *God's Red Son: The Ghost Dance Religion and the Making of Modern America* (New York: Basic Books, 2017), 24, 30.

8. Jeffrey Ostler, "Native Americans against Empire and Colonial Rule," in *Empire's Twin: U.S. Anti-Imperialism from the Founding Era to the Age of Terrorism*, ed. Ian Tyrrell and Jay Sexton (Ithaca: Cornell University Press, 2015), 51–52.

9. Alexis de Tocqueville, *Democracy in America: Historical-Critical Edition of De la démocratie en Amérique*, ed. Eduardo Nolla, trans. James T. Schleifer, A Bilingual French-English Edition (Indianapolis: Liberty Fund, 2010), vol. 3, chap. 8, online source. The passage alludes to the key Enlightenment text about the inevitability of progress, the Marquis de Condorcet's *Sketch for a Historical Picture of the Progress of the Human Mind* (1795).

10. John L. O'Sullivan, "Annexation," *United States Magazine and Democratic Review* 17, no. 1 (July–August 1845).

11. Warren, *God's Red Son*, 47.

12. David Treuer, *The Heartbeat of Wounded Knee: Native America 1890 to the Present* (New York: Riverhead Books, 2019).

13. Richard Koselleck, *Futures Past: On the Semantics of Historical Time* (1979), trans. Keith Tribe (New York: Columbia University Press, 2004), 50.

14. Jonathan Levy, *Freaks of Fortune: The Emerging World of Capitalism and Risk in America* (Cambridge, MA: Harvard University Press, 2012), 4.

15. Daniel Rosenberg and Susan Harding, introduction to *Histories of the Future* (Durham: Duke University Press, 2005), 6.

16. See Chris Jennings, *Paradise Now: The Story of American Utopianism* (New York: Penguin Random House, 2016).

17. Peggy Ann Brown, "Edward Bellamy: An Introductory Bibliography," *American Studies International* 26, no. 22 (October 1988): 37.

18. Thomas Hine, *Facing Tomorrow* (New York: Alfred A. Knopf, 1991), 50.

19. Michael Robertson, *The Last Utopians: Four Late Nineteenth-Century Visionaries and Their Legacy* (Princeton, NJ: Princeton University Press, 2018), 63.

20. Richard C. Michaelis, *Looking Further Forward: An Answer to "Looking Backward" by Edward Bellamy* (Chicago: Rand, McNally, 1890), 122.

21. Justin Nordstrom, "*Looking Backward*'s Utopian Sequels: Fictional Dialogues in Gilded-Age America," *Utopian Studies* 18, no. 2 (2007): 193–221.

22. Alex Zamalin, *Black Utopia: The History of an Idea from Black Nationalism to Afrofuturism* (New York: Columbia University Press, 2019), 36.

23. Frederick W. Betts, *Billy Sunday: The Man and Method* (Boston: Murray Press, 1916), 8.

24. Quoted in Robert F. Martin, *Hero of the Heartland: Billy Sunday and the Transformation of American Society, 1862–1925* (Bloomington: Indiana University Press, 2002), 7.

25. William A. (Billy) Sunday, *The Sawdust Trail* (Iowa City: University of Iowa Press, 2005), 76–77. First published serially in *Ladies' Home Journal* in 1932 and 1933.

26. Betts, *Billy Sunday*, 17.

27. "Billy Sunday Burns up the Backsliding World: Whirlwind Evangelist Swings into Action at Boston to Cure Depression" (Boston, 1926), film, archived at British Pathé, online source.

28. Kenyatta R. Gilbert, *A Pursued Justice: Black Preaching from the Great Migration to Civil Rights* (Waco, TX: Baylor University Press, 2017).

29. Matthew Avery Sutton, *American Apocalypse: A History of Modern Evangelicalism* (Boston: Belknap Press, 2014), 12–19.

30. Sunday, *Sawdust Trail*, 83–85.

31. Quoted in Martin, *Hero of the Heartland*, 61.

32. "The Big Idea: George Bellows Talks about Patriotism for Beauty," *Touchstone* 1 (July, 1917): 270.

33. John Reed, "The Back of Billy Sunday," *Metropolitan* 42 (May 1915): 66.

34. Elizabeth Gurley Flynn, "The Prince of Strike Breakers," *Santa Ana Register* (Orange County, CA), May 14, 1915.

35. George Creel, "Salvation Circus," *Harper's Weekly*, June 19, 1915, 580.

36. *Melting Pot* 3 (April 1915): 5–6, quoted in William G. McLoughlin, *Modern Revivalism: Charles Grandison Finney to Billy Graham* (New York: Ronald Press, 1959), 441.

37. Reed, "Back of Billy Sunday," 9.

38. Quoted in Emily M. Orr, *Designing the Department Store: Display and Retail at the Turn of the Century* (London: Bloomsbury, 2020), 42.

39. Betts, *Billy Sunday*, 59.

40. Stuart Ewen, *Captains of Consciousness: Advertising and the Social Roots of the Consumer Culture* (1976; repr., New York: Basic Books, 2001), 33.

41. Edward Bernays, *Propaganda* (New York: H. Liveright, 1928), 9. Adam Curtis's documentary *Century of the Self* (BBC/RDF Television, 2002), in which Ewen is featured, accords Bernays a central role in developing techniques of mass manipulation.

42. Samuel Hopkins Adams, *The Great American Fraud: The Patent Medicine Evil* (Salt Lake City: Project Gutenberg, 2013), online source. First published in *Collier's Weekly*, 1905.

43. Seymour Eaton, *Sermons on Advertising* (New York: J. Walter Thompson, 1907), n.p.

44. Walter Dill Scott, *Psychology of Advertising* (Boston: Small, Maynard, 1908), 197, 20. Scott's first book on the topic was *The Theory of Advertising: A Simple Exposition of the Principles of Psychology in Their Relation to Successful Advertising* (Boston: Small, Maynard, 1903).

45. Daniel Navon, "Truth in Advertising: Rationalizing Ads and Knowing Consumers in the Early Twentieth-Century United States," *Theory and Society* 46, no. 2 (June 2017): 143–76.

46. Jackson Lears, *Fables of Abundance: A History of Advertising in America* (New York: Basic Books, 2005), 88.

47. Hubert Henry Harrison, "U-Need-A Biscuit," *Negro World*, July 17, 1920.

48. Hubert Henry Harrison, *When Africa Awakes* (New York: Porro Press, 1920), 39.

49. David Levering Lewis, *When Harlem Was in Vogue* (1979; repr., New York: Penguin, 1997), 36. See also Colin Grant, *Negro with a Hat: The Rise and Fall of Marcus Garvey* (London: Vintage, 2009), 193–94.

50. Harrison, *When Africa Awakes*, 93.

51. Marcus Garvey, "The Negro's Greatest Enemy," *Current History* 18, no. 6 (September 1923): 951–57.

52. "The Handwriting Is on the Wall," August 31, 1921, in *Selected Writings and Speeches of Marcus Garvey*, ed. Bob Blaisdell (Mineola, NY: Dover, 2004), 51.

53. Hubert Henry Harrison, "On a Certain Conservatism in Negroes," in *The Negro and the Nation* (New York: Cosmo Advocate, 1920), 44.

54. Jeffrey B. Perry, *Hubert Harrison: The Voice of Harlem Radicalism, 1883–1918* (New York: Columbia University Press, 2009), 244.

55. Reed, "Back of Billy Sunday," 12.

56. Herbert J. Seligmann, "Negro Conquest," *New York World Magazine*, December 4, 1921.

57. "Negroes Will Stop at Nothing Short of Redemption of Motherland and Establishment of African Empire," August 14, 1921, in Blaisdell, *Writings of Marcus Garvey*, 44–47.

58. Tunde Adeleke, *UnAfrican Americans: Nineteenth-Century Black Nationalists and the Civilizing Mission* (Lexington: University of Kentucky Press, 1998), 98–102.

59. "The Resurrection of the Negro," April 16, 1922, in Blaisdell, *Selected Writings of Marcus Garvey*, 48.

60. Lewis, *When Harlem Was in Vogue*, 318. See also Claude McKay, *A Long Way from Home* (1937; repr., New York: Harcourt, Brace, 1970), 109.

61. Anna Julia Cooper, *A Voice from the South, by a Woman of the South* (Xenia, OH: Aldine, 1892).

62. The line was reused in the "Forethought" to W. E. B. Du Bois, *The Souls of Black Folk: Essays and Sketches* (Chicago: A. C. McClurg, 1903). Du Bois later wrote a science fiction story called "The Comet," in which a black man and white woman believe themselves to be the only humans left alive. Romance seems inevitable, until they realize that only New York City has been destroyed; with the arrival of a group of white people, racist social expectations are crushingly restored. W. E. B. Du Bois, "The Comet," in *Darkwater: Voices from within the Veil* (New York: Harcourt, Brace, 1920).

63. W. E. B. Du Bois, "The Conservation of the Races," *American Negro Academy Occasional Papers* 2 (1897).

64. Cooper, "Womanhood: A Vital Element in the Regeneration and Progress of a Race," in *Voice from the South*, 25. See Derrick Aldridge, "Of Victorianism, Civilizationism,

and Progressivism: The Educational Ideas of Anna Julia Cooper and W. E. B. Du Bois, 1892–1940," *History of Education Quarterly* 47, no. 4 (November 2007): 416–46.

65. Cooper, "Has America a Race Problem; If So, How Can It Best Be Solved?" in *Voice from the South*, 151.

66. Cooper, "Has America a Race Problem?" 163–64.

67. Cooper, "The Gain from a Belief," in *Voice from the South*, 303–4. See also Chike Jeffers, "Anna Julia Cooper and the Black Gift Thesis," *History of Philosophy Quarterly* 33, no. 1 (January 2016): 79–97.

68. Cooper, "Womanhood," 31.

69. This was in Du Bois's essay "The Damnation of Women," otherwise a forceful feminist statement, in Du Bois, *Darkwater*, 187. See also Joy James, *Transcending the Talented Tenth: Black Leaders and American Intellectuals* (New York: Routledge, 1997), 44.

70. Cooper, "Womanhood," 29.

71. Barbara Welter, "The Cult of True Womanhood, 1820–1860," *American Quarterly* 18 (Summer 1966): 151–74.

72. Linda K. Kerber, "Separate Spheres, Female Worlds, Woman's Place: The Rhetoric of Women's History," *Journal of American History* 75, no. 1 (June 1988): 9–39.

73. Elizabeth Boynton Harbert, *Amore* (Chicago: New Era, 1892), 205. See also Steven M. Buechler, "Elizabeth Boynton Harbert and the Woman Suffrage Movement, 1870–1896," *Signs* 13, no. 1 (Autumn 1987): 78–97.

74. Charlotte Perkins Gilman, "The Yellow Wall-Paper," *New England Magazine* 11, no. 5 (January 1892), 648–49, 655.

75. Jill Lepore, *The Secret History of Wonder Woman* (New York: Vintage, 2014).

76. Charlotte Perkins Gilman, *Women and Economics* (Boston: Small, Maynard, 1898), 14.

77. Charlotte Perkins Gilman, "The Waste of Private Housekeeping," *Annals of the American Academy of Political and Social Science* 48 (July 1913): 91.

78. John Van der Zee Sears, "Housekeeping Hereafter," *Atlantic Monthly* 48 (September 1881): 331–38. Sears was a Philadelphia journalist who had studied at Brook Farm, the transcendentalist intentional community, in his youth. See also Robert Hardy, " 'Housekeeping Hereafter': The Preservation of Domesticity in a Technological Utopia," *Utopian Studies* 13, no. 2 (2002): 53–66.

79. Gilman, *Women and Economics*, 257.

80. Lawrence J. Olivier, "W. E. B. Du Bois, Charlotte Perkins Gilman, and 'A Suggestion on the Negro Problem,' " *American Literary Realism* 48, no. 1 (Fall 2015): 25–39.

81. Charlotte Perkins Gilman, "A Suggestion on the Negro Problem," *American Journal of Sociology* 14, no. 1 (July 1908),: 78–85.

82. Charlotte Perkins Gilman, "Birth Control, Religion, and the Unfit," *Nation* 134 (January 27, 1932): 108–9.

83. Jason S. Lantzer, "The Indiana Way of Eugenics: Sterilization Laws, 1907–74," in *Century of Eugenics in America: From the Indiana Experiment to the Human Genome Era*, ed. Paul A. Lombardo (Bloomington: Indiana University Press, 2008).

84. Gilman, " 'Suggestion on the Negro Problem,' " 79.

85. The nickname was first given to her by the author Theodore Dreiser in 1906. Helen C. Camp, *Iron in Her Soul: Elizabeth Gurley Flynn and the American Left* (Pullman: Washington State University Press, 1995), 3, 16. Flynn recalled in her memoirs that Bellamy's *Looking Backward* "made a profound impression on me, as it had done on countless others, as a convincing explanation of how peaceful, prosperous and happy America could be under a socialist system of society." Elizabeth Gurley Flynn, *Rebel Girl: An Autobiography; My First Life, 1906–1926* (1955; repr., New York: International, 1973), 47–48.

86. Elizabeth Gurley Flynn, *Sabotage: The Conscious Withdrawal of the Workers' Industrial Efficiency* (Cleveland: International Workers of the World, 1916).

87. *Industrial Worker*, August 1, 1914, quoted in Philip S. Foner, "The IWW and the Black Worker," *Journal of Negro History* 55, no. 1 (January 1970): 47.

88. William D. Haywood and Frank Bohn, *Industrial Socialism* (Chicago: Charles H. Kerr, 1911), 59.

89. Lewis, *When Harlem Was in Vogue*, 109.

90. Hubert Henry Harrison, review of "Terms of Peace and the Darker Races," by A. Philip Randolph and Chandler Owen, *Messenger* 1 (1917): 33.

91. Langston Hughes, "The Negro Artist and the Racial Mountain," *Nation* 122 (June 23, 1926): 692.

92. "Harlem, Mecca of the New Negro," ed. Alain Locke, special issue, *Survey Graphic* 53, no. 11 (March 1, 1925): 629. This special issue included a number of the Harlem Renaissance's key voices, including Locke, who contributed the essay "Enter the New Negro."

93. Walter Everette Hawkins, "The Poets' Corner," *Messenger* 1, no. 11 (November 1917): 27.

94. "Lenine and Trotzky," *Messenger* 2, no. 7 (July 1918): 28, 30.

95. "The March of Soviet Government," *Messenger* (May–June 1919): 9.

96. See Peter Hartshorn, *I Have Seen the Future: A Life of Lincoln Steffens* (Berkeley, CA: Counterpoint, 2011), 315.

97. Lewis, *When Harlem Was in Vogue*, 56; and Joshua Yaffa, "A Black Communist's Disappearance in Stalin's Russia," *New Yorker*, October 18, 2021).

98. Camp, *Iron in Her Soul*, xxvii.

99. Reed's time in Russia is portrayed in Warren Beatty's 1981 film *Reds*.

100. David Bordwell, *The Cinema of Eisenstein* (New York: Routledge, 2005), 81.

101. "Making the World Safe for Democracy," *Messenger* 1, no. 11 (November 1917): 9.

102. Brown, "Edward Bellamy," 40.

Chapter Two: MACHINE

1. Sergei Eisenstein, notebook entry, October 13, 1927, reprinted and translated in "Notes for a Film of *Capital*," *October* 2 (Summer 1976): 4. See also Vance Kepley Jr., "The First 'Perestroika': Soviet Cinema under the First Five-Year Plan," *Cinema Journal* 35, no. 4 (Summer 1996), 31–53.

2. F. T. Marinetti and Fillìa, *The Futurist Cookbook*, trans. Barbara McGilvray (London: Sternberg Press, 2013), 37.

3. F. T. Marinetti, "Multiplied Man and the Reign of the Machine" (1911), in *Futurism: An Anthology*, ed. Lawrence S. Rainey, Christine Poggi, and Laura Wittman (New Haven, CT: Yale University Press, 2009), 90–91.

4. Hirato Renkichi, "Manifesto of the Japanese Futurist Movement," trans. Miryam Sas, *Cabinet* 13 (1921; repr. Spring 2004), online source.

5. Joshua B. Freeman, *Behemoth: A History of the Factory and the Making of the Modern World* (New York: W. W. Norton, 2018), 185.

6. Massimo Livi-Bacci, "On the Human Costs of Collectivization in the Soviet Union," *Population and Development Review* 19, no. 4 (December 1993): 743–66.

7. Roman Jakobson, "On a Generation That Squandered Its Poets" (1931), trans. Edward J. Brown, in *Language and Literature*, ed. Krystyna Pomorska and Stephen Rudy (Cambridge, MA: Harvard University Press, 1987), 300.

8. Boris Groys, *The Total Art of Stalinism: Avant-Garde, Aesthetic Dictatorship, and Beyond* (London: Verso, 2011).

9. Ray T. Tucker, "Is Hoover Human?" *North American Review* 226, no. 5 (November 1928): 513.

10. William E. Akin, *Technocracy and the American Dream: The Technocrat Movement, 1900–1941* (Berkeley: University of California Press, 1977), 34.

11. "400 Leaders Hear Technocracy Plea," *New York Times*, January 14, 1933.

12. Dora Russell, "The Soul of Russia and the Body of America" (1920–21), in *Religion of the Machine Age* (London: Routledge & Kegan Paul, 1983), xv.

13. Russell, *Religion of the Machine Age*, 200.

14. Bertrand Russell and Dora Russell, *Prospects of Industrial Civilization* (1923; repr., London: Routledge & Kegan Paul, 2009), 211, 218.

15. Samuel Butler, "Darwin among the Machines," *Press* (Christchurch, New Zealand), June 13, 1863, 182.

16. Samuel Butler, *Life and Habit* (London: Trübner, 1878), 134. As James Gleick points out, this argument strikingly anticipates that of Richard Dawkins's well-known book *The Selfish Gene*. James Gleick, *The Information: A History, a Theory, a Flood* (New York: Pantheon, 2011), 302.

17. Andreas Huyssen, "The Vamp and the Machine: Technology and Sexuality in Fritz Lang's *Metropolis*," *New German Critique* 24, no. 25 (Autumn 1981): 221–37.

18. Aleksandr Rodchenko, "Charlot" (1922), in *Aleksandr Rodchenko: Experiments for the Future: Diaries, Essays, Letters, and Other Writings*, trans. Jamey Gambrell (New York: Museum of Modern Art, 2005), 147.

19. "Mr. Wells Reviews a Current Film," *New York Times*, April 17, 1927.

20. Darko Suvin, *Metamorphoses of Science Fiction: On the Poetics and History of a Literary Genre* (New Haven, CT: Yale University Press, 1979), 270.

21. James D. Graham, "An Audience of the Scientific Age: *Rossum's Universal Robots* and the Production of an Economic Conscience," *Grey Room* 50 (Winter 2013): 119; William E. Harkins, "Karel Čapek's *R. U. R.* and A. N. Tolstoj's *Revolt of the Machines*," *Slavic and East European Journal* 4, no. 4 (Winter 1960): 312–18; and David Christopher, "Stalin's *Loss of Sensation*: Subversive Impulses in Soviet Science-Fiction of the Great Terror," *Journal of Science Fiction* 1, no. 2 (May 2016): 18–35.

22. "Mechanical Man Startles London," *Modern Mechanix*, January 1929, 60.

23. Amy Sue Bix, *Inventing Ourselves Out of Jobs: America's Debate over Technological Unemployment, 1929–1981* (Baltimore: Johns Hopkins University Press, 2000), 13.

24. Bix, *Inventing Ourselves Out of Jobs*, 22–26, 36.

25. T. Arnold Hill, "The Plight of the Negro Industrial Worker," *Journal of Negro Education* 5, no. 1 (January 1936): 40–41.

26. Robert C. Weaver, "The Employment of the Negro in War Industries," *Journal of Negro Education* 12, no. 3 (Summer 1943): 386–96.

27. Sheldon Cheney, *The New World Architecture* (London: Longmans, Green, 1930), 75.

28. Lewis Mumford, *The Story of Utopias* (New York: Boni and Liveright, 1922), 251.

29. Casey Nelson Blake, *Beloved Community: The Cultural Criticism of Randolph Bourne, Van Wyck Brooks, Waldo Frank, and Lewis Mumford* (Durham: University of North Carolina Press, 1990).

30. Lewis Mumford, "The Drama of the Machines," *Scribner's Magazine* 88, no. 2 (August 1930): 150–61.

31. Lewis Mumford, *Technics and Civilization* (London: Routledge & Kegan Paul, 1934), 216, 218, 389.

32. Mumford, 363.

33. Christine Frederick, *Selling Mrs. Consumer* (New York: Business Bourse, 1929), 155.

34. Janice Williams Rutherford, *Selling Mrs. Consumer: Christine Frederick and the Rise of Household Efficiency* (Athens: University of Georgia Press, 2003), 56; and Danielle Drelinger, *The Secret History of Home Economics* (New York: W. W. Norton, 2021).

35. *The J. Walter Thompson Book* (New York: J. Walter Thompson, 1909), 22, quoted in Jackson Lears, *Fables of Abundance: A History of Advertising in America* (New York: Basic Books, 2005), 160.

36. Justus George Frederick, "Is Progressive Obsolescence the Path toward Increased Consumption?" *Advertising and Selling*, September 5, 1928, 19–20, 44–46. See also Giles Slade, *Made to Break: Technology and Obsolescence in America* (Cambridge, MA: Harvard University Press, 2007), 58.

37. Frederick, *Selling Mrs. Consumer*, 246.

38. Kristina Wilson, *Livable Modernism: Interior Decorating and Design during the Great Depression* (New Haven, CT: Yale University Press, 2004).

39. Aldous Huxley, *Brave New World* (London: Chatto & Windus, 1932), chap. 3. See also Slade, *Made to Break*, 73.

40. "Gwendolyn Wright, "The Model Domestic Environment: Icon or Option?" in *Women in American Architecture: A Historic and Contemporary Perspective*, ed. Susana Torre (New York: Whitney Library of Design, 1977), 20, quoted in Rutherford, *Selling Mrs. Consumer*, 4.

41. Frederick, *Selling Mrs. Consumer*, 22–23.

42. Frederick, *Selling Mrs. Consumer*, 7.

43. Russell Flinchum, *Henry Dreyfuss, Industrial Designer: The Man in the Brown Suit* (New York: Cooper-Hewitt/Rizzoli, 1997).

44. Jeffrey Meikle, *Twentieth Century Limited: Industrial Design in America, 1925–1939* (Philadelphia: Temple University Press, 1981).

45. Glenn Adamson, *Industrial Strength Design: How Brooks Stevens Shaped Your World* (Milwaukee: Milwaukee Art Museum/MIT Press, 2005),

46. Nicolas P. Maffei, *Norman Bel Geddes: American Design Visionary* (London: Bloomsbury, 2018), 120.

47. Norman Bel Geddes, *Horizons* (Boston: Little, Brown, 1932), 222, 4.

48. Bel Geddes, *Horizons*, 24.

49. Norman Bel Geddes, "Ten Years from Now," *Ladies' Home Journal* 48 (January 1931), quoted in Maffei, *Norman Bel Geddes*, 84.

50. Bel Geddes, *Horizons*, 291, 289.

51. Regina Lee Blaszczyk, *The Color Revolution* (Cambridge, MA: MIT Press, 2012), 81.

52. See Philip B. Scranton, ed., *Silk City: Studies on the Paterson Silk Industry, 1860–1940* (Newark: New Jersey Historical Society, 1985).

53. Blaszczyk, *Color Revolution*, 187.

54. Natalie Kalmus, "Color Consciousness," *Journal of the Society of Motion Picture Engineers* 25, no. 2 (August 1935): 143.

55. Natalie Kalmus, color chart (1932), reproduced in Sarah Street, *Chromatic Modernity: Color, Cinema, and Media of the 1920s* (New York: Columbia University Press, 2019), 65.

56. Donald Albrecht, *Designing Dreams: Modern Architecture in the Movies* (New York: Harper and Row/Museum of Modern Art, 1986).

57. Quoted in Blaszczyk, *Color Revolution*, 189.

58. Raymond Loewy, "Selling through Design," *Journal of the Royal Society of Arts* 90 (January 9, 1942): 96.

59. John Mulkern, *Continuity and Change: Babson College, 1919–1994* (Wellesley, MA: Babson College, 1995), 8.

60. Roger W. Babson, "Billy Sunday as an Investment," *Congregationalist and Christian World*, January 4, 1917, 31.

61. Roger W. Babson, *Business Fundamentals: How to Become a Successful Business Man* (New York: B. C. Forbes/Babson Institute, 1923), xi.

62. Roger W. Babson, "Business Forecasting and Its Relation to Modern Selling," *Annals of the American Academy of Political and Social Science* 115 (September 1924): 146.

63. On this earlier generation of economic forecasters, see Jamie L. Pietruska, *Looking Forward: Prediction and Uncertainty in Modern America* (Chicago: University of Chicago Press, 2018).

64. Roger W. Babson, "Tomorrow's Demands on Education," *Journal of Education* 115, no. 14 (June 6, 1932): 420. See also Walter A. Friedman, *Fortune Tellers: The Story of America's First Economic Forecasters* (Princeton, NJ: Princeton University Press, 2014), 43ff.

65. Roger W. Babson, "Ascertaining and Forecasting Business Conditions by the Study of Statistics," *Publications of the American Statistical Association* 13, no. 97 (March 1912): 41.

66. Jonathan Levy, *Freaks of Fortune: The Emerging World of Capitalism and Risk in America* (Cambridge, MA: Harvard University Press, 2012), 2.

67. François Ewald, "The Values of Insurance" (1998), trans. Shana Cooperstein and Benjamin J. Young, *Grey Room* 74 (Winter 2019): 140–41.

68. Wallace Stevens, "Insurance and Social Change," *Hartford Agent* 29, no. 4 (October 1937): 49–50, reprinted in *Wallace Stevens Journal* 4, nos. 3–4 (Fall 1980): 37–39.

69. Stevens, "Insurance and Social Change," 39.

70. Quoted in Pietruska, *Looking Forward*, 15.

71. Quoted in Joseph Harrington, "Wallace Stevens and the Poetics of National Insurance," *American Literature* 67, no. 1 (March 1995): 103.

72. James M. Anderson, Paul Heaton, and Stephen J. Carroll, *The U.S. Experience with No-Fault Automobile Insurance: A Retrospective* (Santa Monica, CA: RAND Corporation, 2010), 23–27; and Caley Horan, *Insurance Era: Risk, Governance, and the Privatization of Security in Postwar America* (Chicago: University of Chicago Press, 2021), 60 (emphasis in original).

73. "America on the Move: Automobile Safety," Behring Center, National Museum of American History, Smithsonian Institution, https://americanhistory.si.edu/explore /exhibitions/america-on-the-move.

74. Horan, *Insurance Era*, 62.

75. Irving Fisher, *How to Live Long* (New York: Metropolitan Life Insurance, 1915).

76. Horan, *Insurance Era*, 49–50.

77. François Ewald, "The Return of Descartes's Malicious Demon: An Outline of a Philosophy of Precaution," in *Embracing Risk, the Changing Culture of Insurance and Responsibility*, ed. T. Baker and J. Simon (Chicago: University of Chicago Press, 2002).

78. Frank H. Knight, *Risk, Uncertainty, and Profit* (Boston: Houghton Mifflin, 1921).

79. Daniel B. Bouk, *How Our Days Became Numbered: Risk and the Rise of the Statistical Individual* (Chicago: University of Chicago Press, 2015).

80. Beatrix Hoffman, "Scientific Racism, Insurance, and Opposition to the Welfare State: Frederick L. Hoffman's Transatlantic Journey," *Journal of the Gilded Age and Progressive Era* 2, no. 2 (April 2003): 150–90.

81. Mary L. Heen, "Ending Jim Crow Life Insurance Rates," *Northwestern Journal of Law and Social Policy* 4, no. 2 (Fall 2009): 360–99; and Horan, *Insurance Era*, chap. 5.

82. W. E. B. Du Bois, *Some Efforts of Negroes for Their Own Social Betterment* (Atlanta: Atlanta University Press, 1898), 20.

83. Walter B. Weare, *Black Business in the New South: A Social History of the North Carolina Mutual Life Insurance Company* (Durham, NC: Duke University Press, 1993), 167.

84. H. G. Wells, *World Brain* (London: Methuen, 1938), 65.

85. George Edward Pendray, *The Story of the Westinghouse Time Capsule* (Pittsburgh: Westinghouse Electric & Manufacturing, 1939), 12–14.

86. Anna Thompson Hajdik, "A 'Bovine Glamour Girl': Borden Milk, Elsie the Cow, and the Convergence of Technology, Animals, and Gender at the 1939 New York World's Fair," *Agricultural History* 88, no. 4 (Fall 2014): 470–90.

87. "The America of 1960: General Motors' Futurama," *Life*, June 5, 1939, 79.

88. Maffei, *Norman Bel Geddes*, 158–59.

89. Bernard Lichtenberg, "Business Backs New York World Fair to Meet the New Deal Propaganda," *Public Opinion Quarterly* 2, no. 2 (1938): 314. Lichtenberg was president of the Institute of Public Relations and a consultant to the World's Fair Corporation.

90. E. B. White, "A Reporter at Large: They Come with Joyous Song," *New Yorker*, May 13, 1939.

91. See Christina Cogdell, *Eugenic Design: Streamlining America in the 1930s* (Philadelphia: University of Pennsylvania Press, 2004); and Carma R. Gorman, "Educating the Eye: Body Mechanics and Streamlining in the United States, 1925–1950," *American Quarterly* 58, no. 3 (September 2006), 839–68.

92. Mabel O. Wilson, *Negro Building: Black Americans in the World of Fairs and Museums* (Oakland: University of California Press, 2021), 196.

93. Wilson, 101.

94. *American Negro Exposition: Official Program and Guide Book 1863–1940* (Chicago: Exposition Authority, 1940), https://libsysdigi.library.illinois.edu/OCA/Books2012-02/americannegroexpooamer/. See also Adam Green, *Selling the Race: Culture, Community, and Black Chicago, 1940–1955* (Chicago: University of Chicago Press, 2007).

Chapter Three: GARDEN

1. Quoted in Marco Duranti, "Utopia, Nostalgia and World War at the 1939–40 New York World's Fair," *Journal of Contemporary History* 41, no. 4 (October 2006): 666. The dinner was held at the City Club of New York and confirmed Mumford as one of the World's Fair planners, along with the industrial designers Henry Dreyfuss and Walter Dorwin Teague, among others. "Fair Planners Selected: Architects and Designers Named for World Exposition," *New York Times*, December 12, 1935.

2. Lewis Mumford, "The Sky Line in Flushing—Genuine Bootleg," *New Yorker*, July 29, 1939, 38.

3. *The City* had at least some international influence, as well; it was, for example, shown to ministers overseeing the development in New Delhi after the war. Rosemary

Wakeman, *Practicing Utopia: An Intellectual History of the New Town Movement* (Chicago: University of Chicago Press, 2016), 119.

4. Karl Schriftgiesser, "Man and His Cities," *New York Times*, April 30, 1939. Mumford's script for *The City* was based on an outline by the New Deal filmmaker Pare Lorenz; the project was funded by the Carnegie Foundation.

5. Catherine Bauer, "Machine-Age Mansions for Ultra-Moderns," *New York Times*, April 15, 1928. See also Gail Radford, *Modern Housing for America: Policy Struggles in the New Deal Era* (Chicago: University of Chicago Press, 1997), 65–66.

6. Bauer, "Machine-Age Mansions," 10.

7. Catherine Bauer, *Modern Housing* (New York: Houghton Mifflin, 1934). A new edition was published by the University of Minnesota Press in 2020.

8. Quoted in H. Peter Oberlander and Eva Newbrun, *Houser: The Life and Work of Catherine Bauer* (Vancouver: University of British Columbia Press, 2002), 48.

9. Lewis Mumford, "Regions—To Live in," *Survey Graphic* 54, no. 3 (May 1, 1925): 151.

10. Jane Jacobs, *The Death and Life of Great American Cities* (New York: Vintage Books, 1961), 17.

11. Lewis Mumford, "Revaluations I: Howard's Garden City," *New York Review of Books*, April 8, 1965, online source.

12. Ebenezer Howard, "Spiritual Influences towards Social Progress," *Light* 30 (April 1910): 195.

13. Ebenezer Howard, *Garden Cities of To-morrow* (London: Swan Sonnenschein, 1902), 18. For Howard's sources, see John Rockey, "From Vision to Reality: Victorian Ideal Cities and Model Towns in the Genesis of Ebenezer Howard's Garden City," *Town Planning Review* 54, no. 1 (January 1983): 83–105.

14. Quoted in Robert Beevers, *The Garden City Utopia: A Critical Biography of Ebenezer Howard* (London: Palgrave Macmillan, 1988), 1.

15. Beevers, *The Garden City Utopia*, 96.

16. Mumford, "Regions," 151.

17. See Steven Logan, *In the Suburbs of History: Modernist Visions of the Urban Periphery* (Toronto: University of Toronto Press, 2021).

18. See Frederick J. Osborn, *New Towns after the War* (London: Dent, 1918); and Mark Clapson, *Invincible Green Suburbs, Brave New Towns* (Manchester, UK: Manchester University Press, 1998).

19. Catherine K. Bauer, "Prize Essay: Art in Industry," *Fortune* 3 (May 1931): 95. See also Radford, *Modern Housing for America*, 71. On Lihotzky's contribution, see Juliet

Kinchin, *Counter Space: Design and the Modern Kitchen* (New York: Museum of Modern Art, 2011).

20. Daniel Schaffer, *Garden Cities for America: The Radburn Experience* (Philadelphia: Temple University Press, 1982).

21. Frank Lloyd Wright, *The Disappearing City* (New York: William Farquhar Payson, 1932), 3, 5.

22. Frank Lloyd Wright, *Broadacre City: A New Community Plan* (New York: Architectural Record, 1935).

23. Lewis Mumford, "The Sky Line: Mr. Wright's City," *New Yorker*, April 27, 1935, 79–80.

24. Quoted in Jason Weems, *Barnstorming the Prairies: How Aerial Vision Shaped the Midwest* (Minneapolis: University of Minnesota Press, 2015), 124, 100.

25. Frank Lloyd Wright, *An Autobiography* (New York: Duell, Sloan and Pearce, 1943), 318.

26. Wright, *An Autobiography*, 318.

27. Wright, *Disappearing City*, 67.

28. Wright, *Autobiography*, 318.

29. Siegfried Giedion, *Mechanization Takes Command: A Contribution to Anonymous History* (New York: Oxford University Press, 1948), 256, 715, 130.

30. Bernard Leach, "American Impressions," *Craft Horizons* 10, no. 4 (Winter 1950): 18.

31. Van Wyck Brooks, *The Confident Years* (London: J. M. Dent and Sons, 1953), 475; and Brooks, "On Creating a Usable Past," *Dial*, April 11, 1918, 337–41.

32. Mabel Dodge Luhan, *Edge of Taos Desert: Escape to Reality* (New York: Harcourt, Brace, 1937), 33, 58.

33. Luhan, 126.

34. Elsie Clews Parsons, *The Social Organization of the Tewa of New Mexico* (Menasha, WI: American Anthropological Association, 1929). Lawrence's visit, which was fraught due to the mutual attraction between himself and Dodge and his reactionary ideas about gender relations, has been the subject of much scholarly attention, as well as a fictionalization by Rachel Cusk. See Frances Wilson, *Burning Man: The Trials of D. H. Lawrence* (New York: Farrar, Straus and Giroux, 2021); and Rachel Cusk, *Second Place* (London: Faber, 2021).

35. Luhan, *Edge of Taos Desert*, 107, 273.

36. Quoted in Lois Palken Rudnick, *Mabel Dodge Luhan: New Woman, New Worlds* (Albuquerque: University of New Mexico Press, 1984), 182.

37. Mabel Dodge Luhan, "A Bridge between Cultures," *Theatre Arts Monthly* 9, no. 7 (May 1925): 297–301.

38. John Collier, *From Every Zenith: A Memoir* (Denver, CO: Sage Books, 1963), 37.

39. Collier, 115. On the Great War's generational effects, see Jon Savage, *Teenage: The Creation of Youth Culture* (London: Penguin, 2007).

40. John Collier, "The Red Atlantis," *Survey* 49 (October 1922): 15–20, 63, 66.

41. Collier, 18, 15.

42. Mary Austin and Ansel Adams, *Taos Pueblo* (1930); and Jonathan Spaulding, *Ansel Adams and the American Landscape: A Biography* (Berkeley: University of California Press, 1995), 78–82. Adams first came to Taos in 1927, O'Keeffe in 1929. See Daniel Worden, "Landscape Culture: Ansel Adams and Mary Austin's Taos Pueblo," *Criticism* 55, no. 1 (Winter 2013): 69–94.

43. Collier, "Red Atlantis," 16.

44. D. H. Lawrence to Mabel Dodge, November 19, 1923, in Mabel Dodge Luhan, *Lorenzo in Taos* (New York: Alfred A. Knopf, 1932), 120.

45. Laura Thompson, *Culture in Crisis: A Study of the Hopi Indians* (New York: Harper & Row, 1950), quoted in Collier, *From Every Zenith*, 265.

46. Elmer R. Rusco, *A Fateful Time: The Background and Legislative History of the Indian Reorganization Act* (Reno: University of Nevada Press, 2000), 148; and *Land Reform in the Navajo Nation* (Tsaile, AZ: Diné Policy Institute, 2017), 11–12.

47. Vine DeLoria Jr. and Clifford Lytle, *The Nations Within: The Past and Future of American Indian Sovereignty* (New York: Pantheon, 1984), 190.

48. Tisa Wenger, *We Have a Religion: The 1920s Pueblo Indian Dance Controversy and American Religious Freedom* (Chapel Hill: University of North Carolina Press, 2009), 121–22.

49. Pablo Abeita, "The Pueblo Indian Question," *Franciscan Missions of the Southwest* 6 (1918): 7–8.

50. Margaret D. Jacobs, "Making Savages of Us All: White Women, Pueblo Indians, and the Controversy over Indian Dances in the 1920s," *Frontiers* 17, no. 3 (1996): 191.

51. Paul Secord, *Albuquerque Deco and Pueblo* (Mount Pleasant, SC: Arcadia, 2012).

52. Quoted in R. Buckminster Fuller and Robert Marks, *The Dymaxion World of Buckminster Fuller* (New York: Anchor Books, 1973), 26.

53. Alec Nevala-Lee, "The Dramatic Failure of Buckminster Fuller's 'Car of the Future,'" *Slate*, August 2, 2022.

54. Eva Díaz, "R. Buckminster Fuller's Strange Bedfellows," *Appalachian Journal* 44, no. 45 (2017–18): 524.

55. Vladimir I. Vernadsky, *The Biosphere* (1926), trans. David Langmuir and Mark McMenamin (New York: Springer, 1998), 9; and Lewis Mumford, *The Culture of Cities* (New York: Harvest/HBJ, 1938), 482.

56. R. Buckminster Fuller and John McHale, *Inventory of World Resources: Human Trends and Needs* (Carbondale: Southern Illinois University, 1963), 3.

57. Alec Nevala-Lee, *Inventor of the Future: The Visionary Life of Buckminster Fuller* (New York: HarperCollins, 2022).

58. Reproduced in Joachim Krausse and Claude Lichtenstein, eds., *Your Private Sky: R. Buckminster Fuller; The Art of Design Science* (Zürich: Lars Müller, 1999), 99.

59. R. Buckminster Fuller, *Nine Chains to the Moon* (Carbondale: Southern Illinois University Press, 1938), 58.

60. R. Buckminster Fuller, *4D Time Lock* (Chicago: privately published, 1928).

61. R. Buckminster Fuller, "Lightful Houses," manuscript, 1928, reproduced in Krausse and Lichtenstein, *Your Private Sky*, 106.

62. Fuller, *Nine Chains to the Moon*, 2.

63. Fuller, *Nine Chains to the Moon*, 9.

64. Philip Johnson to Max Levinson, May 27, 1932, quoted in Nevala-Lee, *Inventor of the Future*.

65. Fuller, *Nine Chains to the Moon*, 2.

66. Nevala-Lee, *Inventor of the Future*.

67. Alistair Gordon, "War Shelters, Short Lived but Living On," *New York Times*, December 31, 2013.

68. Jonathon Keats, *You Belong to the Universe: Buckminster Fuller and the Future* (Oxford: Oxford University Press, 2016), 64.

69. Calvin Tomkins, "In the Outlaw Area," *New Yorker*, January 8, 1966.

70. R. Buckminster Fuller with Kiyoshi Kuromiya, *Critical Path* (New York: St. Martin's Press, 1981), xxiii.

71. R. Buckminster Fuller, "Emergency Through Emergence," *Shelter*, May 1932, 10; and R. Buckminster Fuller, "Streamlining," *Shelter*, November 1932, 78.

72. R. Buckminster Fuller, "Domes," in *Synergetics Dictionary: The Mind of Buckminster Fuller*, ed. E. J. Applewhite (New York: Garland, 1986), 4186. See also Nevala-Lee, *Inventor of the Future*; and Elizabeth Kolbert, "Dymaxion Man," *New Yorker* (June 2, 2008).

73. Barbara Ward, *The International Share-Out* (London: Thomas Nelson and Sons, 1938), 174.

74. Barbara Ward, *India and the West* (New York: W. W. Norton, 1961), 181.

75. Barbara Ward, *Spaceship Earth* (New York: Columbia University Press, 1966), 14.

76. Barbara Ward Jackson, "Interview with Lady Barbara Ward Jackson," c. 1966 (misdated at link), Studs Terkel Radio Archive, audio, 20:46, quote at 0:51, online source.

77. *Ekistics* 4, no. 25 (1957). The editor of *Ekistics* was Jaqueline Tyrwhitt.

78. Wakeman, *Practicing Utopia*, 135.

79. Constantinos A. Doxiadis, "Architecture, Planning and Ekistics," *Ekistics* 7, no. 42 (April 1959): 293.

80. Marshall McLuhan, *The Gutenberg Galaxy: The Making of Typographic Man* (Toronto: University of Toronto Press, 1964).

81. Mark Wigley, "Network Fever," *Grey Room* 4 (Summer 2001): 84.

82. "The Declaration of Delos," *Ekistics* 107 (October 1964): 268–99.

83. Ward, *Spaceship Earth*, 148.

84. Barbara Ward, *The Rich Nations and the Poor Nations* (New York: W. W. Norton, 1962).

85. Barbara Ward, *The Interplay of East and West* (New York: W. W. Norton, 1954), 107. See also Barbara Ward, *Faith and Freedom* (New York: W. W. Norton, 1954), 234.

86. Kwame Nkrumah, *Ghana: The Autobiography of Kwame Nkrumah* (Edinburgh: Thomas Nelson and Sons, 1957).

87. Frances Nwia-Kofi [Kwame] Nkrumah, "Education and Nationalism in Africa," *Educational Outlook* 18, no. 1 (November 1943): 38–40.

88. Kwame Nkrumah, *Africa Must Unite* (New York: Frederick A. Praeger, 1963), 16.

89. Barbara Ward, "The Emerging Africa," *Atlantic*, April 1959, online source.

90. Basil Davidson, *Which Way Africa? The Search for a New Society* (Harmondsworth, UK: Penguin, 1964), 68.

91. See Kwame Nkrumah, *Consciencism: Philosophy and the Ideology for Decolonization* (London: Heinemann, 1964).

92. T. E. Hilton, "Akosombo Dam and the Volta River Project," *Geography* 51, no. 3 (July 1966): 251–54.

93. Sir Robert Jackson, foreword to *The Volta Resettlement Experience*, ed. Robert Chambers (London: Pall Mall Press, 1970).

94. Jean Gartlan, *Barbara Ward: Her Life and Letters* (London: Continuum, 2010), 105.

95. Nkrumah, *Africa Must Unite*, 117.

96. "Students Experience Life in Ghana," *Chicago Tribune*, April 2, 1964; and Buckminster Fuller to Naomi Smith, January 30, 1964, R. Buckminster Fuller Collection, Stanford Libraries.

97. Thomas Turman, interview by author, December 15, 2022. Turman, from the University of Colorado, was one of these recruits; like the others, he spent only two years there: "We didn't want to be colonialists."

98. R. Buckminster Fuller, "Everything I Know: Session 10," Buckminster Fuller Institute, online source. According to Turman, after its display in Accra the aluminum dome was flown up to Kumasi, suspended from a helicopter.

99. Miles Danby, "House Design," in Chambers, *Volta Resettlement Experience*, 164–78.

100. Viviana d'Auria, "From Tropical Transitions to Ekistic Experimentation: Doxiadis Associates in Tema, Ghana," *Positions* 1 (Spring 2010): 42.

101. Łukasz Stanek, "Architects from Socialist Countries in Ghana, 1957–67: Modern Architecture and Mondialisation," *Journal of the Society of Architectural Historians* 74, no. 4 (December 2015): 416–42.

102. Michelle Provoost, "Tema, Ghana, Africa," International New Town Institute, online source. See also Michelle Provoost, "The Flagship of Nkrumah's Pan-African Vision," in *New Towns on the Cold War Frontier* (Delft, Netherlands: International New Town Institute, forthcoming).

103. C. A. Doxiadis, "Ekistics and Regional Science," *Ekistics* 14, no. 84 (November 1962): 197.

104. C. A. Doxiadis, "Ekistics, the Science of Human Settlements," *Ekistics* 33, no. 197 (April 1972): 239.

105. Provoost, "Tema, Ghana."

106. Stephan F. Miescher, "Building the City of the Future: Visions and Experiences of Modernity in Ghana's Akosombo Township," *Journal of African History* 53, no. 3 (2012): 367–90.

107. Ward, *Spaceship Earth*, 2.

108. Doxiadis, "Architecture, Planning and Ekistics," 294.

109. "Declaration of Delos Ten," *Ekistics* 34, no. 203 (October 1972): 230, 234.

Chapter Four: LAB

1. Michael J. Neufeld, "Wernher von Braun, the SS, and Concentration Camp Labor: Questions of Moral, Political, and Criminal Responsibility," *German Studies Review* 25, no. 1 (February 2002): 57–78.

2. Daniel Lang, "A Romantic Urge," *New Yorker*, April 21, 1951, 92. See also Wayne Biddle, *Dark Side of the Moon: Wernher von Braun, the Third Reich, and the Space Race* (New York: W. W. Norton, 2009).

3. Lang, "Romantic Urge," 81.

4. Wernher von Braun, "Crossing the Last Frontier," *Collier's*, March 22, 1952, 25.

5. Werner Wiskari, "Space Conference in Sweden Ends," *New York Times*, August 21, 1960.

6. "Strangelove Reactions," *New York Times*, March 1, 1964.

7. Lewis Mumford, "Gentlemen, You Are Mad," *Saturday Review of Literature*, March 2, 1946, 5–6.

8. Lewis Mumford, "Program for Survival" (1946), reprinted in Mumford, *Values for Survival: Essays, Addresses, and Letters on Politics and Education* (New York: Harcourt Brace Jovanovich, 1972), 96.

9. Mumford, 106.

10. Elizabeth Gurley Flynn, *Alderson Story: My Life as a Political Prisoner* (New York: International, 1963).

11. Jenny Andersson, *The Future of the World: Futurology, Futurists, and the Struggle for the Post Cold War Imagination* (Oxford: Oxford University Press, 2018), 46.

12. Ossip K. Flechtheim, "Teaching the Future," *Journal of Higher Education* 16, no. 9 (December 1945): 465.

13. Andersson, *Future of the World*, 46.

14. Bertrand Russell and Lewis Mumford also advocated a "world government" that would have ultimate authority over the regulation and control of nuclear weapons. See Or Rosenboim, *The Emergence of Globalism: Visions of World Order in Britain and the United States, 1939–1950* (Princeton, NJ: Princeton University Press, 2017), 237–38; and Lewis Mumford, *Atomic War: The Way Out* (London: National Peace Council, 1949).

15. Timothy Stott, *Buckminster Fuller's World Game and Its Legacy* (New York: Routledge, 2022).

16. Alex Abella, *Soldiers of Reason: The RAND Corporation and the Rise of the American Empire* (New York: Harcourt, 2008), 4.

17. Louis Menand, "Fat Man: Herman Kahn and the Nuclear Age," *New Yorker*, June 19, 2005.

18. Bertrand de Jouvenel, "Futuribles," paper delivered to the RAND Corporation, November 30, 1964. For example, he distinguished between point predictions, which posit a quantitative value to be reached at a specific time; interval predictions, which establish a range, no more than x and no less than y; and whole predictive systems, which attempt to describe the dynamic interrelation of interacting forces.

19. Bertrand de Jouvenel, *The Art of Conjecture*, trans. Nikita Lary (London: Weidenfeld and Nicolson, 1967), 54, 74–75. See also Andersson, *The Future of the World*, 62.

20. Daniel Bell, *The End of Ideology: On the Exhaustion of Political Ideas in the 1950s* (Glencoe, IL: Free Press, 1960). The compatibility of Bell's rhetoric with von Braun's, which also asserted the non-ideological character of science, is worth noting; so too is the way that Bell anticipated *The End of History and the Last Man* by Francis

Fukuyama—himself intermittently a researcher at RAND. Francis Fukuyama, *The End of History and the Last Man* (New York: Free Press, 1992).

21. Daniel Bell, "Twelve Modes of Prediction: A Preliminary Sorting of Approaches in the Social Sciences," *Daedalus* 93, no. 3 (Summer 1964): 845–80. Bell was affiliated with Herman Kahn's Hudson Institute, and his example of this last predictive type, the "prime mover," was the discussion of military technology in *On Thermonuclear War.*

22. Bell, "Twelve Modes of Prediction," 846–47.

23. Bell borrowed this phrasing from Dennis Gabor's *Inventing the Future* (New York: Alfred A. Knopf, 1964).

24. Robert Jungk, *Brighter Than a Thousand Suns: A Personal History of the Atomic Scientists* (New York: Harcourt Brace, 1958); and Robert Jungk, *Children of the Ashes: Story of a Rebirth* (New York: Harcourt Brace & World, 1961).

25. Robert Jungk, *Tomorrow Is Already Here* (1952), trans. Marguerite Waldman (New York: Simon & Schuster, 1954), 19.

26. Jungk, *Tomorrow Is Already Here*, 20–21.

27. Jungk, *Tomorrow Is Already Here*, 24.

28. Jungk, *Tomorrow Is Already Here*, 178, 186, 205.

29. Andersson, *Future of the World*, 75.

30. Jungk, *Tomorrow Is Already Here*, 230.

31. Jungk, *Tomorrow Is Already Here*, 235.

32. James Burnham, *The Managerial Revolution: What Is Happening in the World* (New York: John Day, 1941), 99.

33. Toward the end of his life (he died in 2009), McNamara was the subject of a full-dress biography, Deborah Shapley's *Promise and Power*, as well as a profoundly ambivalent documentary film by Errol Morris, *The Fog of War.* McNamara also wrote an autobiography, and participated in another book (much more interesting) in which he and other officials from both the United States and Vietnam raked over the coals of the war, discussing where they had gone wrong and how it might have been otherwise. Most recently, his son has published a heartbreaking memoir, adding a new human dimension to his father's story. Craig McNamara, *Because Our Fathers Lied: A Memoir of Truth and Family, From Vietnam to Today* (Boston: Little, Brown, 2022).

34. David Halberstam, "Dead Wrong," *Los Angeles Times*, April 16, 1995.

35. Paul Hendrickson, *The Living and the Dead: Robert McNamara and Five Lives of a Lost War* (New York: Vintage, 1997), 83.

36. John A. Byrne, *Whiz Kids: Ten Founding Fathers of American Business and the Legacy They Left Us* (New York: Currency/Doubleday, 1993), 40.

37. Quoted in Byrne, *Whiz Kids*, 399.

38. Gabriel Kolko, *Confronting the Third World: United States Foreign Policy, 1945–1980* (New York: Pantheon, 1988), 133.

39. Among them was the assistant secretary of defense Charles Hitch, who had recently coauthored, with Roland N. McKean, *The Economics of Defense in the Nuclear Age* (Cambridge, MA: Harvard University Press, 1960).

40. "M'Namara Agrees to Call It His War," *New York Times*, April 25, 1964.

41. David Halberstam's *The Best and the Brightest* (New York: Random House, 1972) was an important early critique of McNamara and the decision-making that led America into the war.

42. Mai Elliott, *RAND in Southeast Asia: A History of the Vietnam War Era* (Santa Monica, CA: RAND Corporation, 2010). See also Jennifer Kavanagh and Michael D. Rich, *Truth Decay: An Initial Exploration of the Diminishing Role of Facts and Analysis in American Public Life* (Santa Monica, CA: RAND Corporation, 2018).

43. Robert Jungk, *The Everyman Project: Resources for a Humane Future* (New York: Liveright, 1976), 13.

44. Robert Jungk, "Futuribles at Work," *Sunday Times*, April 18, 1965. See also Andersson, *Future of the World*, 74.

45. Jungk, *Everyman Project*, 50.

46. Jungk, *Everyman Project*, 17, 25.

47. Robert Jungk and Norbert Müllert, *Future Workshops: How to Create Desirable Futures* (1981; repr., London: Institute for Social Inventions, 1987).

48. Jungk, *Everyman Project*, 17.

49. Hugo Gernsback, "$300.00 Prize Contest," *Amazing Stories* 3, no. 1 (April 1928): 5.

50. H. G. Wells, *The Shape of Things to Come* (New York: Macmillan, 1933); and Nicolas P. Maffei, *Norman Bel Geddes: American Design Visionary* (London: Bloomsbury, 2018), 59.

51. Louis Kuslan, "New York S-F Convention," *Satellite* (fanzine) 2, no. 8 (August 1939): 4.

52. Damon Knight, *The Futurians* (New York: John Day, 1977). See also A. Brad Schwartz, *Broadcast Hysteria: Orson Welles's War of the Worlds and the Art of Fake News* (New York: Hill and Wang, 2016).

53. Jon Savage, *Teenage: The Creation of Youth Culture* (London: Penguin, 2007).

54. Susan Sontag, "The Imagination of Disaster," *Commentary* 40, no. 4 (October 1, 1965): 42.

55. M. Keith Booker, *Monsters, Mushroom Clouds, and the Cold War: American Science Fiction and the Roots of Postmodernism, 1946–1964* (Westport, CT: Greenwood Press, 2001), 50.

56. Booker, *Monsters, Mushroom Clouds*, 45–46.

57. Isaac Asimov, "Social Science Fiction," in *Modern Science Fiction: Its Meaning and Its Future*, ed. Reginald Bretnor (New York: Coward-McCann, 1953), 188–89.

58. Isaac Asimov, "Evidence," *Astounding Science Fiction* 38, no. 1 (September 1946): 121–40.

59. Judith Merril and Emily Pohl-Weary, *Better to Have Loved: The Life of Judith Merrill* (Toronto: Between the Lines, 2002), 42–43. Pohl-Weary is the granddaughter of Judith Merril and Frederik Pohl. See also Lisa Yaszek, "Stories 'That Only a Mother' Could Write: Midcentury Peace Activism, Maternalist Politics, and Judith Merril's Early Fiction," *NWSA [National Women's Studies Association] Journal* 16, no. 2 (Summer 2004): 70–97.

60. Yaszek, "Stories," 70–97.

61. Judith Merril, "Give the Girls a Break!" *TEMPER!* fanzine (1945), reprinted in Merril and Pohl-Weary, *Better to Have Loved*, 63, 65.

62. Ruth Milkman, *Gender at Work: The Dynamics of Job Segregation by Sex during World War II* (Champaign: University of Illinois Press, 1987).

63. Lisa Yaszek, *Galactic Suburbia: Recovering Women's Science Fiction* (Columbus: Ohio State University Press, 2008), 26.

64. Judith Merril, "What Do You Mean: Science? Fiction? Part Two," *Extrapolation* 8 (December 1966): 3.

65. Elizabeth Cummins, "Judith Merril: Scouting SF," *Extrapolation* 35 (1994): 5–14.

66. Kat Clay, "On Earth the Air Is Free: The Feminist Science Fiction of Judith Merril," in *Dangerous Visions and New Worlds: Radical Science Fiction, 1950 to 1985*, ed. Andrew Nette and Iain McIntyre (Oakland, CA: PM Press, 2021).

67. Kingley Amis, *New Maps of Hell: A Survey of Science Fiction* (New York: Harcourt, Brace., 1960), 83, 48, 60.

68. Colin Greenland, *The Entropy Exhibition: Michael Moorcock and the British "New Wave" in Science Fiction* (London: Routledge, 2013), 10.

69. The cover was designed by the American artist and dandy Richard Merkin, who, like Merril, had come to London to experience it in full swing (he is one of the less well known figures included in Peter Blake's famous record sleeve for *Sgt. Pepper's Lonely Hearts Club Band*). Richard Poynor describes Merkin's proto-postmodern

design as "one of those prescient imaginative leaps into the future that vaulted so far that it disappeared from the historical record." Richard Poynor, "Speculative Fiction, Speculative Design," *Design Observer*, June 28, 2011, online resource.

70. Judith Merril, *England Swings SF* (New York: Ace/Doubleday, 1968), 9–10.

71. Both pieces were originally published in the journal *Ambit*, where Ballard was an editor, in 1966 and 1967, respectively. The former is a tribute to Alfred Jarry's "The Passion of Christ Considered as an Uphill Bicycle Race" (1903).

72. Merril, *England Swings SF*, 103.

73. Quoted in Ian Thompson, "A Futurist with an Urge to Exorcise," *Independent*, September 21, 1991.

74. Isaac Asimov, "Foreword 1—The Second Revolution," in *Dangerous Visions: 33 Original Stories*, ed. Harlan Ellison (Garden City, NY: Doubleday, 1967), xii.

75. Quoted in Greenland, *Entropy Exhibition*, 69.

76. "A Dialogue: Samuel Delany and Joanna Russ on Science Fiction," *Callaloo* 22 (Autumn 1984): 31. Delany did publish a story in *New Worlds*, "Time Considered as a Helix of Precious Stones," in 1969, but said that this was "over editor [Michael] Moorcock's objections" as it could easily have been published in a more standard science fiction publication. "Unfortunately my story went on to win me my fourth Nebula Award," Delany recalled, "and so it managed to establish a spurious link between my name and the New Wave." Delany, interview by Takayuki Tatsumi, *Diacritics* 16, no. 3 (Autumn 1986): 40.

77. Delany's "Aye and Gomorrah" also won the Nebula Award, which had recently been introduced as a means of recognizing literary merit in the field.

78. Samuel Delany, *The Motion of Light in Water: Sex and Science Fiction Writing in the East Village* (New York: Arbor House, 1988), 52

79. Samuel R. Delany, interview by Robert F. Reid-Pharr, *Callaloo* 14, no. 2 (Spring, 1991): 526.

80. Darko Suvin, *Metamorphoses of Science Fiction: On the Poetics and History of a Literary Genre* (New Haven, CT: Yale University Press, 1979), 4.

81. Delany, afterword to Ellison, *Dangerous Visions*, 544.

82. Delany, *Light in Water*, 32.

83. "The Lessons of the Future," *New Worlds* 51, no. 173 (July 1967: 3.

84. Thomas Disch, *Camp Concentration* (London: Rupert Hart-Davis, 1968). Joe Haldeman, who had actually served in Vietnam, built his 1974 novel *The Forever War* around the conflict's most traumatic aspects, depicting futuristic Earth soldiers massacring innocent aliens, then returning home to a society in which they find no place for themselves. Haldeman, *The Forever War* (New York: St. Martins Press,

1974). See also Rjurik Davidson, "Imagining New Worlds Sci-Fi and the Vietnam War," in Nette and McIntyre, *Dangerous Visions*.

85. Frederik Pohl, "On Inventing Futures," *Galaxy Science Fiction* 26, no. 5 (June 1968): 7.

86. Pohl, "On Inventing Futures," 10.

87. Frederik Pohl, "Vietnam Revisited," *Galaxy Science Fiction* 27, no. 4 (November 1968): 4–9.

88. Delany, interview by Reid-Pharr, 526.

89. Ursula K. Le Guin, "Is Gender Necessary?" in *Aurora: Beyond Equality*, ed. Susan J. Anderson and Vonda McIntyre (Greenwich, CT: Fawcett Gold Medal, 1976), revised as Ursula K. Le Guin, "Is Gender Necessary: Redux?" in *The Language of the Night: Essays on Fantasy and Science Fiction* (New York: HarperCollins, 1992), 159.

90. Ursula K. Le Guin, "American SF and the Other," *Science Fiction Studies* 2, no. 3 (November 1975): 209–10.

91. Le Guin, "Is Gender Necessary: Redux?" 158.

92. Ursula K. Le Guin, notebook entry, in Amelia Z. Greene, "Variations on a Theme by William James: Varieties of Religious Experience in the Writing of Ursula K. Le Guin," *William James Studies* 13, no. 2 (Fall 2017): 222.

93. Carl Freedman, "Kubrick's *2001* and the Possibility of a Science-Fiction Cinema," *Science Fiction Studies* 25, no. 2 (July 1998): 303.

94. Renata Adler, "*2001* Is Up, Up and Away: Kubrick's Odyssey in Space Begins Run," *New York Times*, April 4, 1968.

95. Merril and Pohl-Weary, *Better to Have Loved*, 163.

96. Buckminster Fuller, liner notes for Arthur C. Clarke, *The Fountains of Paradise*, Caedmon Records TC 1606, 1979, 33⅓ rpm.

97. Naum Abramov, "Dialogue with Andrei Tarkovsky about Science-Fiction on the Screen" (1970–71), in *Tarkovsky Interviews*, ed. John Gianvito (Jackson: University of Mississippi Press, 2006), 162–65. On Tarkovsky's antipathy to Eisenstein's montage cinema, see Andrei Tarkvosky, *Sculpting in Time: Reflections on Cinema*, trans. Kitty Hunter-Blair (Austin: University of Texas Press, 1986), 118.

98. Le Guin borrowed both this insight and the essay's title from the anthropologist Elizabeth Fisher, who had proposed a "carrier bag theory of evolution" in her book *Women's Creation: Sexual Evolution and the Shaping of Society* (New York: McGraw Hill, 1975).

99. Ursula K. Le Guin, "The Carrier Bag Theory of Fiction" (1986), in *Dancing at the Edge of the World: Thoughts on Words, Women, Places* (New York: Grove Press, 1987), 174.

100. Ursula K. Le Guin, introduction to *The Left Hand of Darkness* (New York: Ace Books, 1976), 1–2.

101. Jerome Agel, ed., *The Making of Kubrick's 2001* (New York: Signet, 1970), 42. Agel also coordinated Marshall McLuhan's book *The Medium Is the Massage* and Buckminster Fuller's *I Seem to Be a Verb*.

102. Amis, *New Maps of Hell*, 83.

103. Daniel Bell, "The Year 2000—Trajectory of an Idea," in *Toward the Year 2000: Work in Progress*, ed. Daniel Bell (Boston: Houghton Mifflin, 1968), 7. Proceedings were also printed periodically in *Daedalus*, the journal of the American Academy, and Kahn published his own book based on the work of commission together with his colleague at the Hudson Institute, Anthony J. Wiener, and an introduction by Bell: *The Year 2000: A Framework for Speculation on the Next Thirty-Three Years* (New York: MacMillan, 1967).

104. Daniel Bell, "Preliminary Memorandum," in Bell, *Toward the Year 2000*, 17.

105. Bell, "The Year 2000," 4; and Daniel Bell, "Alternative Futures," in Bell, *Toward the Year 2000*, 31.

106. The term *paradigm shift* was introduced by Thomas Kuhn in *The Structure of Scientific Revolutions* (Chicago: University of Chicago Press, 1962). The theorist Patricia Waugh has noted the deep uncertainty implied by Kuhn's work, in which scientific development is seen as discontinuous and contingent, "a panorama of serial doom, of transient worlds and their phantom knowledges slipping successively into darkness." Patricia Waugh, "Paradigm," in *Future Theory: A Handbook to Critical Concepts*, ed. Waugh and Marc Botha (London: Bloomsbury, 2021), 102.

Chapter Five: PARTY

1. Arthur C. Clarke, "The Mind of the Machine," *Playboy*, December 1968, reprinted in *Report on Planet Three, and Other Speculations* (New York: Signet, 1972), 117.

2. Clarke, "Mind of the Machine," 122, 128. He put the same point more forcefully in an interview earlier in the year: "The goal of the future is full unemployment, so we can play. That's why we have to destroy the present politico-economic system." Interview with Arthur C. Clarke, *Los Angeles Free Press*, April 26, 1969, 15.

3. "The Lessons of the Future," *New Worlds* 51, no. 173 (July 1967): 3.

4. Eric W. Leaver and J. J. Brown, "Machines without Men," *Fortune*, November 1946, 192–204. See Amy Sue Bix, *Inventing Ourselves Out of Jobs: America's Debate over Technological Unemployment, 1929–1981* (Baltimore: Johns Hopkins University Press, 2000), 238, 247.

5. Roland Barthes, "Plastic," in *Mythologies*, trans. Annette Lavers (Paris: Editions de Seuil, 1957).

6. Alan Watts, Allen Ginsberg, Timothy Leary, and Gary Snyder, "The Houseboat Summit: Changes," *San Francisco Oracle* 1, no. 7 (1967): 10.

7. Quoted in Peter Braunstein and Michael William Doyle, "Historicizing the American Counterculture of the 1960s and 1970s," in *Imagine Nation: The American Counterculture of the 1960s and 1970s* (New York: Routledge, 2002); and Free [Abbie Hoffman], "April 11, 2001," in *Revolution for the Hell of It* (New York: Dial Press, 1968), 86.

8. Quoted in Martin A. Lee and Bruce Shlain, *Acid Dreams: The Complete Social History of LSD* (New York: Grove Press, 1985), 130.

9. Lewis Yablonsky, *The Hippie Trip* (New York: Pegasus, 1968), 36.

10. Yablonsky, *The Hippie Trip*, 26.

11. "2000 A.D. Symposium: Alan Watts, Herman Kahn and Carl Rogers," *San Francisco Oracle* 1, no. 12 (1968): 9.

12. Hunter S. Thompson, "The 'Hashbury' Is the Capital of the Hippies," *New York Times Magazine*, May 14, 1967.

13. "Trip without a Ticket," flyer, 1966–67, reprinted in *The Digger Papers*, August 1968, online source; "Don't Nod!" *Venture*, August 1967, Digger Archives, online source; and "Diggers Don't Just Dig Money," *Palm Springs Desert Sun*, March 20, 1967.

14. Armand Barotti, "Fascist Ideology of the Self: Mailer, Rubin and Hoffman," *Literature and Ideology* 6 (1970), 59.

15. Alan Watts, Herman Kahn, and Carl Rogers, "2000 A.D. Symposium," *Oracle* 12 (February 1968), 27. This was the last issue of the paper; editor Allen Cohen has commented, "It was symptomatic of our failing energy and vision that we used such a canned feature." Allen Cohen, "Notes on the San Francisco *Oracle*," in Tony Bove, "Haight-Ashbury in the Sixties: Allen Cohen and the S.F. Oracle," *Rockument* (blog), online source.

16. Louis Menand, "Acid Redux," *New Yorker*, June 18, 2006.

17. Watts, Ginsberg, Leary, and Snyder, "Houseboat Summit," 15.

18. Watts, Ginsberg, Leary, and Snyder, "Houseboat Summit," 15.

19. Peter Cohon [Peter Coyote], interviewed in Leonard Wolf, ed., *Voices from the Love Generation* (Boston: Little, Brown, 1968), 125–26.

20. Judson Jerome, *Families of Eden: Communes and the New Anarchism* (New York: Seabury Press, 1974).

21. Thompson, "The 'Hashbury,' " 19.

22. Watts, Ginsberg, Leary, and Snyder, "Houseboat Summit," 31.

23. Theodore Roszak, *The Making of a Counterculture: Reflections on the Technocratic Society and Its Youthful Opposition* (New York: Doubleday, 1969), 5, 35.

24. Charles Reich, *The Greening of America* (New York: Random House, 1970), 73, 225. In his analysis of the midcentury generation, Reich was adapting arguments first put forward in David Riesman, *The Lonely Crowd: A Study of the Changing American Character* (New Haven, CT: Yale University Press, 1950); and William H. Whyte Jr., *The Organization Man* (New York: Simon & Schuster, 1956).

25. Lew Welch, "Final City," *San Francisco Oracle* 1, no. 12 (1968): 24.

26. Nat Hentoff, "We Look at Our Parents and . . . ," *New York Times Magazine*, April 21, 1968, 19.

27. Joan Didion, "Slouching toward Bethlehem," *Saturday Evening Post*, September 23, 1967.

28. Tom Wolfe, *The Electric Kool-Aid Acid Test* (New York: Bantam Books, 1968), 64.

29. Gavin Arthur, "The Aquarian Age," *San Francisco Oracle* 1, no. 6 (1967): 6, 20. Arthur, the grandson of President Chester Arthur and author of *The Circle of Sex* (1966), was also a pioneering figure in gay rights activism.

30. Gayla [Rosalind Sharpe Wall], "Aquarian Age Symbols," *San Francisco Oracle* 1, no. 6 (1967): 33.

31. *The New Tarot: Tarot for the Aquarian Age* (Kentfield, CA: Western Star Press, 1970).

32. Wolfe, *Electric Kool-Aid Acid Test*, 11.

33. Helen Swick Perry, *The Human Be-In* (New York: Basic Books, 1970), 75, 85.

34. Danny Goldberg, "All the Human Be-In Was Saying 50 Years Ago, Was Give Peace a Chance," *Nation*, January 13, 2017, online source.

35. Swick Perry, *The Human Be-In*, 4.

36. Allen Cohen, in *Oracle Rising: The Recreation of the Original Haight Ashbury Hippie Psychedelic Underground Newspaper*, dir. Claire Burch, [1994?], partially reproduced as "'The San Francisco Oracle'— documentary film—2000?," Youtube, 24:33, Cohen quote at 14:56, online source.

37. "Highs and Lows of Hippiedom," *Time* 90, no. 1 (July 7, 1967): 24.

38. R. Buckminster Fuller, "Vertical Is to Live—Horizontal Is to Die," *American Scholar* 39, no. 1 (Winter 1969–70): 47.

39. Martin A. Lee and Bruce Shlain, *The Complete Social History of LSD: The CIA, The Sixties, and Beyond* (New York: Grove Press, 1985).

40. Alan Watts, *Joyous Cosmology: Adventures in the Chemistry of Consciousness* (New York: Vintage Books, 1962), 12.

41. Timothy Leary, Richard Alpert, and Ralph Metzner, "Rationale of the Mexican Psychedelic Training Center," in *Utopiates: The Use and Users of LSD-25*, ed. Richard Blum (New York: Atherton Press, 1964), 182.

42. Huxley had taken his title, in turn, from a line of William Blake's: "If the doors of perception were cleansed / everything will appear to man as it is, infinite."

43. Aldous Huxley, *The Doors of Perception* (London: Chatto & Windus, 1954), 20.

44. Gerald Heard, "Can This Drug Enlarge Man's Mind?" *Psychedelic Review* 1, no. 1 (June 1963): 12.

45. Watts, *Joyous Cosmology*, 19, 32. See also Jay Stevens, *Storming Heaven: LSD and the American Dream* (New York: Perennial Library, 1988), 57.

46. William Braden, *The Private Sea: LSD and the Search for God* (Chicago: Quadrangle Books, 1967), 32. Braden also wrote a study of the counterculture, *The Age of Aquarius: Technology and the Cultural Revolution* (Chicago: Quadrangle Books, 1970).

47. "Playboy Interview: Timothy Leary," *Playboy* 13, no. 9 (September 1966); and Frank H. Gawin, "Pharmacologic Enhancement of the Erotic: Implications of an Expanded Definition of Aphrodisiacs," *Journal of Sex Research* 14, no. 2 (May 1978): 107–17. Oral contraceptives were first approved by the Food and Drug Administration in 1960.

48. Lenore Kandel, interviewed in Wolf, *Voices from the Love Generation*, 32.

49. Peter Coyote, *Sleeping Where I Fall*, 117.

50. Lenore Kandel, "With Love," *San Francisco Oracle* 1, no. 4 (1966): 3.

51. Lenore Kandel, *Word Alchemy* (New York: Grove Press, 1967), viii.

52. Kathryn Schultz, *Being Wrong: Adventures in the Margin of Error* (London: Portobello Books, 2010), 37.

53. Dominick Cavallo, *A Fiction of the Past: The Sixties in American History* (New York: St. Martin's Press, 1999), 140.

54. Cohon, interview, 139.

55. Pam Hanna, "Infinite Points of Time: Morningstar Chronicles, Part I," Digger Archives, online source.

56. Timothy Leary and Richard Alpert, "The Politics of Consciousness Expansion," *Harvard Review* 1, no. 4 (Summer 1963): 33.

57. Joseph J. Downing, "Zihuatanejo: An Experiment in Transpersonative Living," in Blum, *Utopiates*, 150, 153.

58. Downing, "Zihuatanejo," 150, 153. Downing, an editor at the *Psychedelic Review*, can be seen working with an LSD subject in the television documentary *Assignment Four*, KRON-TV, San Francisco, 1964.

59. Downing, "Zihuatanejo," 165.

60. Peter Coyote, "Coyote Howl: The Sixties Counterculture as Agent of Change," lecture at Booksmith, San Francisco, August 20, 2009. See also Coyote's memoirs *Sleeping Where I Fall* (Berkeley, CA: Counterpoint Press, 1998) and *The Rainman's Third Cure: An Irregular Education* (New York: Penguin Random House, 2015).

61. Thomas Constantine Maroukis, *The Peyote Road: Religious Freedom and the Native American Church* (Norman: University of Oklahoma Press, 2010), 60.

62. Paul Chaat Smith, *Everything You Know About Indians Is Wrong* (Minneapolis: University of Minnesota Press, 2009), 172–73.

63. Mabel Dodge Luhan, *Edge of Taos Desert: An Escape to Reality* (New York: Harcourt, Brace, 1937), 310.

64. Alice Marriott, "The Open Door," *New Yorker*, September 17, 1954; and R. G. Wasson, "Seeking the Magic Mushroom," *Life* 49, no. 19 (May 13, 1957): 100–102, 109–20.

65. Mike Jay, *Mescaline: A Global History of the First Psychedelic* (New Haven, CT: Yale University Press, 2019).

66. Mark Rozzo, *Everybody Thought We Were Crazy: Dennis Hopper, Brooke Hayward, and 1960s Los Angeles* (New York: HarperCollins, 2022).

67. Quoted in Barry H. Leeds, *Ken Kesey* (New York: Unger, 1981), 21.

68. Ken Kesey, "Who Flew Over What?" in *Kesey's Garage Sale* (New York: Viking Press, 1973), 14. See also Kimberly R. Connor, "Reading from the Heart Out: Chief Bromden through Indigenous Eyes," *Concentric* 37, no. 1 (March 2011): 231–53.

69. Peter Coyote, "The Freefall Chronicles: Playing for Keeps," Digger Archives, online source.

70. Watts, Ginsberg, Leary, and Snyder, "Houseboat Summit," 13.

71. Ward Churchill, "Spiritual Hucksterism: The Rise of the Plastic Medicine Men," *Cultural Survival*, May 7, 2010, online source. See also Richard Ogar, "The Earth around You in Your Storehouse: Interview with Sun Bear," *Berkeley Barb*, April 28, 1967, 8–10.

72. Sherry L. Smith, *Hippies, Indians and the Fight for Red Power* (Oxford: Oxford University Press, 2012).

73. Wallace "Mad Bear" Anderson, quoted in Stan Steiner, *The New Indians* (New York: Harper & Row, 1968), 282.

74. Smith, *Hippies, Indians*, 117.

75. Paul R. McKenzie-Jones, *Clyde Warrior: Tradition, Community and Red Power* (Norman: University of Oklahoma Press, 2015), 46.

76. Clyde Warrior, "Which One Are You? Five Types of Young Indians," *ABC: Americans Before Columbus* 2, no. 4 (December 1964): 3.

77. Robert J. Kett, *Prospects Beyond Futures: Counterculture White Meets Red Power* (Montreal: Canadian Centre for Architecture, 2020).

78. Paul Chaat Smith and Robert Allen Warrior, *Like a Hurricane: The Indian Movement from Alcatraz to Wounded Knee* (New York: W. W. Norton, 1996), 96.

79. Smith and Warrior, 230.

80. Warrior, "Which One Are You?" 3.

81. Vine DeLoria Jr., *Custer Died for Your Sins: An Indian Manifesto* (New York: MacMillan, 1969), 232.

82. Quoted in Stan Steiner, *The New Indians* (New York: Harper & Row, 1968).

83. Collier, *On the Gleaming Way* (1949; Chicago: Sage Books/Swallow Press, 1962), 15.

84. N. Scott Momaday, "The Morality of Indian Hating," *Ramparts* 3, no. 1 (Summer 1964): 30.

85. Patti Jo King, "Time Capsule Hopes to Capture Living History," *Indian Country Today* 26, no. 11 (August 2006): A7.

86. Joseph Tirella, *Tomorrow-Land: The 1964–65 World's Fair and the Transformation of America* (Guilford, CT: Lyons Press, 2014), 197–99.

87. James Farmer, *Freedom—When?* (New York: Random House, 1965), x.

88. "CORE Chief among Scores Arrested on Grounds," *New York Times*, April 23, 1964.

89. Farmer, *Freedom*, 197.

90. Fannie Lou Hamer, *To Praise Our Bridges: An Autobiography* (Jackson, MS: KIPCO, 1967), 15.

91. Floyd McKissick, "The Way to a Black Ideology," *Black Scholar* 1, no. 2 (December 1969): 15.

92. Keisha N. Blain, *Until I Am Free: Fannie Lou Hamer's Enduring Message to America* (Boston: Beacon Press, 2021), 121–23; and Raymond L. Hall, *Black Separatism in the United States* (Hanover, NH: Dartmouth College/University Press of New England, 1978).

93. As always, he kept his true opinions, in all their ugliness, behind closed doors, as when he told his chief of staff, "The whole problem is really the Blacks. The key is to devise a system that recognizes this while not appearing to." Quoted in "Haldeman Diary Shows Nixon Was Wary of Blacks and Jews," *New York Times*, May 18, 1994.

94. Katie Mingle, producer, *99% Invisible* podcast, episode 207, "Soul City," April 5, 2016, online source.

95. Thomas Healy, *Soul City: Race, Equality, and the Lost Dream of an American Utopia* (New York: Metropolitan Books/Henry Holt, 2021).

96. John Szwed, *Space Is the Place: The Life and Times of Sun Ra* (New York: Da Capo, 1998), 316.

97. Dennis McNally, *A Long Strange Trip: The Inside History of the Grateful Dead* (New York: Broadway Books, 2002), 538.

98. John Coney, dir., *Space Is the Place*, written by Sun Ra and Joshua Smith, 1972.

99. Szwed, *Space Is the Place*, 29–30.

100. Robert Mugge, dir., *Sun Ra: A Joyful Noise*, 1980.

101. LeRoi Jones (later Amiri Baraka), *Blues People* (New York: William Morrow, 1963), 181. Baraka would collaborate with Sun Ra on a production of his play *A Black Mass* in 1968.

102. Paul Youngquist, *A Pure Solar World* (Austin: University of Texas Press, 2016), 107.

103. "Language of the Gods" and "Jesus Said, Let the Negro Bury the Negro," reproduced in John Corbett, *The Wisdom of Sun Ra: Sun Ra's Polemical Broadsheets and Street Corner Leaflets* (Chicago: WhiteWalls, 2006), 10, 9.

104. Sun Ra, interview by John and Peter Hinds, October 13, 1984, *Sun Ra Research* 19 (October 1998): 4.

105. Stewart Brand, *Whole Earth Discipline: An Ecopragmatist Manifesto* (New York: Viking, 2009), 214.

106. See Ekow Eshun, *Into the Black Fantastic* (London: Hayward Gallery, 2022); Mark Dery, "Afrofuturism Reloaded: 15 Theses in 15 Minutes," *Fabrikzeitung*, February 1, 2016; and Ytasha L. Womack, *Afrofuturism: The World of Black Sci-Fi and Fantasy Culture* (Chicago: Lawrence Hill Books, 2013).

107. Greg Tate, "Kalahari Hopscotch, or Notes toward a Twenty-Volume Afrocentric Futurist Manifesto," in *Flyboy 2: The Greg Tate Reader* (Durham, NC: Duke University Press, 2016), 334.

108. See Lisa Corrigan, *Black Feelings: Race and Affect in the Long Sixties* (Jackson: University Press of Mississippi, 2020).

109. Tricia Rose, interview by Mark Dery, "Black to the Future: Interviews with Samuel R. Delany, Greg Tate, and Tricia Rose," in *Flame Wars: the Discourse of Cyberculture*, ed. Dery (Durham, NC: Duke University Press, 1994). Dery, who is white, has told me that "the reason to sit down with three leading Black intellectuals was also to serve as an isometric object that they could push against intellectually (which Delany in particular did do), not as a straw man for white tone-deafness, but as a proxy for white readers, woefully but not willfully ignorant." Author's interview with Mark Dery, February 22, 2022.

110. Kodwo Eshun, "Further Considerations of Afrofuturism," *New Centennial Review* 3, no. 2 (2003): 287–88.

111. Rick Theis, interview with Sun Ra, 1984, in Youngquist, *Pure Solar World*, 107; and Mugge, *Sun Ra: A Joyful Noise*.

112. John Corbett, *Extended Play: Sounding Off from John Cage to Dr. Funkenstein* (Durham, NC: Duke University Press, 1994), 8.

113. George Clinton, "The Hair of the Dog," interview by John Corbett, in Corbett, *Extended Play*, 290.

114. Dery, "Black to the Future," 182

115. George Clinton, "The Atomic Dog," interview by Greg Tate with Bob Wisdom, in Tate, *Flyboy in the Buttermilk: Essays on Contemporary America* (New York: Simon & Schuster, 1992).

116. Greg Tate, "Yo! Hermeneutics!" in Tate, *Flyboy in the Buttermilk*, 154.

117. Scott Hacker, "Can You Get to That? The Cosmology of P-Funk," *Stuck between Stations*, January 11, 2011, online source.

118. Jorge La Torre, quoted in Tim Lawrence, *Love Saves the Day: A History of American Dance Music Culture, 1970–1979* (Durham, NC: Duke University Press, 2003), 27.

119. Mancuso was using Timothy Leary, Ralph Metzner, and Richard Alpert's *The Psychedelic Experience: A Manual Based on the Tibetan Book of the Dead* (1964), which is structured according to successive "bardos," stages of heavenly transcendence.

120. Lawrence, *Love Saves the Day*, 24.

121. The last glory days of New York's ball scene are documented in Jennie Livingston, dir., *Paris Is Burning*, 1990.

122. Andrew Holleran, *Dancer from the Dance* (New York: William Morrow, 1978), 40.

123. Michael Gomes, quoted in Lawrence, *Love Saves the Day*, 53.

124. Turner was covering a 1958 chart by Ray Charles. See Alice Echols, "Shaky Ground: Popular Music in the Disco Years," in *Shaky Ground: The '60s and Its Aftershocks* (New York: Columbia University Press, 2002), 180–81.

125. Tan Lin, "Disco as Operating System, Part One," *Criticism* 50, no. 1 (Winter 2008): 87.

126. The image was later used as the cover for Jones's 1985 greatest-hits album *Island Life*, the title referring to both her Caribbean origins and her relationship with Island Records.

127. The cover of Monaé's 2010 album *The ArchAndroid* bears an image of the singer in neo-Egyptian garb, intended as an explicit tribute to Sun Ra. See John Calvert, "Black Sky Thinking: Janelle Monáe," *Quietus*, September 2, 2010.

Chapter Six: FLOOD

1. Jerry Blumenthal, Sheppard Ferguson, James Leahy, and Alan Rettig, dirs., *Shulie*, 1967.

2. Elisabeth Subrin, "Trashing Shulie: Remnants from Some Abandoned Feminist History," in *F Is for Phony: Fake Documentary and Truth's Undoing*, ed. Alex Juhasz and Jesse Lerner (Minneapolis: University of Minnesota Press, 2006).

3. Alice Echols, *Daring To Be Bad: Radical Feminism in America, 1967–1975* (Minneapolis: University of Minnesota Press, 1989), 21.

4. The term *consciousness-raising* was coined by Kathie Sarachild (born Kathie Amatniek), another leader of the New York Radical Women, who also invented the slogan "Sisterhood is powerful." See Breanne Fahs, *Firebrand Feminism: The Radical Lives of Ti-Grace Atkinson, Kathie Sarachild, Roxanne Dunbar-Ortiz, and Dana Densmore* (Seattle: University of Washington Press, 2018).

5. Shulamith Firestone, ed., "When Women Rap about Sex," in *Notes from the First Year*, ed. Firestone and Anne Koedt (New York: New York Radical Women, 1968), 11.

6. Shulamith Firestone, "Love," in *Notes from the Second Year*, ed. Firestone and Anne Koedt (New York: New York Radical Women, 1970), 16–22, 25–27.

7. Firestone and her coeditor Anne Koedt seem to have been the first to employ this phrase, using it as the title for an essay by Carol Hanisch, "The Personal Is Political," in Firestone and Koedt, *Notes from the Second Year*, 76–78.

8. Shulamith Firestone, *The Dialectic of Sex* (New York: William Morrow, 1970), 1–3.

9. Ti-Grace Atkinson, foreword to *Amazon Odyssey* (New York: Links Books, 1974), xxii.

10. The event was held in response to Mailer's essay "The Prisoner of Sex," published in *Harper's Magazine*, March 1971. He had attacked feminists for trying to bring about a future in which "virility had become a quality blank as plastic, an abstract power over the employment of techniques." See D. A. Pennebaker and Chris Hegedus, dirs., *Town Bloody Hall*, 1979.

11. Jill Johnston, *Lesbian Nation: The Feminist Solution* (New York: Simon & Schuster, 1973), 258.

12. Donna Haraway, "A Cyborg Manifesto: Science, Technology, and Socialist-Feminism in the Late Twentieth Century," *Socialist Review*, no. 80 (1985): 65–108, reprinted in

Donna Haraway, *Simians, Cyborgs and Women: The Reinvention of Nature* (London: Routledge, 1990), 149–82.

13. Caroline Bassett, "Impossible, Admirable, Androgyne: Firestone, Technology, and Utopia," in *Further Adventures of "The Dialectic of Sex": Critical Essays on Shulamith Firestone*, ed. Mandy Merck and Stella Sanford (New York: Palgrave Macmillan, 2010), 85–110; and Madeline Lane-McKinley, "The Dialectic of Sex, after the Post-1960s," *Cultural Politics* 15, no. 3 (2019): 331–42.

14. Freeman quoted in Alice Echols, "Totally Ready to Go: Shulamith Firestone and *The Dialectic of Sex*," in *Shaky Ground: The '60s and Its Aftershocks* (New York: Columbia University Press, 2002), 103; and Jane Gebhard, *The Dinner Party: Judy Chicago and the Power of Popular Feminism, 1970–2007* (Athens: University of Georgia Press, 2013), 45.

15. Shulamith Firestone, *Airless Spaces* (Los Angeles: Semiotext[e], 1998), 61.

16. Susan Faludi, "Death of a Revolutionary," *New Yorker*, April 15, 2013, 126.

17. Echols, *Daring to Be Bad*, 11.

18. Betsy Warrior, "Man as an Obsolete Life Form," in *Women's Liberation: Blueprint for the Future* (New York: Ace Books, 1970), 45–47. See also Greta Rensenbrink, "Parthenogenesis and Lesbian Separatism," *Journal of the History of Sexuality* 19, no. 2 (May 2010): 288–316.

19. Alice Echols, "Nothing Distant about It: Women's Liberation and Sixties Radicalism," in Echols, *Shaky Ground*, 87.

20. Firestone, *Dialectic of Sex*, 233. See also Echols, "Nothing Distant about It," 88.

21. Firestone, *Dialectic of Sex*, 274.

22. Thomas Robertson, *Malthusian Moment: Global Population Growth and the Birth of American Environmentalism* (New Brunswick, NJ: Rutgers University Press, 2012).

23. Paul [and Anne] Ehrlich, *The Population Bomb* (New York: Ballantine Books, 1968), xi, 18, 8 (emphasis in the original).

24. Ehrlich, *Population Bomb*, 151.

25. [Thomas Malthus], *An Essay on the Principle of Population* (London: J. Johnson, 1798).

26. Jay W. Forrester, *Urban Dynamics* (Cambridge, MA: MIT Press, 1969), 115, 129.

27. Jay W. Forrester, interview, January 26, 2009, Infinite MIT, https://infinite.mit .edu/video/jay-forrester-sm-%E2%80%9945-part-1.

28. Hasan Ozbeckhan, *The Predicament of Mankind: Quest for Structured Responses to Growing Worldwide Complexities and Uncertainties; A Proposal* (Rome: Club of Rome, 1970), 9–10.

29. Jay W. Forrester, *World Dynamics* (Cambridge, MA: Wright-Allen Press, 1971).

30. Donella H. Meadows, Dennis L. Meadows, Jørgen Randers, and William W. Behrens III, *The Limits to Growth: A Report for the Club of Rome's Project on the Predicament of Mankind* (New York: Universe Books, 1972), 142.

31. Meadows, Meadows, Randers, and Behrens, *Limits to Growth*, 142.

32. Meadows, Meadows, Randers, and Behrens, *Limits to Growth*, 134.

33. Herman E. Daly, ed., *Toward a Steady-State Economy* (San Francisco: W.H. Freeman, 1973).

34. Edward Goldsmith, *Blueprint for Survival* (Boston: Houghton Mifflin, 1972), 11.

35. Paul Ehrlich, interview, in *On Growth*, ed. Willem Oltmens (New York: Capricorn Books, 1974), 79.

36. Quoted in Mauricio Schoijet, "Limits to Growth and the Rise of Catastrophism," *Environmental History* 4, no. 4 (October 1999): 520.

37. Quoted in Robert Gillette, "The Limits to Growth: Hard Sell for a Computer View of Doomsday," *Science* 175, no. 4026 (March 10, 1972): 1092.

38. John Maddox, *The Doomsday Syndrome: An Attack on Pessimism* (New York: McGraw-Hill, 1972), 284, 23–24.

39. Peter Passell, Marc Roberts, and Leonard Ross, "The Limits to Growth," *New York Times*, April 2, 1972; and W. Patrick McCray, *The Visioneers: How a Group of Elite Scientists Pursued Space Colonies, Nanotechnologies, and a Limitless Future* (Princeton, NJ: Princeton University Press, 2012), 35.

40. Christopher Freeman, "Malthus with a Computer," in *Models of Doom: A Critique of the Limits to Growth*, ed. H. S. D. Cole, Christopher Freedman, Marie Jahoda, and Keith Pavitt (New York: Universe Books, 1973), 8.

41. Peter Thiel, *Zero to One: Notes on Startups, or How to Build the Future*, with Blake Masters (New York: Random House, 2014), 194.

42. Mary Harrington, "Peter Thiel on the Dangers of Progress," *UnHerd*, December 30, 2022, online source.

43. Donella Meadows, Dennis Meadows, and Jørgen Randers, *Limits to Growth: The Thirty-Year Update* (White River Junction, VT: Chelsea Green, 2002); and Ugo Bard and Carlos Alvarez Pereira, *Limits and Beyond* (London: Exapt Press, 2022).

44. Donella Matthews, "Chicken Little, Cassandra and the Real Wolf: So Many Ways to Think About the Future," *Whole Earth* 96 (Spring 1999): 111.

45. McCray, *Visioneers*, 38.

46. Barbara Ward and René Dubois, *Only One Earth: The Care and Maintenance of a Small Planet* (New York: W. W. Norton, 1972), 214.

47. Robert Jungk, interview, in Oltmens, *On Growth*, 118.

48. Daniel Bell, *The Coming of Post-Industrial Society: A Venture in Social Forecasting* (New York: Basic Books, 1973), 464, 21, 14.

49. Lewis Mumford, *The Myth of the Machine, II: The Pentagon of Power* (New York: Harcourt, Brace, Jovanovich, 1970), 172, 72, 180.

50. Alvin [and Heidi] Toffler, *Future Shock* (New York: Bantam Books, 1970).

51. Paul Ehrlich's "Eco-Disaster!" was originally published in *Ramparts* (September 1969), and reprinted in Alvin Toffler, *The Futurists* (New York: Random House, 1972).

52. John Markoff, *What the Dormouse Said: How the Sixties Counterculture Shaped the Personal Computer Industry* (New York: Penguin, 2005), xxii.

53. Markoff, 6.

54. Vannevar Bush, "As We May Think," *Atlantic* 176, no. 1 (July 1945): 101–8. Engelbart read a condensed version that appeared in *Life,* September 10, 1945, 112–24.

55. Quoted in Thierry Bardini, *Bootstrapping: Douglas Engelbart, Coevolution, and the Origins of Personal Computing* (Stanford, CA: Stanford University Press, 2000), 16.

56. Doug Engelbart, "Microelectronics and the Art of Similitude," in *1960 IEEE International Solid-State Circuits Conference, Digest of Technical Papers* (Philadelphia: IEEE, 1960), 76.

57. Douglas Engelbart, *Augmenting the Human Intellect: A Conceptual Framework* (Menlo Park, CA: Stanford Research Institute, 1962).

58. Markoff, *What the Dormouse Said*, 174.

59. Fred Turner, *From Counterculture to Cyberculture*: *Stewart Brand, the Whole Earth Network, and the Rise of Digital Utopianism* (Chicago: University of Chicago Press, 2006).

60. Markoff, *What the Dormouse Said*, 56.

61. John Markoff, *Machines of Loving Grace: The Quest for Common Ground between Humans and Robots* (New York: HarperCollins, 2015), 62.

62. Bardini, *Bootstrapping*, 167.

63. Stewart Brand had created a spinoff called the *CoEvolution Quarterly* in 1974, mainly devoted to exploring the symbiosis between people and computers. He later commented, "As it turned out, psychedelic drugs, communes and Buckminster Fuller domes were a dead end, but computers were an avenue to realms beyond our dreams." Mark Dery, *Escape Velocity: Cyberculture at the End of the Century* (New York: Grove Press, 1996), 27.

64. Bardini, *Bootstrapping*, 174.

65. Walter Isaacson, *Steve Jobs* (New York: Simon & Schuster, 2011), 41.

66. Steve Wozniak, "Steve Wozniak Tells Us Why He's Never Done LSD," *Business Insider*, July 17, 2012, online source.

67. Isaacson, *Steve Jobs*, 115.

68. The ad agency Chiat/Day had originally developed the 1984 concept for an Apple II print advertisement, then adapted it for television for the introduction of the Macintosh.

69. Isaacson, *Steve Jobs*, 165.

70. See, for example, Giuliana Bruno, "Ramble City: Postmodernism and *Blade Runner*," *October* 41 (Summer 1987): 61–74; and Will Brooker, ed., *The Blade Runner Experience: The Legacy of a Science Fiction Classic* (New York: Columbia University Press, 2006).

71. Neville Wakefield, *Postmodernism: The Twilight of the Real* (London: Pluto Press, 1990), 118.

72. The term was initially popularized by architectural theorist Charles Jencks in *The Language of Post-Modern Architecture* (London: Academy Editions, 1977). See also Perry Anderson, *The Origins of Postmodernity* (London: Verso, 1998); and Glenn Adamson and Jane Pavitt, eds., *Postmodernism: Style and Subversion, 1970 to 1990* (London: V&A, 2011).

73. Jean Baudrillard, *Simulacra and Simulation* (1981), trans. Sheila Faria Glaser (Ann Arbor: University of Michigan Press, 1994), 1.

74. Baudrillard, *Simulacra and Simulation*, 87.

75. Baudrillard, *Simulacra and Simulation*, 12. Here Baudrillard adapts Michel Foucault's conception of the "heterotopia," a place where norms of behavior are suspended in such a way as to confirm the legitimacy that lies all around it. Foucault, "Of Other Spaces: Utopias and Heterotopias" (1967), trans. Jay Miskowiec, *Diacritics* 16, no. 1 (Spring 1986): 22–27. See also Umberto Eco, *Travels in Hyperreality*, trans. William Weaver (New York: Harcourt Brace Jovanovich, 1986).

76. Thomas Dyja, *New York, New York, New York* (New York: Simon & Schuster, 2021), 6.

77. *Keith Haring: Future Primeval* (New York: Abbeville Press, 1990), 11.

78. *Keith Haring Journals* (New York: Viking, 1996), 88–89.

79. Keith Haring, artist's statement, *Flash Art* 116 (March 1984): 24.

80. Baudrillard, *Simulacra and Simulation*, 123.

81. "Talking Heads," *Spin*, June 1985, 39.

82. Dick Hebdige, *Hiding in the Light: On Images and Things* (London: Routledge/Comedia, 1988), 239.

83. Jean-François Lyotard, *The Postmodern Condition: A Report on Knowledge* (1979), trans. Geoff Bennington and Brian Massumi (Minneapolis: University of Minnesota Press, 1984), 38.

84. Alex Ross, *The Rest Is Noise: Listening to the Twentieth Century* (New York: Picador, 2007), 315.

85. Devon Powers, *On Trend: The Business of Forecasting the Future* (Champaign-Urbana: University of Illinois Press, 2019), 56.

86. Faith Popcorn, *The Popcorn Report* (New York: Doubleday, 1991).

87. John Naisbitt [and Patricia Aburdene], *Megatrends: Ten New Directions Transforming Our Lives* (New York: Warner Books, 2002). Aburdene was credited as Naisbitt's coauthor in several sequels, including *Megatrends 2000: Ten New Directions for the 1990s* (New York: Avon Books, 1990); and *Megatrends for Women* (New York: Villard Books, 1992).

88. Nicholas Wade, "Not a Clue," *New York Times*, March 1, 1998.

89. William Sherden, *The Fortune Sellers: The Big Business of Buying and Selling Predictions* (New York: John Wiley & Sons, 1998), 196–97.

90. Theodore Roszak, *The Cult of Information* (Berkeley: University of California Press, 1986), 163.

91. Sherden, *Fortune Sellers*, 196–97.

92. Sherden, *Fortune Sellers*, 259.

93. Sherden, *Fortune Sellers*, 216.

94. Bell, *Post-Industrial Society*, 97–98.

95. Ulrich Beck, *Risk Society: Towards a New Modernity* (1986), trans. Mark Ritter (London: Sage, 1992), 13.

96. Beck, *Risk Society*, 56. See also Giddens and Scott Lash, *Reflexive Modernization: Politics, Tradition and Aesthetics in the Modern Social Order* (Stanford, CA: Stanford University Press, 1994).

97. Robert A. Kagan, *Adversarial Legalism: The American Way of Law* (Cambridge, MA: Harvard University Press, 2001).

98. François Ewald, "The Return of Descartes's Malicious Demon: An Outline of a Philosophy of Precaution," trans. Stephen Utz, in Tom Baker and Jonathan Simon, eds, *Embracing Risk: The Changing Culture of Insurance and Responsibility* (Chicago: University of Chicago Press, 2002), 291–93.

99. Beck, *Risk Society*, 29.

100. Quoted in Carolyn S. Davidson, "The Science Fiction of Octavia Butler," *Sagala* 2, no. 1 (1981): 35.

101. Gerry Canavan, *Octavia E. Butler* (Champaign-Urbana: University of Illinois Press, 2016), 17.

102. Octavia E. Butler, "A Few Rules for Predicting the Future," *Essence*, May 2000, 31.

103. Interview with Gregory Jerome Hampton, *Changing Bodies in the Fiction of Octavia Butler: Slaves, Aliens, and Vampires* (Plymouth, UK: Lexington Books, 2014), 135.

104. Stefanie K. Dunning, "Learn or Die: Survivalism and Anarchy in Octavia Butler's *Parable of the Sower*," in *Human Contradictions in Octavia E. Butler's Work*, ed. Martin Japtok and Jerry Rafiki Jenkins (New York: Palgrave Macmillan, 2020), 183.

105. Interview with Charles Brown, "Octavia E. Butler: Persistence," *Locus* 21, no. 10 (October 1988), reprinted in Consuela Francis, ed., *Conversations with Octavia Butler* (Jackson: University Press of Mississippi, 2000), 288.

106. Butler, "Rules for Predicting the Future," 31.

107. Randall Kenan, interview, *Callaloo* 14, no. 2 (Spring, 1991): 504.

Conclusion

1. Press release for *Manifest Destiny*, Library Street Collective, Detroit, 2019.

2. Wendell Berry, *The Art of Loading Brush: New Agrarian Writings* (Berkeley, CA: Counterpoint, 2017), 8–9, 101–2.

3. Berry, *Art of Loading Brush*, 61.

4. Vernor Vinge, "Technological Singularity," *Whole Earth Review* (Winter 1993): 89. See also John Markoff, *Machines of Loving Grace: The Quest for Common Ground between Humans and Robots* (New York: HarperCollins, 2015).

5. In Fredric Brown's two-page sci-fi story "Answer" (1955), "all the monster computing machines of all the populated planets of the universe" are networked together into one vast "supercalculator." When asked, "Is there a God?" it replies, "Yes, *now* there is," and destroys its own off switch.

6. Arthur C. Clarke, *Profiles of the Future* (1962; repr., New York: Harper & Row, 1972), 235.

7. Erica Thompson, *Escape from Model Land: How Mathematical Models Can Lead Us Astray and What We Can Do About It* (London: Basic Books, 2022), 71, 108.

8. Jaron Lanier, "Agents of Alienation," *Journal of Consciousness Studies* 2, no. 1 (1995): 76–81. See also Lanier, "There Is No AI," *New Yorker*, April 20, 2023.

9. Adrienne Marie Brown, *Emergent Strategy: Shaping Change, Changing Worlds* (Chico, CA: AK Press, 2017), 21.

10. Peter Adamson, *Don't Think for Yourself: Authority and Belief in Medieval Philosophy* (Notre Dame, IN: University of Notre Dame Press, 2022), 2. See also Stephen Turner, "What Is the Problem with Experts?" *Social Studies of Science* 31, no. 1 (2001): 129.

11. John Brockman, ed., *This Will Change Everything: Ideas That Will Shape the Future* (New York: Harper Perennial, 2010), 59.

12. Arjun Appadurai, *The Future as Cultural Fact: Essays on the Global Condition* (London: Verso, 2013), 286–87.

INDEX

Note: Italic page numbers refer to illustrations.

A NOTE ON THE AUTHOR

GLENN ADAMSON is a curator and cultural historian. His books include *Craft: An American History*; *Fewer, Better Things*; and *The Invention of Craft*. His work has been published in *Art in America, Antiques, Apollo,* and numerous other periodicals and museum catalogues. He is currently curator at large at the Vitra Design Museum, and was previously director of the Museum of Arts and Design, New York, and head of research at the Victoria and Albert Museum, London. He divides his time between London and the Hudson Valley.